SAVAGE CHILDREN

PETER BOLAND

Savage Children (John Savage Action Thriller Book 3).
Copyright © Peter Boland 2019.

ISBN: 978-0-9935695-3-1

This novel is entirely a work of fiction. The names, characters and incidents portrayed in it are the work of the author's imagination. Any resemblance to actual persons, living or dead, events, locales or organisations is entirely coincidental.

All rights reserved. No part of this book may be used or reproduced in any form or by any means without the prior permission of the author.

PROLOGUE

"I want you to draw a picture for me," the Archangel says. The voice is strange and unfamiliar to the girl, as is the room. It's dark and cramped and smells weird, like that chemical smell in the swimming baths, mingled with something more vinegary. The girl is called Sally and she doesn't know how she got here, sitting at a desk, staring at a blank piece of paper and a shiny new set of colouring pencils arranged neatly beside it. She tries to send her mind back to the point where she arrived at this place or stopped being where she was before, but the memory has been rubbed out, like her school work when she knows she's done it wrong.

She squirms in her seat and says, "I want to go home." A tear makes itself known at the corner of her eye. More quickly follow. Soon a whole procession chase each other down her hot, red cheeks. "Please. I want my mum," she sobs.

"I want you to draw a picture for me." The Archangel's voice is more insistent now. A tinge of impatience colouring every word.

"I want my mum," Sally repeats, her voice growing smaller with each syllable. She doesn't dare turn around to look at her captor—she's too terrified—so she keeps her eyes front, focused on the small pool of light from a lamp next to her; the only light in the room.

Behind her the Archangel exhales, a sigh of resignation. "Yes, of course, you'll see Mummy soon. But first, let's draw her a lovely picture. The best work you can possibly do. Better than anything you've ever done."

"I want to go home." Sally's fear switches to desperation, her sobs threatening to become screams. "I want to go home."

"Have another lolly," says the Archangel.

Over her shoulder, a slender hairless arm places the odd-shaped confection in the centre of the paper. She's had one of these before. It's about the only thing she can remember about this place. She liked it a lot. Sally takes it in her small, trembling hand and examines it, turning it over in her soft fingers. Most lollies she buys from the sweet shop have a thin little stick and a big bulbous boiled sweet stuck to the end. But this lolly is the opposite. The sweet part is small and cone-shaped, almost like a tiny lamp shade, while the stick is large, made of flattened plastic. Without thinking she pops it in her mouth. A fruity, syrupy fizz floods her tongue. It's nice. Comforting. Taking her mind off where she is.

After a few minutes of sucking, she says, "These lollies are funny."

"Funny in what way?" asks the Archangel.

"They make me feel all warm and tingly inside."

"It's nice, isn't it?"

"I feel sleepy," Sally adds. "And floaty. Like I'm flying."

"Well," says the Archangel. "That's lucky, because I want you to draw a picture of an angel. A very special angel."

"Why's it special?"

"It's special because the angel is going to be you."

CHAPTER 1

DCI NICK SUTCLIFFE WASN'T WHAT YOU'D call a happy man. In fact, if asked, he'd be hard pressed to pinpoint a moment in time when he remembered the headiness of joy, or the rush of laughter, or the sweet honey of elation. For his was a life defined by degrees of glumness. A scale that ranged from feeling low at one end to total misery or volcanic anger at the other. In recent months, this had been exacerbated by relentless insomnia, the pressures of the job acting like a powerful amphetamine on his frayed brain. Sleep eluded him, and the second he would shut his eyes, images of everything he'd seen and heard from all his years on the job would jam up his head like junk emails. He'd seen the worst humanity had to offer, and his head was a septic tank, overflowing with the vileness that people managed to inflict on each other.

In the past, he'd fed off it, thrived off it. The chance to right wrongs and make a difference, be a force for good, just like the police recruitment ads had promised. But the force for bad had pushed back and was now winning. Like a Dementor from Harry Potter, it'd sucked every last drop of hope or positivity he possessed. Some coppers turned to drink to blot it out. Sutcliffe had refused to be another cliché. So instead he just didn't sleep, and became a perpetual grump, as opposed to an insufferable drunk.

Sutcliffe swivelled his legs out of bed, picked up his sleep diary and scrawled 'Sweet FA' in it, or tried to, but the pen had run out so he threw both pen and diary across the room. The diary had been his therapist's idea. She'd said it would identify his sleep patterns. But he already knew his patterns of sleep. He never got any. Committing it to paper wouldn't make a difference.

This time of year didn't help. Sutcliffe hated all times of the year, no matter what month showed on the calendar, but he hated this one more than most. Late spring. Tormenting for an insomniac. Why the sun felt the need to rise at four thirty in the morning he could never fathom; light spearing through the curtains when it should be dark; bloody birds outside chirping away like winged crack addicts. The dawn chorus, indeed. People got all doe-eyed about it, as if it were designed for humans to serenade us into wakefulness. In reality, it was nothing more than Mother Nature being anti-social; birds showing off how hard they were, warning other birds to get lost—"look how noisy and strong I am, now back away from my branch or you'll be sorry". The bird equivalent of strutting around on a Saturday night being loud and obnoxious with your tattooed guns out. No one would put up with it if it were people making that racket. He'd march out there and slap ASBOs on all the trees if some idiot in Whitehall hadn't done away with them.

He reached for his phone. The screen informed him he'd missed a voicemail from Roberts.

"Godammit!" he shouted.

She'd called forty minutes ago, but his bloody phone hadn't rung. He kept telling his mobile phone provider that the signal had started dropping out where he lived but all they'd said was they'd tested it, and everything seemed fine. Of course they'd say that. He needed to change phone companies but when would he get the time to do that? And why was Roberts in work before him? He knew why. To make him look bad. The young, female DI, keen and smart, getting the jump on the worn-out old dog. He'd seen that before, he'd *been* that before. Got promoted by being better than his boss when he was her age. Well, he wasn't out of it yet, sleep or no sleep.

He hit the play button and his phone's recorded robotic voice shamed him by reminding him again that he had one missed call. "Yes, I know. Get on with it," he said to the disembodied voice.

Roberts' message played in his ear. "Sir, we've got another one. Girl by the name of Sally Woodrow. Parents reported her missing two days ago. Disappeared from a park in Tooting Bec on May 22nd. Parents received a drawing in the post. Same scenario. I've texted a shot of it to you. The drawing's at the lab for analysis. Thought it was best to get the ball rolling."

Sutcliffe swore. Then swore again a few more times. He checked his phone. No text had come through. Bloody rubbish phone company. But he already knew what the image would be. A child's drawing in coloured pencil, drawn by Sally Woodrow of herself as an angel, complete with wings and halo, her name written in the top right-hand corner.

The serial child abductor they'd nicknamed the Archangel had been busy again. So far, no bodies had turned up, so they were keeping an open mind. But with a person who took kids and made them draw pictures of themselves as heavenly creatures, it wasn't difficult to see where this was going.

CHAPTER 2

Two weeks later

SAVAGE WATCHED THE ONLINE RETAIL giant, or Lev as he was better known, drive up onto the pavement. Savage called him the online retail giant because of his dimensions—six-foot-six and square as a house—and because he delivered goods for an online retail giant. Savage got excited whenever he saw Lev's Sprinter van rattling up his road, past the line of handsome Edwardian terraced houses, converted into flats. For Savage there was no greater pleasure of living in the twenty-first century than being able to prod a picture on a screen one day, and have its real-life counterpart turn up on your doorstep the next.

Lev parked his van at a jaunty angle, straddling Savage's next-door neighbour's driveway. Something that Savage heartily encouraged him to do because he knew it annoyed the hell out of his neighbour. And Lev was only too happy to oblige.

Lev slid out of the cab clutching a large box and a handheld delivery device. Before Lev even had a chance to knock, Savage had the door open, smiling.

"John, I bring gift for you," Lev said, smiling back and passing him the box. Savage took it in one hand and made a quick squiggle on the screen of Lev's device with the other.

"Thanks, Lev. My new T-shirt. Couldn't have come at a better time. Going to put it on and sit in my garden."

"Yes, is very nice day."

Savage tore open the box and delved inside. There was far too much packaging for his liking, especially considering what the box held; three items of clothing, one of which was a T-shirt. But it wasn't just any old T-shirt. A T-shirt of Savage's favourite band, *The Jam*. He fished around, pushing aside the twisted lengths of brown packing paper and pulled out a neat, flat, folded square sheathed in cellophane. Savage put down the box, split open the cellophane and unfurled the crisp white T-shirt, revealing the distinctive logo of the band, a simple spray-painted design. He proudly held it aloft.

"Best band in the world."

"Meh," Lev muttered.

"What do you mean, 'meh'?"

"Jam is good. Clash is better."

"Oh, no," said Savage. "Oh, no, no, no. Don't get me wrong. I love The Clash. But The Jam has the edge on them, easily."

Lev shook his head. "No, no. *London Calling*. Is best record."

Savage could feel one of their doorstep debates coming on, which he relished. Savage liked nothing better than a good, friendly bit of banter about which music or movie was best. And he knew Lev did too, probably to the annoyance of all the people who were waiting for their packages to be delivered.

"*London Calling* is a sublime record," said Savage. "I have several copies of it myself. But you can't compare it to *Going Underground*. It's an urban hymn. The youthful anger of the suburbs. Whereas, *London Calling* is more melancholic."

"Melancholic?"

"You know, sad."

Lev screwed his face up. "Is not sad. Is Clash. Is punk rock. Angry too."

"Yes, but in a different way."

Savage patiently listened to Lev exploring why The Clash's lyrics were better, until the portly figure of his next-door neighbour appeared in his field of vision. Frank stood on his doorstep, pot belly sagging over his boxer shorts, stained T-shirt and dressing gown hanging open to let every passer-by see the result of a man who had no direction in life. He held an Xbox controller in one hand, like he always did when he came to the door.

"Hey," said Frank. "I've told you not to park over my driveway, you Polish idiot." Frank always got up in arms whenever someone parked over his driveway, which Savage could completely understand except that Frank didn't have a car, unless you counted the decaying Ford Mondeo that sat on his potholed concrete drive, resting on its axles because it had no wheels and no engine. It had an engine once, but they had parted company long ago and the engine now resided in Frank's back garden, along with several other of Frank's abandoned projects, which included a conservatory (still in pieces), the carcass of a Volkswagen Beetle, a moulded plastic pond (full of green water) waiting to be sunk into the ground, and mountains of discarded building products Frank had taken from skips because it was "free stuff" and he could make something out of it. The one common denominator all this detritus had was that he *never* made anything of it, and once it had entered Frank's garden it was doomed to stay there, the grass growing up around it.

Looking at this eyesore every day had led Savage to grow what he called the "Berlin Wall" in his back garden. An eight-foot-high privet hedge to block out the graveyard of abandoned rubbish that resided next door.

"I want you to move it now," Frank demanded, waving his Xbox controller in the air.

Lev winked at Savage, then turned to Frank. "I sorry. I move for you. I go now."

"Lev is working, Frank," Savage called to him. "You remember work, don't you?"

Frank nearly threw his controller on the ground. "Hey, I've been signed off with stress. Doctor says I'm not allowed to work." Frank used to be a drill-press operator, making holes in steel all day. It ranked in the top ten of the least stressful jobs you could do alongside being an ice-cream taster and testing cuddly toys for softness. "Anyway," Frank continued. "Doesn't look like he's working. Looks like he's talking crap with you again about that rubbish music you like. And anyway, Savage, you don't work either."

"It's called retirement," Savage replied. "It's what you do after working."

Frank mouthed the word *wanker* under his breath and went

inside, slamming the door behind him. Savage waved goodbye to Lev, telling him their debate would be continued.

Inside his flat he opened the plastic wrapping of his other package. He had ordered himself what he called some house trousers. Like a person finally accepting they needed glasses, Savage had succumbed to the joyful pleasure of an elasticated waistband for mooching around his flat. Two pairs for twenty quid, both sky blue. A bargain. He slipped out of his jeans and pulled a pair on, then gave a sigh of satisfaction as he stood in front of his bedroom mirror. Then he tried on his new T-shirt and tucked it in. Not the trendy way to wear a T-shirt, but he didn't care. Both fitted perfectly; roomy and comfortable, though both in a slightly larger size than he would have once chosen. Though Savage was a regular at the gym and liked to keep in shape and watch what he ate, he had to admit that his midriff was increasing, having made some sort of Machiavellian deal with his hair; as his belly got thicker, his hair got thinner. What's more, as the hairs fled from his head, they had no trouble appearing in places where they really weren't wanted, like out of his ears or nostrils. What evolutionary purpose this served he couldn't fathom, other than to broadcast to females that this male was well past his sell-by date, and was best avoided.

Savage shrugged in the mirror. He didn't care. The only woman he had ever loved, his wife Dawn, had died, taken by that wretched disease, cancer. She was the only woman for him and was irreplaceable. He'd stay single for the rest of his life. Stay faithful to her even in death.

His daughter Kelly had also passed away, on the battlefield in Afghanistan. Blown to pieces by a roadside bomb.

The only two people he cared about had gone, leaving a void he knew would never be filled by anyone else. But it did get filled by something quite unwanted. All the guilt and remorse he'd buried deep in the darkest corners of his mind had swept in like a storm to fill the vacuum they'd left. It grew and grew, threatening to blot out any happiness Savage had left, which wasn't much. It had grown so strong that it spoke to Savage when he was at his lowest and most desperate. Taking the form of a berating voice in his head, it flung torments at him, goading him to take his own life to atone for all the people he'd killed on his SAS missions. How many had he killed? Savage had lost count. It was definitely in the hundreds. A fact that the sneering voice would remind him of whenever it got the chance.

He'd grown so accustomed to the voice, he'd given it a name—Jeff Perkins. Somehow, naming the voice had made it sound less threatening, and now whenever Jeff Perkins went off on a malicious diatribe, Savage would imagine a stiff, pencil-necked man in a shirt and tie. An uptight creature who hated himself, which wasn't far from Savage's own truth, as Jeff was almost certainly the personification of Savage's self-loathing. Nevertheless, Jeff Perkins was a dangerous influence and had to be managed and corralled to stop Savage wanting to kill himself. Jeff had almost succeeded once, and Savage had put a gun to the side of his head, but had seen sense and got help.

Today however, the voice of Jeff Perkins couldn't be further from his mind. A warm spring sun filled the sky and all Savage wanted to do was slip on his Crocs, sit in the fragrant air in his new T-shirt and elasticated-waist trousers, gulping down buckets of strong tea and reading his doorstep-sized book on ancient Rome.

Outside in his back garden, Savage pulled up his deckchair and flopped into it, slightly spilling some of the precious beverage he held in his hand. No matter. This would be the first of many cups he'd suck down, because in Savage's mind there was nothing finer than sitting outside drinking copious quantities of tea, his face gently warmed by the sun, watching birds flit in and out of his hedge, and reading about how Romans invented central heating and concrete. Simple pleasures.

Simple pleasures that ended rather too quickly.

Savage sniffed the air and caught the unmistakable stench of smoke.

CHAPTER 3

IT WAS A BONFIRE. AND Savage hated bonfires.

Why was it in England that the moment the sun came out and it was safe to sit outside without your nether regions shrinking to the size of ball bearings and disappearing up into your chest area, someone would always want to pollute the air by burning stuff outside? Bad enough, but what made it worse for Savage is that it reminded him of war.

War smelt of many things, including the pungent stench of the rotting flesh of dead soldiers, but more than that it smelt of smoke. In war everything burned. Houses, cars, people, animals. Even the ground burned, hot and scorched beneath your feet. Wherever there was war there was smoke. Lots of it. Thick and black and noxious. It got in your eyes, in your hair, up your nose and in your mouth, and stank out your uniform. Even after returning to base, showering, scrubbing and changing, you still imagined you could smell it surrounding you. Engulfing you.

Savage could put up with most things, but smoke was not one of them. And he knew just who was responsible. The wafts of smoke drifting over the top of his giant privet 'Berlin Wall' hedge originated from Frank's garden. The guy was doing it to wind up Savage, like he always did, knowing that a bonfire was sure to push his buttons. From the smell, Frank wasn't just burning plain old wood either. He was burning the painted and plastic-coated varieties, the toxic fumes making Savage choke.

Savage went into his shed and took out his large aluminium step ladder. He set it up as close to the hedge as he could then went back to his shed to retrieve his garden hose, attaching one end to the outside tap. Taking the nozzle and unfurling the hose as he went, Savage climbed to the top of the step ladder, where he had a good view of Frank throwing offcuts of laminated chipboard into a glowing brazier. Frank was still in his dressing gown and boxers even though it was nearly five o'clock in the afternoon. Without warning, Savage twisted the nozzle and sent a powerful jet of water into the flames. Frank nearly fell over backwards in shock. He quickly regained his balanced, swearing every second.

"What the hell are you doing?" screamed Frank. "You mad, old idiot."

"Putting out a fire," Savage called back, innocently. Savage had perfect aim but pretended to lose control so some of it went over Frank.

"Turn that hose off, it's a bonfire you maniac."

"Bonfire?" Savage asked. "Oh no, it can't be a bonfire. Bonfires aren't allowed until after six o'clock. So, technically, it's a fire, and I'm putting it out."

Frank did a kind of angry dance, then stood in front of the brazier in an attempt to shield it from the effects of Savage's hose, getting himself drenched in the process. "Turn it off now. Or I'm calling the police."

"Be my guest," said Savage. "Did you know the word bonfire is actually Celtic, derived from *bone fire*, when they used to burn animal bones to ward off spirts."

"I don't care, turn it off."

"As a concerned citizen I can't allow it," Savage said grinning.

"Right, I'm coming round there." Frank marched—or rather squelched—out of his garden. Savage turned off the hose, having doused the flames, then descended the step ladder so he could confront his neighbour. As he approached his front door, Savage could hear Frank shouting through the letterbox. "You've gone too far this time, Savage. The police are going to hear about this. I'll write to my MP."

Savage opened the door to find Frank on his knees at the level of the letterbox, water pooling around him as if he'd peed himself. "You look like you've had a bit of an accident," Savage remarked.

Frank got to his feet and tried to regain a modicum of dignity. Pretty impossible when you were wet through, wearing boxer shorts and a dressing gown. "You had no right."

"I had every right. You were breaking a by-law. I had to act or the whole neighbourhood would have gone up."

Frank was preparing his rebuttal when a car they both recognised pulled up. It was Frank's ex-wife Julie and her mother, Celia. They worked together and lived together, Julie having moved back with her mother after she and Frank had split up.

Julie was the polar opposite of Frank. Smart, hard-working and ambitious. Savage liked her and was sad when she'd moved out. Her presence next door had cancelled out Frank's lack of charm—he had about as much of it as a depleted uranium rod—and all his other shortcomings, which were numerous. She'd been a good influence on her husband, keeping him in check, making him work. Soon after she'd moved out, Frank had got himself signed off sick so he could play video games all day, and let the house and garden descend into chaos. Strangely, the courts had awarded Frank custody of their one and only son Callum, probably because Frank was at home all day, whereas Julie worked full time to pay for everything. Ironic that a parent should be punished for having a job.

She stepped out in a smart business suit, her shoulder-length chestnut hair had been cut into a sharp bob. She did not look happy. "Frank, is Callum ready?"

Savage could tell just by Frank's expression that he was not.

"What?" asked Frank's dumb face, as he turned to watch Julie march up Savage's pathway. Celia got out of the car too, following her daughter at a safe distance, sensing a big bust up about to take place. She looked like an older version of her daughter, hair a similar shape and length, except she'd let it go completely grey.

"I've got Callum this weekend," said Julie. "You promised you'd have him ready, bag packed."

"You're late," said Frank. "Supposed to be here at four. It's now five."

"Would it have made any difference? Is he ready? Bag packed?"

"Er, no."

"No? You had one job, Frank. One job. What have you been doing all day, and why are you soaking wet?"

"That's his fault." Frank pointed at Savage childishly, as if he were in front of the headmaster. "He sprayed me with his garden hose and—"

"Good. Maybe, it'll wake you up. So I'm assuming Callum's bag's not packed."

"I'll do it right now." Frank went to leave.

Julie pulled him back. "No, you will not. I can't trust you to do anything. I'll do it. You tell Callum I'm here and that we're leaving in five minutes."

"He's not here," Frank said quietly.

Julie put her hands on her hips. "Not here? Well, where is he?"

"I dunno. Up the park I suppose."

Julie closed her eyes like she had the world's worst migraine. "I told you not to let him go up that park. I don't know how many times I've said it."

"Stop worrying, woman. He goes up there after school and nothing ever happens."

"Frank may have a point," said Celia. "You have to give kids a bit of freedom."

"Mum, stay out of this. You're not helping."

Feeding off Celia's support, Frank seized the advantage. "You mollycoddle him too much. God, when I was a lad the nonsense we used to get up to."

"Yeah and look how you turned out," said Julie.

Savage laughed.

"I'll go and get him," said Frank.

"No you will not," Julie replied. "Not looking like that. Knowing you, you'll go via the kebab shop, or the bookies, then forget what you went out for."

Savage interrupted. "Why don't I go and fetch him. Then you can pack his things."

Julie turned to Savage. "Oh, John, would you? That would be great."

"I'll come with you," said Celia.

"Great." Savage closed his front door. Frank gave him a filthy look as he passed.

Together, Celia and Savage walked towards the park at the end of his road, leaving Julie and Frank time to sort out their differences, which would be never.

"Smart move," said Savage.

"Yeah," said Celia. "I wasn't going to hang around while those two had another argument. Seen enough of those already. Thought it might have got better since the divorce."

"How's Julie doing?"

"Oh, you know. Same old Julie. Works too much. We were supposed to be having a half day today. Finish at twelve. Get back to my place, get it ready for Callum to stay. Buy his favourite food. I kept going into her office, telling her we had to go. She kept saying five more minutes, five more minutes. Five minutes turned into hours. That's why we were late."

"I think she just cares about what she does," said Savage. "She's passionate."

"Yes, but she needs to learn to put family first. Work will always be there. But kids grow up fast, and you can never get those years back. I keep telling her. She never listens. Just carries on working. I don't know how to get through to her."

After doing a degree, Julie had followed in her mum's footsteps by becoming a social worker. Soon after qualifying, she quickly rose through the ranks to become a manager. It wasn't long before she'd worked her way up to senior management and then just a couple of years ago got promoted to the position of the Director of Children's and Family Services.

"How does it feel to have your daughter as the boss?" asked Savage.

"Well, I'm only part-time these days. But she's made a lot of changes."

It was a non-committal answer. He'd expected her to say how proud she was of her daughter and her achievements, of the career heights she'd reached. Maybe Celia wasn't fond of the changes Julie had made. People didn't like change, he knew that much, and if it were your daughter doing the changes, then Celia would be in a tricky predicament; having to support her daughter's decisions even if she didn't agree with them.

"You know," said Celia, "I was in line for a director's position. Same as her."

"Really? What happened?"

"Julie happened. I left to be a mum, put my efforts into bringing her up."

"Any regrets?" asked Savage.

"Not for a second. Best decision I ever made. Loved every minute of it. I can't understand why Julie doesn't feel the same."

"I suppose it's her decision. And she sees Callum quite a lot."

"Not nearly enough if you ask me. Leaving him with that idiot of a father. Now that was one of her worst decisions, marrying Frank."

"Yeah, that is a mystery."

"I knew he was a wrong-un the moment I met him, but you can't say that to your kids, can you? I mean, it's their life."

Savage knew that all too well. He'd tried to interfere with his daughter's life. Pleaded with her not to join the army. It had only strengthened her resolve and made her want to join even more. Savage wondered if she'd still be alive if he hadn't tried to control her life. Maybe she would have lost interest, got distracted by all the other things the world had to offer. And still be with him today.

They reached the T-junction at the end of Savage's street. On the other side sat two bland warehouses built too close together, the only thing separating them a dank, narrow alley, which led into the park. It was barely wide enough to allow two small people to pass through at once. Celia and Savage crossed the road and were about to enter it, when a short teenager coming out of the alley, wearing a red Adidas T-shirt, nearly bumped into them. He wasn't looking where he was going and had the default posture of most young people these days; head bowed, shoulders hunched over. Savage and Celia had to side-step him, as he continued his course unperturbed, like an automaton in casual sportswear.

Savage and Celia exchanged glances then carried on walking into the narrow alleyway, the crunch of broken glass underfoot and the lingering stench of pee. "You wouldn't want to walk down here in the dark," Celia remarked as they passed through it.

Out the other side, they reached their destination, which was not so much a park, more of a scrubby, compact rectangle of grass pretending to be a park. Yes, it had a couple of benches, some swings, a roundabout, a litter bin and a dog-poo bin, but that was as far as the similarities went. "Prison exercise yard" would've been a better description, if prisoners were allowed swings and roundabouts to play on. The park itself was hemmed in on three sides by the solid, featureless walls of the warehouses. The fourth side of the park was formed by the back of a petrol station on the main road, separated by a brutal-looking, high metal fence made up of pointed spikes as long as eight-feet pike-staffs.

Every available wall and surface in the park was covered in gang tags. The same one repeated over and over. The litter and dog-poo bins overflowed, spewing their contents on the ground. One of the benches had been set alight at some time or other, and sat blackened and charred. Only one of the three swings worked, the others had snapped chains that dangled uselessly, and the lopsided roundabout looked ready to topple off its mountings. It wasn't a place you could spend quality time with the kids.

And Callum was not there.

"No sign of him," Celia remarked. "Let's try the petrol station, he might have gone to buy sweets."

They headed back out the way they came, looping round to the main road and into the petrol station. Crossing the busy forecourt, packed with cars, Celia and Savage stepped inside the pay kiosk, which doubled as a convenience store. The cashier stood behind a protective grille and a line of impatient motorists waited to pay for their fuel before getting home for the weekend. Celia and Savage did a quick circuit of the store. Callum was not in there.

As they hurried back home, a small seed of panic grew in Savage's belly.

Down the road, Julie leant against the bonnet of her car, prodding at her phone, a small rucksack by her feet, presumably full of Callum's things. He could see the worry on her face when she looked up and realised that Callum wasn't with Savage and Celia. They quickened their pace.

Before they reached her, Savage called out, "Callum's not at the park. Is he with you?"

Julie's eyes widened. "No. He's not here either."

CHAPTER 4

"**D**ID YOU CHECK THE PETROL station? He sometimes goes there to buy snacks." Julie tried her best to remain calm, but Savage could hear the fragility in her voice.

"We looked, he wasn't there," said Celia.

Frank came out of his flat, now dressed slightly better in jogging bottoms and a football jersey. "Callum's missing!" Julia shouted at him. "I told you not to let him go up that park."

"Relax, he's fine," said Frank, hands in his pockets. "Probably round a mate's house. See, now if you'd let him have a phone, we could've called him. Found out where he is."

"Frank, he's ten. This is your fault for letting him go up there."

"Take it easy, Jules," said Celia. "He'll turn up. Probably lost track of time."

Julie shook her head. "He knows I was coming to pick him up."

"Well, maybe if you'd been on time," said Frank.

She threw a spear-like glare at her ex. "You shouldn't have let him go up the park. You knew we were coming to pick him up. If anything happens to him, it's your fault."

Frank rolled his eyes at Savage hoping for some support, as if to say *women, eh*? He wouldn't get anything of the sort from Savage.

"Is there anywhere else he'd go?" Savage asked. "A friend's house nearby?"

"That's what I just said," Frank remarked.

"He never goes round friends' houses, not unless it's arranged in advance. You know, like a play date," said Julie.

"Parents these days," said Frank, tutting. "Have to arrange everything. In my day, we could just turn up at a mate's, 'You comin' out?' And that was that. None of this synchronising-diaries nonsense."

"Okay, Frank, that's no help whatsoever," said Savage.

"Did he come home from school?" asked Julie. Frank nodded. "And then he went straight up the park with his football?"

"Yeah, pretty much," Frank added.

"I tell you what we do. We phone his friends," said Julie. "All of them. Mum, could you drive my car back to yours on the off chance that he's already there?"

"But Celia's is miles away in Greenwich," said Frank. "I doubt if he'd have trekked over there."

"We need to be sure."

"I'll go right now," said Celia. "Call you when I get there." Julie's face was a map of worry. "Don't worry, love. He'll turn up." They hugged. Celia took Julie's keys, got in the car and started it up. U-turned and drove off.

"Okay," said Julie. "Now we need to get on the phone. Call his friends, school. Anyone or anywhere he might be. Then if there's no sign, we call the police."

"Now, steady on," said Frank. "That's a bit drastic. We don't want to waste their time."

Julie closed the gap between her and Frank, so their noses were nearly touching. "Waste their time? This is your son you're talking about."

"I didn't mean it like that. I meant we should give it a bit longer. You know how boys are. He could've gone into Peckham or Camberwell, to McDonald's or Subway, spend his pocket money."

"You never give him any pocket money," Julie said.

Frank ignored her jibe. "Don't you have to wait twenty-four hours before you call the police?"

"That's a myth," said Julie. "You can call them as soon as you think a child is missing. If he's not round a friend's, we have to call the police."

"How come you're suddenly the expert?" Frank asked.

Julie rounded on him. She looked as if she was about to punch him in the mouth. "Because I work for social services. How long were we married? You still don't have a clue about my job, do you?"

"Yeah, you look after naughty kids."

"Vulnerable kids. I look after *vulnerable* kids, and there's nothing more vulnerable than a child who's gone missing. We even have a missing-persons team at work. That's how I know so much about it."

"So, pull a few strings. Get them out looking for Callum."

Now it was Julie's turn to roll her eyes. "It's not that sort of team. Police do that. It's more about support and sharing information. Liaising with them."

Frank sneered. "Still got to do it by the book, even though it's your own son."

Julie snarled at Frank. "Obviously you know more about it than I do. Playing bloody Playstation all day."

"It's Xbox, actually," Frank said.

"I don't care! All I care about is finding Callum!"

"What, and I don't?"

"It doesn't seem like it!"

"Okay," said Savage, stepping between them like a ref in a boxing match. "Let's all calm down. Why don't you both start making calls, and I'll make you a nice cup of tea."

Over the next half an hour, Julie and Frank called anyone who knew Callum, from the vaguest friends and acquaintances, to his school and his junior football club. Savage made them hot drinks and plied them with biscuits. Julie didn't touch any. Frank, on the other hand, had no problem slurping Savage's tea and stuffing biscuits into his big gob, his front strewn with crumbs, clearly not worried as to the whereabouts of his son. During that time Celia called to confirm that Callum wasn't at her home waiting for them. Savage noticed Frank's casual abandon had been replaced by something else. Not exactly worry. Maybe the absence of indifference. The pair continued making calls until they'd exhausted every possible contact.

Julie then immediately called the police.

While they waited for the police to show up, Savage sat on the front steps with Julie and Frank, attempting to offer words of comfort. A pointless task seeing as the only words they wanted to hear were that Callum had been found.

The idea of Callum going missing was worrying Savage. He had grown fond of the lad and would often have him round his flat after school, usually because his idiot father had locked him out, and he had nowhere else to go. To avoid him hanging out at the park on his own, Savage would invite Callum in, make him a cup of tea and a sandwich, and they'd talk about tanks and planes or have a kickabout in his back garden. The poor lad had nowhere to play, what with Frank's garden being a death trap. Savage had become Callum's surrogate father of sorts. The thought of Callum out there all alone in London made bile rise up in Savage's throat and gloom enshroud his mind.

The police arrived. Out stepped two uniformed officers from the London Met. A couple of modern coppers, young, lean and healthy-looking. Probably had specialist degrees. Not like the coppers from Savage's youth who were sweaty, overweight and drunk on prejudice. As they introduced themselves, Savage decided to make himself scarce, heading back into his flat. Best to stay out of the way. They'd want to interview the parents alone to get a clear picture of the events leading up to Callum's disappearance. No point in muddying the water.

Savage sat in his front lounge and waited, knowing that Julie would be going through seven circles of hell at the moment. As for Frank, he couldn't be sure what the guy was thinking. Or if he was even capable of thinking. He wasn't taking it seriously, that was clear. Maybe he would after the two coppers had left. One thing was for sure, even though Savage couldn't stand Frank, he wouldn't wish this on him.

Savage got up and paced the hall, wondering what he could do. Go out looking, perhaps? He'd already done that. Plus, randomly wandering the streets wasn't the most efficient way of tracking down missing people. He needed clues, motivations. Maybe Callum had been bullied at school and Julie and Frank didn't know, although that was highly unlikely. Julie dealt with abused kids every day and would know the signs. Maybe it was a lot simpler than that. What if Frank had been getting nasty, taking out his frustrations on Callum? Didn't seem likely, either. For one, Julie would've spotted a change in Callum's behaviour, and two, Frank was extremely happy with his life. He was doing what he always wanted to do—nothing. He sat around all day eating junk food and playing video games while benefit cheques rolled in. Life couldn't be better.

"*It's probably a kiddie fiddler, you know,*" said Jeff Perkins, the voice in Savage's head. "*Right now, he'll be miles away from here in some basement. Or maybe even dead. They prefer a shallow grave these paedos. Never a deep grave. Haven't got the stamina to dig one. That's because they're all unfit. Fat, greasy guys in sweatpants. I mean, you never hear of a well-groomed paedo who works out, do you? Goes to the gym.*"

"Shut up, Jeff."

"*Oh, come on, Savage. You know it's true, you just don't want to admit it. It's so obvious. Kid goes up a park. A park of all places? It's almost a cliché. Gets snatched. Then left for dead in a wood or an allotment a few days later. It's just statistical probability.*"

"How do you know?"

"*How many cases do you know where a kid goes missing, and they're found alive and well? Apart from that dopey couple who claimed their daughter had been abducted so they could rake in money from an appeal. Do you remember? They found her under the bed at her uncle's house. That's the exception. Though by the looks of Frank, I wouldn't rule that out. He looks stupid enough to try something like that to make a bit of money to put on the horses. All I'm saying is, don't go getting their hopes up. I know what you're like, you're all 'I'm John Savage. I'm ex-SAS. I'm good at finding people.' Then as time goes on, people start winding up dead around you. Face it, Savage, the chance of them finding Callum, well, it ain't going to happen.*"

"Listen, Jeff. You need to leave now. I need to think. Work out a way of helping these people find their son."

"*Now you know I can't do that, Savage. You know it's my duty in life to make your life miserable, and if I can't do that, then I have to obstruct you in every way I can."*

"Okay then. Time to call Tannaz."

"Why are you calling her?"

"Because whenever she's around you disappear. And she might be the only person who can find out what happened to Callum."

CHAPTER 5

Savage sauntered over to the window of his lounge, gently nudging back the net curtains. He had heard two car doors slam and looked out to see that another police car had arrived. A third one turned up seconds later and out stepped a female officer. The two police officers who'd been inside Frank's flat came out and joined her on the pavement. She looked as if she were in charge, as everyone gathered round her, listening to her every word.

Things were getting serious.

The search for Callum had begun.

While the police were co-ordinating their search, fanning out, going house to house, Savage left his flat and nipped round to Frank's and knocked gently on the door. Rapid footsteps came from the other side. Frank opened the door wide.

"Oh, it's you. We thought it might be Callum."

"Sorry," said Savage.

Frank didn't ask Savage to come in but he didn't slam the door in his face either. Savage took that as an invitation of sorts. He followed Frank down the hallway and into his front lounge. Julie sat on the scruffy, sunken leather sofa that dominated the small room, and was surrounded by gaming paraphernalia. A plasma TV perched on the wall, far too big for the proportions of the room. There was a crowded coffee table holding more gaming gear mixed with dried-up coffee cups. Julie didn't look at Savage. From where he stood he could see her eyes were red and raw.

"How did it go?" he asked.

"Bloody waste of time," Frank said. "Do you know, those two

coppers searched in the loft for him. I said, you won't find him up there, you know."

"They have to be sure he's not in the house," Julie spoke in a quiet, small voice.

Frank ignored her and continued. "What a joke. They even looked under his bed and in his chest of drawers. I said he won't fit in there."

"They have to be sure," Julie's voice gained in volume. "Imagine if they do a full-scale search and it turns out he's hiding in his bedroom."

"Do they think we're stupid?" asked Frank. "I mean what sort of parents do they think we are?" He shot a look at Julie expecting her to throw back a response like a hand grenade. She didn't speak. This had gone beyond personal blame or fighting now. She just wanted her son back. And so did Frank. The guy just had a weird way of showing it.

"So that's the missing-persons team outside, I take it?" asked Savage.

Julie nodded.

"Hope they're not going to waste time looking in people's lofts and under the floorboards," said Frank. "He's out there somewhere. On the street. They need to be checking CCTV and all that sort of thing."

"Listen," said Savage. "That's what I wanted to talk to you about. I think I might have someone who can help you."

"Yes?" said Julie, a flicker of hope in her voice.

"It might be a bit... unconventional."

Julie stood up. "Don't care. Who is this person?"

They trooped next door to Savage's flat and into his lounge. Tannaz sat surrounded by several laptops she'd arranged on the dining table. Cables snaked everywhere. It was a makeshift command centre.

"This is Tannaz," said Savage.

"Alright," said Tannaz through a mouthful of chewing gum.

Savage had met Tannaz a couple of years ago. Actually, he'd sought her out when he needed help of the online variety. She

Savage Children

wasn't just the smartest person in the room, she was the smartest person in the postcode—the smartest person in whatever postcode she happened to be standing in. A programmer with gymnastic hacking abilities. There weren't many places Tannaz couldn't get into. With her quick wits and sharp tongue, the young Iranian immigrant had quickly become Savage's best friend, not to mention his best student—over time he'd taught her everything he knew about combat, and Tannaz had soaked it up like an ocean full of sponges, becoming a formidable fighter.

Frank took one look at her. "Oh, no. I don't want her sort helping us."

Tannaz looked at Savage. Stood up and started pulling out leads and folding up laptops, slotting them into bags. "Okay, looks like we're done here," she said.

"No, please," said Julie. "He didn't mean it. Did you, Frank?"

"I did mean it," Frank replied.

Julie gave him a shove. "You stupid racist. This young lady's offering to help find our son and you're worried about the colour of her skin."

"No," Frank pleaded. "I didn't mean *that*. Look at her. She's one of them Elizabeth Salamander cyber-hacker types. Hair all shaved up the sides and tattoos."

"You mean Lisbeth Salander," Tannaz corrected. "And you're no oil painting yourself, mate."

"She'll have our PIN numbers off us," Frank continued. "Empty our accounts into some Nigerian bank."

"I might still do that," Tannaz said, shoving another laptop into her bag.

Savage grabbed Frank by the scruff of the neck. "Sorry to do this, Julie."

"No, you go right ahead."

Kicking him in the back of the knee, Savage forced him into a kneeling position. "Now you apologise to the nice lady who's offering to find your lost son completely free of charge even though you are being a complete asshole, and this is probably all your fault."

Frank groaned. "This is assault, Savage. And Julie was late…"

"You need to apologise and ask her nicely to switch her equipment back on that she's lugged halfway across London, all to help find your son."

"Do it, Frank," said Julie. "We need to find Callum. We need all the help we can get."

"Fine," said Frank. "I'm sorry."

"And the rest," said Savage.

"Please, can you help us? I apologise."

"That's better." Savage hauled Frank to his feet.

Tannaz stopped what she was doing and took her equipment back out.

"Tannaz, thank you," said Julie. "I apologise for my idiot ex-husband."

Tannaz shrugged and sat down, plugging leads back into her array of computer equipment. She switched them back on and started typing. "Gather round."

Savage, Julie and Frank stood behind Tannaz, gazing at the bewildering lines of computer code on each screen.

"Okay," said Tannaz. "I'm guessing the coppers who came to visit you mentioned several things they would do as part of their search for Callum, one of them viewing CCTV footage."

"That's right," said Julie.

"What they probably didn't tell you is their access to CCTV is limited, restricted to local-authority cameras."

Julie and Frank looked at each other, confused.

Savage said, "Police have instant access to public CCTV. But privately owned cameras are a different matter. It's a bit like me coming round your house and demanding to watch Netflix on your telly. They have no legal right to look at cameras that are on private property. They have to ask permission. And that takes time. And time is of the essence. Tannaz has found a camera that overlooks the park's one and only entrance, the narrow alley between the warehouses at the end of the road. There's no way in or out of that park without passing that camera."

"But it's on business property, privately owned," Tannaz added.

"So how do we get a look at it?" asked Julie.

"I hack into it," said Tannaz.

"See, I told you," Frank said smugly. "She's a hacker, and this is illegal."

"Do it," said Julie.

"Just hold on a minute," Frank said. "Why don't we wait until the police get access to that camera."

"How long will that take?" asked Julie.

"Who knows?" Savage replied. "Could be minutes, hours, days, weeks. I can't answer that. But it's late Friday afternoon, the weekend. Warehouse is all closed up. Could take them a while to get in touch with the owners of that camera. Monday the earliest."

"Do it," said Julie.

"Don't I have a say in this?" asked Frank.

"No," Julie replied. "Tannaz, you have my permission."

Frank groaned and his shoulders sagged in defeat.

"Okay, here goes." Tannaz's fingers whizzed across the keyboard of one of her laptops, pulling up streams of code. Seconds later a grainy black-and-white video popped up on the screen of the laptop next to the one Tannaz was typing on. Tannaz immediately switched to that laptop. The image was a side-on shot of the front door of one of the warehouses, and beyond the entrance to the alley that led into the park. "That's the view at the moment. What time did you say Callum went up there?"

"Just after school," said Frank. "About four o'clock, I suppose."

Tannaz rewound the footage in a blur and hit pause. The grainy image froze. "Okay, I've gone back to three thirty, just to be on the safe side." Tannaz played the footage, speeding it up and then slowing it down whenever anyone entered the gap. A handful of kids went in first, then later a mum with a push chair and a fearsome weapon dog by her side. Tannaz sped the footage up again. One by one, all the people who had gone in drifted back out again. Savage wasn't surprised, there wasn't that much to do in the park. And it clearly wasn't the safest place to hang around. Savage looked at the timestamp. It now showed 4.05 p.m. Tannaz slowed the footage right down again, as a gang of eight youths wearing black hoodies went into the gap single file. They were in their mid to late teens, possibly early twenties. One of them was pushing a BMX bike, his mate sitting on the handlebars. A couple of them had their hoods up over their heads, including the guy sitting on the bike, making him look like E.T.

"I don't like the look of them," said Frank. "I bet they're something to do with it."

"Now do you see why I don't like him going up that park," Julie remarked.

Frank shook his head. "I knew it, he's got in with a gang."

Julie glared at Frank. "What do you mean, *you knew it*. You were all like, he's fine, *let him get on with it...*"

"Guys, please." Tannaz held up her hand to silence them both. She continued scrolling through the footage. Then at 4.11 p.m., Callum walked into the frame.

"Oh, my baby," Julie said, bursting into tears.

"Callum," Frank said, as if he were calling out to him, hoping he might hear him and step out of the screen.

"Okay, so we definitely know he went to the park," Savage remarked. "That's good."

The angle of the camera caught the top half of Callum, dressed in a blue T-shirt with a football under his arm. He walked towards the gap between the two warehouses, not a care in the world. A second later, he'd disappeared into the narrow alley. Tannaz wound it back so they could watch it again, slowed it down as if some clue would jump out at them. It didn't. All they saw was Callum going in again.

"So he's gone into the park and the only people in there is that gang," said Frank. "I bet they've taken him off somewhere, probably to be one of their drug mules. You know, moving product for them because no one suspects a ten-year-old, I saw this program on it—"

"Frank, shut up," said Julie. "We need to watch the footage."

When they were satisfied there was nothing else to see, Tannaz scrolled the footage forward slowly.

"You mark my words," said Frank. "In a second we'll see him leaving with that gang. Drug mule, that's what he is."

"Frank, let's just watch the footage and see, eh?" said Savage.

Savage Children

At 4.42 p.m. the gang emerged from the gap, exactly the same way as they went in, single file. Same eight guys. Same BMX.

Callum was not with them.

CHAPTER 6

"You were saying?" Julie remarked.

Frank ran his fingers through his limp hair. "I was sure they'd have something to do with it. That still doesn't let them off the hook. Maybe they attacked him. Left him for dead up there."

"Don't talk like that, Frank," said Julie.

Once the gang had left the shot, Tannaz sped the footage up again, expecting the next person appearing on camera to be Callum. Twenty minutes later, according to the time stamp, Savage and Celia came into view, walking towards the alley between the two warehouses. At the same time, the teenager in the red Adidas top emerged from the gap, nearly bumping into Celia and Savage going the other way.

"I don't get it," said Savage. "Callum should still be in there or we should've seen him leave. After Celia and I went in, the park was empty. That short guy in the Adidas top was the last one to leave."

"Are you sure?" asked Frank.

"Positive. You saw the footage; Callum's gone in but hasn't come out."

"How's that possible?" asked Julie. "He can't just disappear into thin air."

"I bet there's another way out," said Frank.

Savage shook his head. "There's no other way out. It's surrounded on all sides by high walls and fences."

"Can you scroll back, Tannaz?" asked Julie. "Watch it all again. Maybe we missed something."

"Of course." Tannaz wound the footage back. This time she

went back to three p.m. Grabbing a pen and paper, she made a note of the time each person went in and the time they left. As she moved the footage forward, every time someone left the park she crossed them off the list. She counted them in and she counted them out again. "This doesn't make sense," she said. "Everyone's accounted for. No one else is in there, apart from Callum. He should still be there."

After the point where Savage and Celia entered the park, she replayed the footage again. This time going back to two p.m., two hours before Callum entered the park. Again, she noted who went in and out. Once more, everyone was accounted for. Every person she wrote down who had gone in the park, had also come out again. Except Callum.

"I tell you, there's another way in and out." Frank stated his theory again.

"Sorry, Frank," said Savage. "It's surrounded on all three sides by solid walls and the spiked fence of the petrol station."

"What about the petrol station?" asked Julie. "Does that have any CCTV?"

"Lots," said Tannaz. "But none of it points towards the park."

"Any other CCTV anywhere?" asked Savage.

"Not in the immediate vicinity."

"Maybe there's a secret door," Frank chipped in, still adamant about his theory.

Savage sighed. "This isn't Narnia, Frank. I tell you there's no other way in or out. We looked."

Frank folded his arms and shook his head. "The only explanation is another exit. People can't walk through walls."

"Frank, shut up, will you," said Julie. "You heard John. There's only one way in and out."

Frank then found an unlikely ally.

"Er, that might not be exactly true," said Tannaz, who had been quietly running the footage backwards and forwards while the others had been arguing.

"How come?" asked Savage.

"This guy." Tannaz froze the video image on the teenager in the red Adidas T-shirt, who nearly collided with Savage and Celia. "I thought I'd accounted for everyone. I write them down as they go in, then cross them off when they leave. It always tallies. However, this guy leaves, but no matter how far back I go, there's no footage of him going in."

"Really. You sure?" asked Savage.

"Positive. There're no images of him going in that park through the alley."

"Told you," said Frank smugly.

Julie turned and faced him. "Frank. Will you shut up."

"How far back have you gone?" asked Savage.

"So far, back to one p.m."

"Go back further," said Savage. "We need to be sure."

"He's probably a drug dealer," said Frank. "Been hanging out there all day to sell drugs."

"Despite what you think," said Julie. "Not every young person that hangs out in a park is a drug dealer."

Tannaz kept running the footage back earlier and earlier, but they never caught a glimpse of the lad in the Adidas top going in. "This is weird," said Tannaz. She'd taken the footage back to the small hours of the morning, right back to sunrise at five thirty a.m. "Still no sign of him going in."

"Could the footage have been tampered with? You know, edited," asked Julie.

"Yeah, it's possible. I'm no expert. There's a guy I know that can run it through analytical software. It'll show up any tampering."

"We need to know," said Savage.

"I'll send him the footage," Tannaz replied.

"Come on," said Frank. "This is ridiculous. There has to be another way in and out. That's the only explanation."

"Well, there's only one way to be sure," said Savage. "We go back up there and look for it."

"At last," said Frank. "Sense has prevailed."

"I'll come with you," said Tannaz.

"Before you do," said Savage. "Can you get some screen grabs of the guy in the Adidas top and the gang, and send them to my phone? Right now, they're the only people who might have been in the park at the same time as Callum. They're our best witnesses."

"I'll have a copy too," said Julie.

"Me too," said Frank.

"Sure," said Tannaz. She took Frank and Julie's numbers, and a few clicks later had transferred the images to everyone's phones.

Frank and Julie led the way to the park with Tannaz and Savage a few paces behind. Tannaz leant over to Savage and spoke quietly. "I've been meaning to ask you something."

"What's that?" asked Savage.

"What are you wearing?" She pointed to his light-blue elasticated-waist trousers and his Crocs. "You look like you're about to disinfect a hospital floor."

"These?" said Savage. "These are my house trousers."

"But you're wearing them outside."

"Well, 'house trousers' is a loose term."

"What, like the fit?"

"Don't you like them?" Savage asked. "They're dead comfy, just like sweatpants but even more comfy."

"Karl Lagerfeld said sweatpants are a sign of defeat, that you've lost control of your life."

"I bet Karl Lagerfeld used to slip into something like this when he was at home. You should try them before you knock them. Hey, my new Jam T-shirt's cool, though."

Tannaz looked unsure. "Ye-ah, but I'm sure The Jam never imagined their T-shirt would be paired with Crocs and elasticated-waist trousers."

"Then I must be unique."

"You're definitely something."

The four of them reached the alley and entered the little park, finding it bleak and empty. There was no sign of the police. Probably been and gone, satisfied that there was nothing more to be learnt, and moved on to searching elsewhere.

Frank stood in the centre of the small space, wheeling around, confounded at how secure and enclosed it appeared. High walls confronted him on three sides, with not so much as a window to break the continuous boundary. He immediately made for the back of the petrol station and the towering heavy-duty spiked metal fence. One by one, he rattled each individual spike, hoping to find some concealed way in or out, a secret gate, perhaps. Savage watched him as he desperately tried to loosen the unyielding metal.

"There has to be another way in," he muttered. "Has to be."

Like a caged rat, Frank then moved onto the walls of the warehouses, pounding his hand along the length of each one. Every square inch, permanent and unmovable masonry. He stared up at the roof of each building in turn. There was no way anyone would be able to scale them unless they'd brought a twenty-foot ladder with them. Savage left Frank to it.

Scanning the ground like a Terminator, Savage searched for any clue as to what had happened to Callum. He had no idea what he hoped to find. Signs of a scuffle, maybe. Blood. A patch of dirt that had been kicked up. Clutching at straws was the phrase that kept popping into his head. Nothing revealed itself, apart from a light scattering of litter. He noticed Tannaz and Julie doing the same, looking around but not quite sure what they were looking for.

Callum had vanished into thin air.

Just when he thought all possibility of finding a clue had diminished, he heard echoing voices behind him—lots of them—plus the tinny sound of grime music being played too loudly through a mobile speaker that wasn't designed to be played that loud. Savage swung round. A gang entered the park.

He analysed them as they headed to the park's only useable bench. Dressed in red sweat tops and trainers, they plonked themselves down, some of them singing along to the track, others doing what young lads do when they're in groups—mocking and making fun of each other. Savage counted ten of them.

Out the corner of his eye, he noticed Frank making a beeline for the boys, quick march, eyes full of determination and a building rage, a look that demanded answers. "Hey, you!" he said. "I'm talking to you."

The good-natured banter of the gang ceased. Swiftly replaced

Savage Children

by faces that said they were ready for a confrontation. One by one, they got to their feet, poised for a fight. And possibly to pull out concealed weapons.

CHAPTER 7

Savage rushed over to Frank, getting in between him and the gang, blocking his path. Savage immediately turned to the group, hands up in surrender. "Sorry, very sorry. I apologise, my friend just thought he recognised you."

Frank struggled to move Savage out of the way. His years spent sitting on a sofa while gaming not really helping him in a shoving match. "What are you doing?" Frank said. "That's the gang we saw in the footage."

Tannaz and Julie came over. The gang looked ready for violence. Shoulders hunched. Fists clenched.

Savage spoke in a low, calm volume. "That's not them. They're different guys."

"How do you know?"

"Frank, I'm ex-SAS," he said quickly. "Trained to take in details, especially when it comes to ID-ing targets, and that's not them. Now if we're nice to these guys, they might tell us who's in the footage."

"John's right," said Julie.

"Listen, it's best if you leave," said Savage. "Let me and Tannaz talk to them. You may've spooked them."

"Don't be daft," said Frank. "I doubt they're frightened of anything."

Julie grabbed Frank by the arm. "Come on, we're going back home." She dragged Frank by the arm towards the exit to the park. He kept looking over his shoulder, eyeing the gang suspiciously. Once they were in the alleyway, Savage could hear Frank's protestations echoing off the walls.

Savage turned and slowly approached the gang with Tannaz by

his side. They were still standing, faces mean, still expecting an altercation. Their bodies were coiled and ready to spring. Something that was second nature to them. They wouldn't get a fight today. Not if Savage could help it.

"Very sorry about that," Savage said. He had his hands held up again.

"You need to keep that dog on a leash," said the biggest one of them. He had swirly patterns shaved into his temples.

"Yes. I'm sorry. His son's gone missing, and he's desperate to find him."

"Nothin' to do with us, man."

"No, no. Of course not. But I was just wondering," Savage held up his phone. "Could I just show you a couple of pictures. Would that be okay?"

Swirly Hair thought for a moment, eyes running up and down Savage, analysing him for threat potential. His shoulders eventually relaxed. "Sure," he said.

Savage came closer and showed them the screen grab on his phone of the other gang entering the park. "Do you recognise these guys?"

"Hey, they're trespassing," one of them said.

"No right being here," said another. "This is Red Crew territory."

"The Red Crew. Is that your gang name?" asked Tannaz.

"Damn right," said Swirly Hair. "Look around. Our tags are everywhere."

Tannaz and Savage surveyed the graffiti. The guy with the swirly hair was right. In amongst the colourful jumble of art and words, were interlocking Rs and Cs, scrawled in marker pen and sprayed in paint.

"I'm John and this is Tannaz. Thank you for allowing us to be on your territory." In this neighbourhood, these guys were the local kings. Deference was the way to keep on their good side. It was all about showing respect, especially if he were hoping to get information out of them. And nobody knew what went on in a neighbourhood better than the local gang.

"S'alright," said the guy with swirly hair. "I'm Snake Eyes."

Savage nearly offered his knuckles out for a fist bump but saw sense at the last moment, and pulled them back.

"So, the gang in the picture," said Tannaz. "You don't know them."

Snake Eyes shook his head.

"Are there any other local gangs around here?" she asked.

Snake Eyes and the others sniggered. "Just a bunch of losers called the Mojos."

"Oh, like the penny sweets," said Savage. Everyone looked at him confused, including Tannaz. "Sorry, no one under forty-five is going to know what that is."

Tannaz went to speak. Snake Eyes got there first.

"Before you ask, it ain't them neither," he said. "We kicked their asses out of this park a week ago." He high-fived his nearest gang member. There were whoops of triumph from his mates.

"Are they your rivals around here?" asked Savage.

"They wish," Snake Eyes replied. "They think they're all badass. Try and take the park. Sometimes they do. Cover up our tags with theirs. But we always come back stronger. Take it back, cover up their weak-ass tags."

All the gang members agreed, saying *yeh-yer*.

Savage showed them a picture of Callum on his phone. "This is the lad who went missing we were telling you about. He came into the park this afternoon but never came out."

Snake Eyes peered at the screen. "Oh, yeah, I recognise him. Seen him up here. Kicks a ball against the wall on his own."

"Do you know of anyone who's been in here looking suspicious?"

"Listen, bruv. We don't allow no pervs or nonces in our park. We don't pick on little kids, neither. Nothin' big about that."

"No, of course not," Savage replied. "What about this guy?" Savage swiped the screen and showed them the shot of the lone teen in the red Adidas T-shirt.

"Never seen him neither," said Snake Eyes. The other assembled gang members peered in at the screen then shook their heads.

Savage Children

"Er, can I ask a stupid question?" said Savage. "Is there another way in or out of this park, apart from that alley?"

Snake Eyes scrunched up his face in confusion. "You must be trippin'. Look around, bruv. S'all concrete and steel."

Savage pulled a ten-pound note out of his wallet and held it out. "If it's not too much trouble, would you mind keeping your ears to the ground, maybe ask around? See if anyone knows anything."

Snake Eyes stared down at the tenner as if it was a rotten fish.

Tannaz cleared her throat a little too loudly. "Excuse us one second," she said, taking Savage to one side. Keeping her voice low, she said, "Savage, what are you doing?"

"Enlisting their help. Offering them an incentive."

"With ten pounds?"

"What's wrong with ten pounds?"

"That's barely enough to top up a phone. Or maybe you thought they would nip off to the sweet shop and buy some Mofos."

"They're called Mojos."

"Whatever. Savage, when was the last time you hired an informant, 1975?"

"Okay, you suggest a figure."

"How much have you got in your wallet?"

Savage retrieved his wallet from his back pocket. Tannaz snatched it out of his hand and dived in, retrieving a fistful of tenners and twenties adding up to about a hundred pounds.

"Savage, is this all you have?"

"Wait, I'll just check my second wallet I keep handy for bunging people cash. Oh, wait, I don't have one."

"Okay, no need to be sarcastic." She plucked the remaining tenner from Savage's hand and returned to the gang who were now sitting on the bench. Savage joined her. She pushed the wedge of cash into Snake Eyes' hands and smiled. "For your trouble," she said. "We'll pop back in a day or two. If you hear anything, we'll double your money."

"You mean my money," Savage said under his breath.

"We'll be here," said Snake Eyes. "We'll ask around."

Savage and Tannaz left the park and headed home, stopping to call on Frank. They stood on his doorstep, filling in him and Julie about what they'd found out. Which wasn't much. Actually, it wasn't anything, but at least they had a local neighbourhood gang keeping an eye out for Callum. Better than nothing.

Julie looked as if she'd aged several years, or was on the brink of shutting down. Frank, on the other hand, couldn't keep still, as if a sandstorm whirled inside him. As he stood next to the door, he fiddled with the latch one minute, the next, he clawed at his neck, leaving long red scratch marks. Strange how stress affected people in different ways.

"We'll find him." Savage tried to offer some comfort. "Tannaz and I are going to crack on. Explore some other possibilities." His words had no effect whatsoever, sounding hollow and paper thin.

"The police called round again," Julie said quietly. "We've got a family liaison officer now. Said she's on-call for us twenty-four hours if we need anything."

"Oh, that's good," said Tannaz.

"Is it?" Julie replied. "A family liaison officer means things are getting more serious. Worse. She's there to hold our hands. Manage our misery, basically."

"You don't know that, Julie," said Frank.

"Yes, I do. I know about these things. Been through it before with families. I know the drill. You don't."

"Well, I'm not staying here, doing nothing," said Frank. "I'm going out looking."

"I think it'd be best if you stayed with Julie," said Savage. "You know, support each other."

"Listen, Savage. My son is out there somewhere. I'm damned if I'm going to sit on my ass waiting for him to come home."

"Savage, why don't you go with Frank," said Tannaz. "Julie can stay at yours with me. I'm going to do some digging on the Internet. Try some facial-recognition software, try to ID the guy in the red Adidas top and the mysterious gang. I could do with some help."

Julie's face brightened a little at the thought of doing something constructive other than waiting for a phone call that might never come. Or perhaps it was the thought of spending some time away from Frank in someone else's company.

"That's a great idea," said Savage.

In fact, he hated the idea of pairing up with Frank. However, he knew it made sense. Frank had nearly got himself into a fight by rubbing up the local gang without trying too hard. Imagine what he'd be like approaching people on the street. He needed someone with him, to look out for him. The guy was an idiot. If Savage just let Frank get on with it, with his current state of mind, he was likely to get himself killed before the night was over. If they did get Callum back safe and sound, Savage wanted him to grow up with a father, no matter how useless he was.

"What are you going to do?" asked Julie.

"Ask around," Savage replied. "Show pictures of Callum. See if anyone's seen him. Maybe show pictures of the gang and the guy in the red Adidas top."

"Shouldn't we tell the police about them?" asked Frank.

Savage shook his head. "Not without admitting we hacked a CCTV camera. Besides, they'll get a look at them soon enough."

They went their separate ways—Frank and Savage scouring the streets; Tannaz and Julie scouring the Internet. Both came up empty handed. No one around Peckham had seen Callum or the gang or the guy in the red Adidas top.

When Savage returned home just before midnight, Julie had left and gone next door to stay at Frank's, sleeping on the sofa. He found Tannaz in one of her volatile moods.

The facial recognition had drawn a blank. The footage wasn't good enough; the low-resolution of the warehouse CCTV camera to blame. To make matters worse, the camera had caught everyone going in through the alley in profile, or at best a three-quarters angle, and the fact that most of the gang had their hoodies up hadn't helped. Facial recognition was very good at full-frontal faces. A nice clean passport-style head-shot worked best for mapping features and comparing the positions of eyes in relation to the nose and the mouth. As soon as the face was at an angle or partially obscured, or captured on low-quality CCTV footage, the software struggled.

Even with Tannaz tweaking it and adding in her own code to try and improve it, she couldn't get anywhere near a match. Her friend had also got back to her, analysed the footage for editing and tampering, and had found no evidence that it had been altered. Her evening had yielded a big fat zero. A total waste of time.

And she had run out of cigarettes.

Hurricane Tannaz was about to make landfall.

As Savage stepped into the lounge, a laptop whistled past his ear. It smashed against the wall, splintering the casing and sending bits of computer innards across the carpet. For anyone else the loss of a laptop would be a minor crisis. Not for Tannaz. She'd just salvage the bits and build herself another one. After she'd calmed down.

Savage offered the only solution he could think of. "Would it help if you punched me in the face?"

Tannaz balled her fist and launched it at Savage. He didn't even see it coming; she had ridiculously fast reflexes.

Her fist stopped just short of his nose. Retracting her hand slowly, a shameful look spread across her face. She'd just nearly punched her best friend in the head. Tannaz shrank; some of the fire subsiding from her eyes. "Sorry," she said. "I just get frustrated. And sorry about your wall."

"Don't worry. Nothing a bit of Polyfilla won't fix. Why don't I make you a coffee," Savage offered.

"Yes. I mean no. I've had enough caffeine to give myself several heart attacks."

"Why don't we start again tomorrow."

"I can carry on. I've got more laptops I could use." She said it as though they were a disposable item, like hand towels in a public toilet.

"Let's not risk it, shall we? Getting angry won't help us find Callum, but getting some rest will."

Tannaz agreed but was far too wired to sleep, so Savage put on a film, *Lord of the Rings*, to help her wind down. Savage loved the film but Tannaz hated it, and complained that she found fantasy movies far-fetched.

Savage Children

"That's the whole point," Savage replied. "Bit of escapism. You need something to calm you down. Come on, we'll watch it together on the sofa."

At first, Tannaz fidgeted and squirmed like a wasp in a puddle of Coca-Cola, the world of fantasy not sitting well with her. Tannaz was more down-to-earth than Middle Earth. But she persevered until Frodo and friends left the Shire. A minute later she was out cold; eyes clamped shut, breathing heavily like a pair of bellows. Savage put a blanket over her, then retired to his bed and drifted off quickly.

He awoke with a start. Not sure how long he'd been asleep. A series of rapid loud bangs came from the front of the house like a cluster bomb going off.

Someone was kicking in the front door.

CHAPTER 8

Callum's eyes flicked open.
Adjusting to the dim light he took in his surroundings. It didn't take long for him to realise this wasn't his bedroom. From what little light was provided by the lamp next to the bed he was lying on, he could see this wasn't the spare room at his gran's either, where he sometimes stayed over the weekends. Her ceilings were high and had those fancy shapes running along the tops of the walls that looked like icing on a cake. The ceilings in this room were far too low and cramped, curving in at the edges. The windows had no curtains either. It must be night-time, thought Callum. Blackness filled the glass from corner to corner, except this black seemed too solid, too artificial. Even night-time wasn't totally black, it had stars and streetlights. Not like this black, which seemed like a wall. As he looked closer, he could see the glass had a texture to it. Paint. The glass had been painted over.

Fear passed through him like a ghost, chilling him to the bone.

Callum jumped out of bed. Made for the door. That too had strange curved corners and an odd porthole window, also painted black.

Before he got to the door he was yanked back. His left arm had snagged on something. In horror, he looked down to see his wrist had a thick chain tightly wrapped around it, the other end disappearing under the bed. With both hands, Callum pulled hard. The chain snapped taut. Unyielding. Again, he pulled. Again, the chain won. He heaved and heaved but his ten-year-old muscles were no match for the hard steel links.

Callum took another approach and scrambled under the bed,

desperately reaching out with his fingers in the dusty darkness only to find the end of the chain had been bolted to the wall. Like an animal in a trap, he struggled against his bindings, banging his head against the underside of the mattress until he was breathless and sticky with sweat. He gave up and slid out from under the bed, slumped against it on the floor and began to cry.

Instinctively, he called out for his mum and his dad, great big sobbing wails. He cried out until his voice was hoarse and his cheeks were drenched in tears. How long this went on for he couldn't tell. Thankfully, the tears subsided, and he began to examine his surroundings again, in more detail. The low ceiling, the strange curved walls and odd-shaped windows. There were a few small cupboards too and a little table. Everything looked dark, compact and cramped. He was in a caravan.

Callum got to his feet and went over to the little table, the chain dragging along behind him. A bottle of water sat next to a bread roll sheathed in Cellophane. Next to these were a few sheets of paper and some colouring pencils. Placed exactly in the middle of the paper on top of a Post-it Note was a lollipop. A weird-looking lollipop with a conical top that seemed too small, too out of proportion for the stick it perched on. Callum picked up the bottle of water and took a long drink. Then he popped the lolly in his mouth. The taste was familiar. Fizzy, fruity and tingly. He definitely remembered having one of these before. It had made him feel all warm inside, chasing away any bad thoughts in his mind. He liked these lollies.

Callum peeled the Post-it Note off the white sheets of paper and began to read:

> *Hope you like the lolly. If you want another one, draw me your best picture of you as an angel flying in heaven. Make sure you write your name in the corner.*
> *Your friend, the Archangel.*

Yes, he would like another one, thank you very much. These lollies were great. The drowning distress and panic he'd experienced minutes ago began to subside, receding far into the background. He was sure the lolly wedged in his cheek had something to do with it. In fact, he now had the complete opposite feeling, he was content and sort of cosy. Callum gave a deep wide yawn. The lolly also made him drowsy. Sleep wasn't far away. He'd better get started if he wanted to make sure the Archangel left him another lollipop.

Callum slotted himself at the table, emptied the colouring pencils out of their wrapper and began to draw.

CHAPTER 9

IT SOUNDED AS IF A battering ram were trying to break down the door. Savage sprang from his bed, noted the time on his bedside clock. It read seven thirty in the morning, Saturday. Then he heard the voice of Julie calling out his name.

"John, John. Please open the door," she cried, as if the house were on fire.

"Hurry up, Savage. Open up." Frank was outside too.

In a second, Savage was out in the hallway and turned the lock and opened the door. If Frank and Julie had been worried yesterday, they now looked terrified. Julie held a sheet of paper in her hands, about the size used in a photocopier. "This came through the door," she said.

She lifted it higher for Savage to see. He reached out to take it.

On the crisp white paper, in coloured pencil, was a child's drawing of an angel with wings, short yellow hair and big blue eyes. The angel wore a football top with red-and-blue stripes and blue shorts—the kit of Callum's favourite football team, Crystal Palace. His name was written in one of the corners. Callum had a shock of blond hair and big blue eyes, and was good at art. The likeness was clear. He'd drawn himself as an angel. But why?

"When did this arrive?" asked Savage.

"Don't know," said Julie. "I dozed off on the sofa, woke up around six, got up to make a cup of tea and saw it lying on the doormat. Someone must have shoved it through the letterbox last night."

"What does it mean?" asked Frank. "That's Callum's name and his handwriting. Do you think it's from his school, a teacher maybe or from Callum himself? Why would he put it through the letterbox and not come home?"

Savage wasn't fully awake, but awake enough to know there was a third possibility. One that Frank and Julie had probably thought of but didn't want to acknowledge out loud. More than likely, considering how hard they'd banged on his door.

"Who's touched this?" asked Savage.

"Just you, me and Julie," Frank replied.

Tannaz came wandering through the hallway and appeared behind Savage. Still in her clothes and dozy-eyed, an unlit cigarette hung from her mouth. She'd lost all control of her tousled hair. "What's going on?" she asked.

"Tannaz. Get a clear plastic sandwich bag from the drawer by the sink." She turned slowly like a wind-up toy and shuffled towards the kitchen, too sleepy to protest.

"Why do you need a plastic bag?" asked Frank.

"To put this drawing in it. There's a chance, and I'm not sure about this, but a chance this has come from the person who's got Callum. It could have his fingerprints on it. Your police family liaison officer, you need to call her immediately."

The police who showed up on Frank's doorstep weren't the same as the ones who called yesterday. They had been young, uniformed coppers. The ones who now sat in Frank's lounge sipping tea that Julie had probably made because Frank's teas were disgusting, were plain-clothes officers. An odd couple. A young, attractive female detective. No makeup and blonde hair tied back in a loose ponytail. She wore a fairly bland, black trouser suit; a cheap one judging by the way it hung baggily around her slight frame. The other one looked more like the coppers of Savage's youth. Sweaty and badly dressed, like a used-car salesman. He wore a dreary shirt and tie with a sensible waterproof jacket—unzipped, which looked as if it would stay that way for the foreseeable future because it didn't make it all the way around his considerable midriff. A thick, healthy mane of salt-and-pepper hair, perhaps the only thing that was healthy about this individual, flopped either side of a tired and miserable face.

Ever since Savage had seen them go into Frank's flat over an hour ago, he had known it wasn't a good sign. They'd turned up quickly and the fact that they were plain-clothes police—detectives no less—instead of uniforms, meant that Callum's missing-child status had just been elevated to something more serious. Not that a missing child wasn't serious, but it didn't merit a couple of senior detectives. Not at this early stage. The drawing had been key; got their attention. Savage feared his hunch had been right and Callum had been abducted.

"Come away from the curtain," said Tannaz.

Savage had become a bit of a curtain twitcher since this had all started. Yes, he was being nosey, but it was for a reason. He wanted to pounce on the two detectives as they left. Ask them questions. Knowing what coppers were like they wouldn't tell Frank and Julie the whole story about what was going on for a number of reasons. One, not to scare them. Two, not to put ideas into their heads that could skew the investigation. And three, they didn't want sensitive information about an investigation getting out into the public domain. So they'd play their hands close to their chests, asking more questions than they gave answers. It made sense. Whatever was happening out there, or what they thought was happening out there, they would want to keep a lid on, not allow it to leak out, especially not to the press, not until they were ready. Information getting out about an investigation too early created speculation and gossip, and gossip turned into panic and fear, and before you knew it, gangs of vigilantes would be roaming the streets demanding justice and suspecting their neighbours without a shred of evidence to back up their actions.

"Celia's here," said Savage, peering out the window. He watched as Julie's mum climbed out of her daughter's car, a big bag of shopping in one hand. "I better bring her in here, probably best if she doesn't interrupt them."

Julie had phoned her mum several times last night, filling her in about everything so far. But she didn't know about the drawing of Callum yet.

As Celia crossed the pavement, about to climb the stairs to Frank's flat, Savage whipped open the door and beckoned for her to come in. She looked at him confused as he came down and took the shopping bag from her. "Police are talking to Frank and Julie. There's been a bit of an update. Come and have a cup of tea."

They sat down in Savage's lounge. He made tea for three and introduced Celia to Tannaz, and told her about the drawing, half wondering if he was doing the right thing, or whether he should've left that up to Julie. He figured Julie had enough on her plate already.

"A drawing?" Celia asked.

"Yes," said Savage. "Of an angel. Julie thinks Callum drew it."

"Did anyone see who delivered it?"

"No one," said Tannaz. "It just appeared on Frank's doormat this morning."

Celia's face screwed up. "How odd."

"Odd?" said Tannaz bluntly. "I think it's chilling."

"How was the traffic getting over here?" Savage changed the subject, figuring that Celia hadn't had time to process the information and therefore, had not come to the horrific conclusion that the drawing was probably from the person who'd abducted Callum.

"Fine," Celia replied with a shade of worry. "You know, I think if we hadn't turned up late yesterday. Callum wouldn't be missing."

"You can't think like that," said Tannaz. "You didn't know this would happen."

Savage nodded his head in agreement. "Tannaz is right. If you think like that, I'm also to blame. Callum usually plays football in my garden after school, but he didn't on Friday. If I'd invited him in instead of waiting for a delivery he'd still be here."

Celia fell silent, sniffed back a tear. She took a tentative sip of tea then put the cup down. "I suppose you're right."

Savage gripped her shoulder reassuringly. "Don't worry, Celia. We'll find him."

"Er, Savage," Tannaz said, looking out the window, "Coppers are leaving."

Savage leapt to his feet. "Sorry to rush out on you. Me and Tannaz are just going to ask the police a few questions. Stay here if you like."

"Thanks, but I'll go next door. Take this shopping round to them. Doubt Frank's got anything remotely edible in his flat."

Savage smiled. "Of course. Come on Tannaz."

Out on the road, the two detectives stood talking beside a forgettable four-door sedan, no doubt discussing what they'd just learnt from Frank and Julie. The female detective held Callum's drawing in one hand, now secured in a proper police evidence bag. They went silent as soon as Savage and Tannaz appeared, the older of the two coppers already visibly irritated at the sight of two members of the public approaching them.

"Hi," said Savage, holding out his hand for a shake. The older copper didn't reciprocate. "I'm John Savage and this is Tannaz. I'm Frank's neighbour. Just wanted to know if there was any news about Callum."

Up close, Savage could see the guy's eyes were bloodshot and watery, as if they'd just been poked. Blackened semi-circles hung underneath them. He looked on the edge, held together by caffeine, bad tailoring and bitterness. He smiled. Not a genuine smile. More of a politician's smile. Forced and rehearsed because he'd probably been to a training seminar that told him to do that when engaging with the public to show empathy. Obviously, they'd warned against shaking hands. Too friendly. Or maybe he didn't like the look of Savage. "I'm afraid, I'm not at liberty to discuss cases with the public." He spoke in a gravelly voice. Ex-smoker maybe, which would explain why he looked so cantankerous. Tannaz always looked like that when she'd run out of cigarettes. "I'm DCI Sutcliffe and this is DI Roberts."

DI Roberts' hand automatically shot out to shake both John and Tannaz's. Sutcliffe gave DI Roberts a disapproving look, as if she'd made him look bad. Roberts was just being polite; an impulsive British knee-jerk reaction, like saying sorry when someone's bumped into you. By the look on Sutcliffe's face he didn't see it that way. He'd bollock her for that later. *If I don't shake their hands, you don't shake their hands. We're not here to make friends.*

"You're a DCI?" said Savage. "Then it must be serious. More than a missing-persons case now."

"As I said, I'm not at liberty to discuss cases with the public." Again, he flashed a fake grin that was about as convincing as a shark with a smiley emoji pasted on its face.

"You said you're Callum Leighton's neighbour." DI Roberts spoke for the first time. She sounded calm and intelligent. Sutcliffe must hate that, thought Savage. "Could I ask, when was the last time you saw him?"

"I think it was Thursday. He came round my house after school to play football in the garden."

"Really?" said Sutcliffe. "What's wrong with his own garden?"

"Have you seen Frank's garden? It's not what you'd call spacious." Savage was being diplomatic. The garden was a tip.

"That happen a lot?" asked Sutcliffe.

"What?" Savage replied.

"Having Callum in your flat."

Savage really wanted to say it happened all the time because his dad was an idiot and often locked him out. "Yeah, I sort of look after him when Frank's not around."

"Like a friendly uncle?" Sutcliffe said it as a question but he really meant it as a statement, laced with the tiniest hint of sarcasm. Savage could see where this line of questioning was going. "And what do you do together in your flat?"

"I just told you, play football in the garden."

"Okay, no need to be defensive Mr Savage."

"I wasn't. Just stating a fact. A fact that I told you earlier."

"Did you now?"

"Yes, he did. About ten seconds ago." Tannaz spat out each word with venom.

"And who are you?"

"I'm Tannaz. He told you that as well. Are you sure you're a detective?"

Savage put a calming hand on Tannaz's arm.

Sutcliffe eyed Savage's hand on Tannaz's arm, then grinned. This time it was genuine. "She's a bit young for you, isn't she?" he said.

Roberts rolled her eyes. Attempted to salvage the conversation. "I think what my colleague means is to ask what is your relationship with each other."

"We're friends."

"Isn't that interesting," Sutcliffe said, smugly. "What's the age gap between you two? She's young enough to be your daughter wouldn't you say, Mr Savage?"

"Yes, she is. She's almost the same age as my daughter."

"And where is your daughter?" Sutcliffe asked, smirking.

"In the ground. Buried. She died. Blown up by a roadside bomb in Afghanistan."

The smirk on Sutcliffe's face vanished. "What regiment was she?" Sutcliffe asked, testing him. Making sure his story was true and not fabricated on the spot to cause him embarrassment. Simplest way coppers did that was to ask for more details. Lying on the spot was easy, making up details was not.

"Royal Engineers," Savage answered without hesitation. Sutcliffe didn't offer his condolences. Savage didn't give him time. "You're from the Major Crime Unit, aren't you? That means this is a kidnapping case."

Sutcliffe feigned shock. "Whatever gave you that idea?"

Savage shrugged. "Simple bit of reason and deduction. And there's a clue in the name Major Crime. You only show up for the serious stuff. Murders, kidnappings, fraud, rape. And this isn't fraud, rape or murder—at least, I hope not. So it must be a kidnapping. Possibly part of an ongoing case, judging by how quickly you responded when that picture landed on their doorstep. I mean, feel free to correct me if I'm wrong."

Sutcliffe's face darkened. He closed the gap between him and Savage, and with a firmer tone he said, "I meet people like you all the time. Jumping to conclusions. Think you can do our jobs better than we can. Well-meaning amateurs. Seen a few episodes of

Luther or *CSI*, have we? Read some Val McDermid novels. Thing is, people like you haven't got the knowledge or the stomach for it. Never seen a dead body in your life."

Tannaz snorted out a laugh.

"What's so funny?" Sutcliffe asked.

Normally Savage hated revealing anything about his military past. Kept it firmly under wraps. And he couldn't stand guys that wanted to have pissing competitions with him. It was childish and immature; the sign of a small, underdeveloped mind. But he would make an exception for Sutcliffe. The guy had an attitude problem and had stepped over the line. He'd insinuated that Savage was in some mucky relationship with Tannaz and had invited Callum into his house for nefarious reasons. So instead of holding up his hand to silence Tannaz, he stood back and let her give it to Sutcliffe. With both barrels.

Tannaz became serious. Fixed the nasty old copper with a couple of eyes like Molotov cocktails. "Do you know who you're talking to?"

Sutcliffe didn't answer.

"This is John Savage. Used to be a captain in the SAS. He's seen more dead bodies than you've got unpopped blackheads on your fat ugly nose. He's been in the worse places imaginable. Fought his way out of hellholes, outnumbered, outgunned. Been tortured. Escaped an Iraqi prison. Walked across the desert without food or water. Hunted down Serbian war criminals in the Balkans. And you think he's just some well-meaning amateur."

Sutcliffe stared at Tannaz, emotionless. "We'll see," he said, then turned and got in the car. Before he shut the door he added, "We'll be back to take a statement from you both. Don't go anywhere. Roberts! Get in the car."

The DI turned on her heel to follow Sutcliffe then turned back. Handed Tannaz her card. "If you think of anything that could help us find Callum, my number's on there."

Tannaz took the card. They watched the two policemen drive away.

Savage elbowed Tannaz gently. "Your speech. Very touching."

"That burn-out had it coming, talking to you like that."

"He did have good hair, though."

"That prick insulted you and all you're thinking about is his hair."

"Well, I do tend to notice hair, seeing I've got about as much of it as Homer Simpson."

"Don't be getting all jealous on me now. You're rocking that receding hairline look."

"I didn't know it was possible to rock it, but thank you. Seriously though, I was a bit stupid. I allowed him to get under my skin when I should've been buttering him up."

"Why did you want to do that?"

"To get some info out of him about the case. Something we could go on. I suppose we could talk to Frank and Julie, see if those two detectives revealed anything. But I really want to give them a bit of space at the moment. Things will be very raw for them. Wouldn't be good to go in firing questions at them."

"I can get us plenty of info," said Tannaz.

"How will you do that?"

"She's just given me the keys to the kingdom," Tannaz said, holding up Roberts' business card.

CHAPTER 10

THE ARRAY OF LAPTOPS STILL sat on Savage's dining table like the skyline of a miniature city, minus the one Tannaz had thrown against the wall. Tannaz had gathered up all the pieces and stuck them in a carrier bag to take home and reuse in another laptop. She took a seat in front of the remaining computers and stuck DI Roberts' card in the corner of one of the screens with Blu Tac. She cracked her knuckles and prepared to hack Roberts' mobile phone, email and anything else she could get into without being detected.

"Right, DI Roberts," she said. "Let's find out what you know."

Tannaz's fingers danced across the buttons of one laptop, then she'd shift over and do the same on the laptop next to it, reams of code appearing before her eyes. She reminded Savage of a prog-rock keyboardist, playing a stack of instruments at once.

"Is there anything I can do?" he asked.

"Bring me coffee. Lots of it."

By late Saturday evening, Tannaz had extracted everything about the case that Roberts had ever sent or received by email or text, including voicemail. The two of them began the gargantuan task of sifting through the mountain of information, collating and classifying everything Tannaz had obtained. Sitting side by side, a laptop each, they split the data between them and carefully analysed each message, stripping it of content. Anything irrelevant got deleted. The rest they filed, arranging in date order so they could read back through it chronologically, building up a picture of what had happened. They worked through the night and into the morning, never stopping, fuelled by tea and coffee and biscuits, with

Savage Children

Tannaz nipping out the back for a cigarette every now and then. By Sunday lunchtime Savage's lounge stank of Tannaz's nicotine breath and stale coffee. A small price to pay, seeing as now they knew what Roberts knew, as far as everything that had been communicated electronically was concerned. Of course, the information was patchy. Like Swiss cheese there were plenty of holes in it, but it gave them more than enough to go on.

They gleaned the following facts: Four children, including Callum, had been abducted by someone the police had dubbed the "Archangel", because he or she made the victims draw a picture of themselves as an angel, which was dropped through the parents' letterbox a day or two after the abduction. No bodies had turned up yet. All the victims were ten years old and had disappeared in parks in south London near to where they lived. And like Callum, CCTV had yielded nothing. They'd seemed to just vanish.

First victim: Leo Bright. Disappeared from a park in Clapham on April 18th.

Second victim: Olive Foley. Disappeared from a park in Forest Hill on May 6th.

Third victim: Sally Woodrow. Disappeared from a park in Tooting Bec on May 22nd.

The fourth victim was Callum Leighton, who they already knew had been taken from his local park in Peckham on Friday June 7th. That made two boys and two girls so far. One child abducted roughly every two weeks since April 18th. Was that relevant? A timetable, perhaps, or just the amount of time it took this evil devil to plan his next abduction. Or was it coincidence? Was the guy an opportunist, seizing the chance to snatch a kid whenever it presented itself? All the kids had disappeared on weekdays, after approximately four o'clock in the afternoon, presumably having gone up to their local park after school. None of them had been wearing school uniform.

Tannaz pulled up pictures of all the missing children, including Callum, and put them on a screen to the left of her. Then she opened a map of London and stuck virtual pins on the locations of all the abductions. Joined up they made the shape of a distorted parallelogram, each side about four miles long, give or take a mile.

Savage tried to remember the formula for working out the area of a parallelogram. Was it the same as calculating the area of a rectangle? Or did he need to do something fancy with the angles? He couldn't remember. Tannaz with her smarts came to his aid.

"That's a rough parallelogram," she said. "Sides about four miles long. Area of a parallelogram is base times height. Estimating the height as three miles, that's an area of twelve square miles."

"Did you say CCTV didn't yield anything."

"That's what all of Roberts' texts said."

"Can you get hold of the footage so we can have a look?"

"Already on it." Tannaz began hacking, searching local-authority systems. "Damn it," she said. "Files have gone. Police have confiscated them as evidence."

"That's a setback."

"For anyone else. Not for us. Nothing ever gets truly deleted, remember? I'll get it, somehow."

An hour later Tannaz had the CCTV camera footage of the other three missing children. Plus Callum's.

First, they watched the footage related to Leo Bright. They saw a small park in Clapham with two entrances; CCTV cameras overlooking both. Tannaz had both camera feeds up on a split screen so they could watch them simultaneously. She scrolled through the footage carefully. Into the frame of the left-hand screen came a ten-year-old boy, Leo Bright, entering the park. Stripy T-shirt, unkempt curly hair and not a care in the world. Savage wished he could somehow reach into the screen and stop him going into the park. Prevent the horrible act that was about to befall him.

Tannaz fast-forwarded the footage on both screens. Seconds, then minutes, then hours. Just like Callum, Leo Bright never emerged. He never left the park.

"Maybe he got out another way," said Tannaz.

"Park has a high fence running around it," Savage replied. "And it's locked at night, presumably to stop kids hanging out there, getting up to no good. But there's always the possibility he got over the fence, which is why CCTV at both entrances didn't capture him. Any CCTV cameras on the adjacent roads?"

"There are loads around that area. There's no way he could've left that park without one of them picking him up." Tannaz hacked away, got more illegal footage of the surrounding streets. They scrutinised every second of it, searching for signs of Leo and his abductor. Nothing. They checked and rechecked it. Leo Bright had vanished into thin air.

Next, they watched the footage of Olive Foley going into a park in Forest Hill. A small, compact area of green in a densely built-up area, there was only one way in and out, and only a single camera pointed at the entrance. Like Callum and Leo, the doomed little girl went in but never came out. Tannaz found another single camera on the road outside belonging to a newsagent. She hacked into it for any signs of Olive passing by after she'd gone in the park. Nothing.

Lastly, they watched Sally Woodrow walk into a park in Tooting Bec, and just like all the others, never walk out.

They watched all three sets of footage back again, hours either side of the time each child disappeared, searching for signs or clues to what had happened. They analysed the footage to see if the gang who had followed Callum into the park had been in the vicinity, or the guy in the red Adidas top. No one suspicious appeared before their eyes, just random people going in and out of each park. Tannaz made notes of all of them, and just like Callum's video she accounted for all of them; everyone who went in came back out again—without an abducted child.

"They just vanished into thin air," said Tannaz.

"Send the footage to your friend. Get him to check it for manipulation."

"On it."

Savage was being thorough. He already knew what Tannaz's friend would say. He'd come back with a flat "no". The police techies would have already checked it; they'd intercepted a text to Roberts' phone that had told them as much. Savage had a feeling every avenue they tried would just be going over old ground that the police had trod and dismissed. They were doubling up. Wasting time.

"I've found something else. A text from the forensics lab," said

Tannaz. "It reads, 'Re: Leo Bright drawing. Positive for *Traces of fentanyl*.' What's fentanyl?"

"It replaced morphine on the battlefield as a painkiller."

Tannaz googled it. Up popped pages and pages of hits. She clicked on the one at the top and began reading. "Fentanyl is a powerful opiate, similar to morphine except a hundred times more powerful. Effects on the brain include extreme happiness, drowsiness and sometimes unconsciousness."

"Ideal for keeping a child calm and sedated," Savage added.

"Look at this." Tannaz pulled up images showing the different forms of fentanyl, one of which was a strange-shaped lollipop on a plastic stick.

"Jeez," said Savage. "It's almost a cliché. This Archangel's offering kids sweets in a park."

"Except these sweets make them compliant. Hell of a lot easier to abduct that way. Like spiking someone's drink with Rohypnol." Tannaz went back through the information they'd gathered. "Traces of fentanyl on all three drawings. Bet Callum's will come back positive too."

"This is a sick individual, that's for sure. Plying them with a sedative shaped like a lolly, then making them draw pictures of themselves as angels to give to their parents. Still doesn't explain how he gets them out of a park unseen."

"Guy's a psycho and some sort of David Blaine."

"In the emails and texts, have you come across any profiles the cops have come up with?"

Tannaz shook her head. "Nah, nothing."

"Me neither. Shame. Might be helpful if we had an idea about the guy's personality, background."

"Guy's got a thing for angels. Religion would seem an obvious one. Someone with strong beliefs."

"Could you check the backgrounds of each family? See if they were religious."

"Sure." Tannaz began hacking, mostly the social-media accounts of the children's parents.

"I'll make more drinks." Savage disappeared into the kitchen. By the time he returned Tannaz had completed her search.

"Okay, so I've left the Leightons out of this. I'm assuming Frank's not a churchgoer," said Tannaz.

"Safe assumption," Savage replied. "Neither is Julie."

"Same with Leo Bright's family and Sally Woodrow's. They don't show any evidence of having religious beliefs. Which might point to Archangel having some kind of punishing-the-unbeliever angle. However, Olive Foley's family are regular churchgoers, members of St Stephen's church in Forest Hill and Olive goes to a church school."

"Okay, what about the art angle? Callum's good at art. What about the other three kids?"

Tannaz got busy, head down hacking into school records. She came up frowning. "No good. Callum may be A-grade but Olive Foley is average and the other two are below average."

"That's a blow," said Savage, sighing deeply. "Thought there might be a connection there. What about someone in healthcare? I mean, they'd need access to pharmaceuticals to get their hands on fentanyl."

Tannaz did a Google search and pulled up some more pages. "Don't need to be in healthcare. Fentanyl can be bought on the street real easy." She showed him an online article featuring a picture of the singer Prince and read the annotation below it. "Prince had extremely high levels of fentanyl in his blood when he died, according to the toxicology report."

"And this guy's giving it to children."

"We need to catch him, Savage."

"Too right."

"What's the next step? How do we use this information?"

"Not sure." Savage sat back, blew out through his teeth.

"What about the police?" asked Tannaz. "What will that asshole Sutcliffe and his little sidekick Roberts be doing right now?"

"Well, Callum's a new victim, which will give them loads of legwork to do. Knocking on doors, interviewing everyone in this street, and the next street and the one after that."

"Sounds tedious. And Sutcliffe and Roberts will do that?"

Savage shook his head. "Nah, they'll have a big team of uniforms doing the grunt work. It's massively time-consuming but that's how the police catch people; collecting tons and tons of data until something stands out. Everyone even remotely connected with Callum will be questioned. Us included. Every car that drove through this neighbourhood on that day they'll trace with ANPR cameras, identify the drivers, do PNC checks."

"That's the police database, right?"

"Yep. They'll check everyone who was in the vicinity at the time for any previous convictions. If they don't like the look of them, they'll haul them in. The park up the road is probably out of bounds too, taped off, being fingertip-searched. Which will attract the attention of the media. Actually, have a quick search online, see if there're any news reports on the abductions. This'd be a big story for them. I'd love to know how a media-unfriendly character like Sutcliffe is handling the press."

Tannaz did a quick search.

"Nothing," she said.

"Nothing?" Savage replied. "Really? You sure? Nothing gets the attention of the press like a police fingertip-search."

"Oh, wait, hold on. Tiny piece about a knife attack in a park in Bushey Hill Road, Peckham. That's our park, right?"

"Ah," said Savage. "Sutcliffe's fobbed them off. Sold them a story about a knife attack. This city's got knife crime coming out of its ears. No story there. Best way to get the press to lose interest."

"Should we tell the press what we know? We could tell them the real story."

"Not a good idea. Would only hamper things. Plus, think what it would do to Julie. Press would be camped outside, hounding her. Wouldn't wish that on anyone."

"So what should we be doing? Interviewing everyone, like the police are?"

Savage stood up and stretched his back, making a few joints pop. Through a cavernous yawn he said, "No point. For a start, their gang is much bigger than ours, we won't even make a dent in the hundreds, maybe thousands of people they need to trace. Even with your skills, it'd be like Sean Locke says, turning up after an earthquake with dustpan and brush. More importantly, though, I doubt they'll find anything."

"What makes you say that?"

"They've been through this whole process before, with the three other victims. Hasn't uncovered anything. Still haven't caught the guy. This asshole has outsmarted them each time. Evaded CCTV. Unless he makes a really big mistake, he's not going to leave behind any clue or lead to follow. I think that's why Sutcliffe was acting like such a prick. Looked ready to pop. I bet it's because he's under pressure from above, and he's got nothing to show for weeks of work. No leads. Only thing in his favour is the whole thing hasn't gone public, causing him even more embarrassment."

"So what do we do?"

Savage sat back down, pulled up the picture of Callum's angel drawing on his phone that he'd taken before Frank and Julie handed it over to the police. "This picture is annoying me."

"Annoying you? I think it's chilling."

"Screams serial killer, doesn't it?"

"Damn right. What's your point?"

"Seems like the guy's trying a bit too hard. Bit over the top. Flashing serial-killer credentials in our faces."

Tannaz fished through her biker jacket and popped an unlit cigarette in the corner of her mouth, ready to light when she went outside. "Again, what's your point?" The cigarette flipped up and down as she spoke.

"Well, if I were a serial killer, which I'm not by the way."

"Reassuring. Go on."

"I've often thought it'd be really easy to send the police on a wild goose chase. Do something divisive like this, while covering up the real reason for your killing."

"But doesn't a serial killer have a compulsion to kill? Like scratching an itch. They get no peace until they kill."

"Yes, exactly. But as far as I understand it, it's more to do with why they kill and whom, or perhaps the way they kill. Making victims draw a picture of an angel and sending it to their parents has nothing to do with that. It seems over the top. Melodramatic. Almost like the killer is saying, 'Look I'm a serial killer and my motivation is something to do with art or religion or both.' Then the police go scuttling off, following their procedure, thinking they're looking for a religious or artistic killer. Pretty good way of getting them to waste their time while it's really hiding the true reason this guy's killing."

"We don't know if it's a serial killer yet. No bodies have turned up."

"Okay, let's hope it stays that way. Serial abductor, then."

"So how do we approach this?"

"Look for other connections."

Tannaz got back on her laptop. "That, I can do. Tell me some things about Callum. What's he into?"

"Average kid, really. Likes superhero movies. Cars. Good at football. Very good, in fact. Plays for a local under-12s club. Try sports. See if the other three are athletic at all."

Tannaz got busy hacking. She already had access to their school reports and came back with a result immediately. "Yep, there's a connection alright. The other three are also good at sports. Olive Foley's a gymnast. Leo Bright is a good swimmer. And Sally Woodrow is also good at football. Let's see if they're members of clubs like Callum."

Minutes later, Tannaz turned to Savage and grinned impishly. "All four kids are members of a sports club."

"Do the clubs have websites?"

Tannaz had the homepages of the four junior sports clubs each child belonged to up on her screen. Two football clubs, a swimming club, and a gymnastics club. All of them were in south London. Savage got up the same four pages on his laptop.

"What are looking for?" asked Tannaz.

"Try going into the gallery pages. Check the photos. I'll take the gymnastics and swimming club. You take the two football clubs."

A sea of amateur photographs, posted by proud parents, littered the screens of both laptops. Action shots of their sons and daughters at matches and swimming galas and gymnastic competitions, interspersed with them holding up trophies and medals, their hair plastered down with sweat or chlorinated water.

After about the tenth page of images, Savage announced, "I think I've found our guy."

CHAPTER 11

Tannaz scooched over so she could get a closer look at Savage's screen. He had the gymnastic club's gallery page side by side with the swimming club's. He enlarged two images from both.

"Ignore the kids in the shot," he said. "Look at the crowd behind. This guy's in both." He pointed to a rather portly Asian man standing in a sports hall, his spectacled eyes fixed on a young girl in a sequinned leotard going through her floor routine. Then he moved the cursor across to another web page of the swimming club Leo Bright belonged to. Savage clicked on a picture of a line of young male swimmers, poised and ready to dive in off the starting blocks at a swimming gala. In one corner of the picture stood the same man. Savage enlarged the image, focusing on him alone. He wore the same glasses and polo shirt in both shots.

"Maybe he's a parent with kids in both the gymnastic and swimming clubs," Tannaz suggested.

"Does he appear in any of the shots of the football clubs?"

Tannaz shifted over to her screen and began scrolling back through the shots of both football clubs simultaneously, carefully scrutinising everyone in each photo. After several minutes she shouted, "Bingo!" and pointed at the overweight man standing on the sidelines at a football match.

"There he is again." Tannaz's hand shot out, pointing at the screen. It was an image of Callum, going in for a sliding tackle. Standing on the edge of the photo, smiling at him, stood the same man in the same glasses and polo shirt. Tannaz scrolled further down the pages of each football club. Sporadically, the man appeared again, not many times, but enough.

"I think we've got a solid lead," said Tannaz. She held her hand up for a high five. Savage slapped it a little half-heartedly. Tannaz looked at him, puzzled. "Come on, Savage. This is good, isn't it?"

"Yeah. I'm just a little cynical."

"Why?"

"It's taken us a matter of minutes to find this guy. Surely the police would have discovered this connection. I mean, it's not exactly hidden."

"Like you said, the whole thing with the drawings could be a smokescreen. Send the cops the wrong way, while he's hiding in plain sight. Besides, we still need to follow through and identify him. Maybe we get a screen grab of this guy and ask Frank or Julie. Surely they must go and watch Callum play football."

"Okay, let's check," said Savage. He made a screen grab of the best image he could find and transferred it to his and Tannaz's phones, then got up, ready go next door.

He sat down again almost immediately. "You know, I don't think that's such a good idea."

"Why not?"

"I'm starting to realise why coppers like Sutcliffe hold back information about a case. What if we show them this picture and the guy's completely innocent, and Frank goes off on one and decides to take matters into his own hands... Or what if it turns out to be a dead end? I don't want to get their hopes up. We need to find another way of ID-ing him. What about facial recognition?"

"Images aren't sharp enough. I've got a better idea," said Tannaz. "And that jacket he's wearing is going to help us." She pointed to an image of the Asian guy at a football match, one of the few shots where he wasn't in a polo shirt. Instead he wore a large, oversized bomber jacket in distressed brown leather.

On her screen she found the contact details of Leo Bright's swimming club. She called the mobile number of the club's chairman. He answered after two rings. "Oh, good afternoon," said Tannaz. "This is Manchester Aquatics Centre. We think someone in your club may have left a rather expensive leather jacket behind after the swimming gala a couple of weeks ago. It's a brown bomber jacket, distressed leather, fleecy collar. Think it may have belonged to an Asian gentleman."

"Ah, yes, that would be our physio, Vikram." The chairman of the club was brusque and well-spoken.

"Your physio?"

"Yes, that's right."

"Oh, sorry. I've never heard of a youth swimming club having a physio." Tannaz raised her eyebrows at Savage, questioningly. He shrugged back.

"Yes, we're very lucky."

"Can I just ask..."

"Very sorry but I'm in a bit of a rush. Do you need me to call him?"

"No," said Tannaz. "That's okay. We can do it if you give us his number."

"I'm afraid we can't give out the contact details of anyone associated with the club."

"No, no of course not."

The line went quiet then the chairman said, "Tell you what. How about you address it to me, care of our local pool in Greenwich. I'll make sure it gets back to him."

"Yes, that sounds good." Tannaz didn't bother taking down the address, just played along with it then hung up. "This is too easy. Okay, Vikram the physio. Let's find out who you are." Tannaz scoured the Internet for a London physio named Vikram. Nothing came up. "That's weird. A big zero."

"Not really," said Savage. "If he is a suspect and is hanging around junior sports clubs looking to abduct kids, I doubt he'd use his real name. He's probably not a real physio. Pity that club chairman didn't give us his last name, although that's probably false too. What about trying some different search combinations, like Vikram, physio, football or Vikram, physio, swimming."

Tannaz got onto it.

Again nothing.

Savage Children

She pushed her fingers through her black curls. "This guy's suddenly looking very suspicious. I'm starting to think you're right. The physio thing is a front to get in with junior sports clubs. Let me try something else."

She typed in: "Vikram sports". A search page popped up with a positive hit. The home page of a freelance sports-performance video analyst called Vikram Murthy. She clicked on it, and there was their suspect smiling out from the top of a home page in a highly posed head-and-shoulders shot, totally corporate, apart from the fact he was still dressed in a brandless polo shirt. Like most people's profile shots, vanity had got the better of him and he'd used one of himself from years ago, when he was younger and thinner.

"What's a sports-performance video analyst?" asked Tannaz.

"I guess it's someone who uses video to analyse sports performance."

"Really?" Tannaz said, her voice thickly laden with sarcasm. "That's just the same words rearranged."

"You're so easy to wind up. I have no idea."

"Idiot."

Tannaz went back to her screen and clicked on the *About me* button and began reading. "With my in-depth knowledge of video, editing, tracking hardware and software, I can help improve your performance in virtually any sport. Through both notational and motion analysis, I can give the team or the individual the edge blah, blah, blah..." She scrolled down the page past all the sales waffle. There was a shot of an altogether more slender, leaner and healthier Vikram Murthy on a running track. She continued reading from the blurb. "I used to be a middle-distance runner and know the demands placed on an athlete to perform... In my spare time I work with local junior sports clubs offering my skills as a physio free of charge at the weekends."

"That's why we couldn't find him as a physio," said Savage. "He just does it voluntarily, a little sideline. But his day job is video analytics. Handy for editing himself out of any CCTV footage that happened to catch him snatching a kid. I think we've found our man."

Tannaz got a ping on her mobile phone. Checked her messages. Looked doubtful.

"What's wrong? This is a breakthrough," said Savage.

"Got a text from my video expert. Big negative on the CCTV footage of the other kids. He says nothing's been tampered with."

"Oh. How good is your guy?"

"The best. If it'd been manipulated, he'd have spotted it."

"Okay. Well, I still think we need to pay this Vikram a visit."

"Definitely."

Several clicks later and Tannaz had found the guy's address in Balham, just a handful of miles away.

Savage's little van headed past Balham's local Waitrose, busy with Sunday afternoon shoppers stocking up on nice food for the week ahead. A sure-fire sign of the town's affluence, Waitrose was a supermarket that, like other supermarkets, sold an essential range for people on a budget, except their classification of essential was not milk, bread and eggs, but vermicelli nests, artichoke hearts and Brussels pâté.

"Balham's alright," remarked Tannaz. "Didn't Adele go to school here?"

"I have no idea. Great singer, though."

A few turns off the high street and they were on a suburban road lined with handsome and expensive Victorian houses. Each one had been immaculately refurbished. Period features brought back to life in all their glory; original tiled pathways and ornate, curly wooden eaves painted crisp white and roofs of inky Welsh slate. Vikram Murthy lived off this posh road, in something altogether more vulgar. A garden-grabbed cul-de-sac, where the back gardens of three homes had been sacrificed to squish in a new development of four modern tiny townhouses shunted together with barely enough room between them to slot a tobacco rolling paper. The thin modern houses looked odd, like they had no right to be there, as if they were squatting. Thankfully garden grabbing had now been halted by most local councils.

Savage Children

Tannaz and Savage parked the VW out on the road and walked up to the first house in the cul-de-sac, Vikram Murthy's home, and pressed the button on the intercom. A CCTV camera stared down at them impassively. Shiny and unweathered, it looked recently installed. The place was clean and well-maintained, sills recently wiped down and even the Yale lock in the door had been buffed to a shine. First impressions: Vikram Murthy ran a tight ship.

"What do you want?" through the speaker came a harsh Indian voice, clipped and abrupt.

"Mr Vikram Murthy," said Savage. "We'd like to talk to you about the physio work you do."

"Are you the police?" asked the voice.

Savage and Tannaz exchanged confused glances. "No," said Savage. "We're looking for…"

"Then go away. Leave me alone." The speaker crackled then went dead. Savage pressed the buzzer several times but Vikram Murthy didn't answer.

"Looks like he's not talking. What do we do now?" Tannaz and Savage walked back to the van out on the road, pausing by its side.

"Set up an OP and wait for him to come out."

"OP is observation post."

"Correct. We'll sit in the van, move it a little further down the road, so we can keep an eye on his house, but he can't see us."

"It could be ages before he comes out."

"I'll nip home, stock up on provisions and come back. You wait here. Find somewhere inconspicuous you can keep an eye on him, play on your phone or something. Call me if he comes out. Follow him if he does but don't engage until I come back. You want anything?"

"Nah, I'm good."

"You sure. We could be a while."

"You could get me another pack of Marlboros."

"I'm not buying you cigarettes so you can kill yourself, I like you too much."

"Aw, sweet. Honestly. I'll be fine. Still got a few smokes left."

When Savage returned, he found Tannaz sitting on a bench, one hand in her pocket, phone in the other, cigarette wedged between her lips. As he pulled up beside her in the van, she flicked away the cigarette and got in.

"Anything?" said Savage.

"Nothing. Guy hasn't moved a muscle."

Savage drove a little way down the road and parked up. From their position, they could see the front door of Vikram Murthy's house in the near distance. Savage reached around his seat and lifted over a rucksack from the back of the van. "I just grabbed a load of food from the flat, help yourself. I got biscuits, some chocolate, a few crusty cheese rolls..."

"I'm good thanks."

"Well, it could be a long time we're waiting. Got to keep your energy up." Savage delved into the backpack and pulled out a flask. Not the trendy stainless-steel type that modern hikers used, but an old-school plastic one in avocado green with a large yellow screw-in cup on the top. A relic from the late seventies, covered in dirty scratches like war scars.

"What the hell is that?"

"A flask."

"I can see that."

"This big fella can hold twenty cups. Been with me through thick and thin, this has," Savage proudly announced.

"Where you get it from, a second-hand store?"

"Hatfield Woolco."

"Woolco? What the hell's a Woolco?" Tannaz sneered.

"Like Woolworth's only bigger. You remember Woolworth's?"

"Vaguely. Went in there once. Weird place. Sold wood glue, CDs and loose sweets."

"That's the one. Got it from Woolco's in 1979. It's not there anymore." Savage unscrewed the yellow cup and poured himself a cup of strong rust-coloured tea. "Nothing better than tea from a flask. Especially one as old as this, gives it a nice tang. Like whisky from an aged oak barrel."

"You are such a nerd."

"Hey, don't disrespect a man and his flask." Savage waved it in front of her. "Or I won't let you have any."

"Yuk, no thanks."

Hours drifted by and still Vikram Murthy didn't emerge from his house. It was now early evening. The sun had dipped in the sky and the temperature dropped. The little cab of the VW became cold and claustrophobic.

"My phone's dead," said Tannaz. "Do you have a charger?"

"I don't I'm afraid."

"Can I use your phone? I'm bored."

"Nope. I don't want your Internet history showing up on it."

"I can get rid of that."

"I'm sure you can, but I'd rather not. Besides, I'm running low too."

"Can't we come back tomorrow? This is boring."

"That's the nature of surveillance, I'm afraid. Wait and watch. Thing is, we know he's in there. If we leave now and he takes off somewhere, we could've lost our one and only suspect."

In front of them, several little girls emerged from a house in pretty party dresses, carrying goody bags in one hand and plastic fairy wands in the other. The end of a birthday party. Followed by their well-dressed yummy mummies and dishy daddies, they skipped along the pavement and clambered into the backs of expensive SUVs.

"This is such a nice neighbourhood," Tannaz remarked.

"Very pleasant." Savage unscrewed the cup from the top of his flask and poured out another steaming hot cup of strong tea. Tannaz licked her lips. "Can I have some of that?"

Savage took a long gulp and pushed out a long and contented "Ah."

"Well, can I have some?" Tannaz asked.

"Nope."

"Why not?"

"You made fun of my flask earlier, called me a nerd."

"I was only joking."

Savage turned to her. "Never joke about another man's tea. Almost as bad as insulting their wife or football team."

"Okay, fine. Come on. Let's have a cup."

"No."

"You're kidding me."

"Haters don't get tea."

"Oh, come on, Savage."

"No. Don't take the piss out of my flask and then expect me to give you some."

Tannaz folded her arms and thrust her back into her seat, sulking. Savage passed the tea to her. She took a sip. "Oh, urgh," she said, screwing her face up. "That is disgusting. Tastes like your socks have been stewing in it." She handed it back.

Savage smiled. "If it doesn't leave a layer of brown in the cup then you're not making it right."

Tannaz began to fidget and then whined, "I'm still bored."

"Okay. Here's an interesting fact. I've been reading up on Roman history and did you know the Romans invented concrete?"

"You're winding me up. Wasn't concrete invented in the forties?"

"Nope. Romans invented it, except they called it pozzolana. Well, technically the Greeks discovered it, but it was the Romans that used it to make concrete. Clever buggers, weren't they?"

Tannaz yawned.

"Am I boring you?"

"No, I'm just a high-stimulation kind of person. I need my energy levels kept up otherwise I crash."

"Have you run out of cigarettes?"

"Yes, but that's got nothing to do with it."

Savage sniggered sarcastically. "And you haven't had coffee for about two hours."

"I had some of that drain cleaner you call tea."

"How about we play a game?"

Tannaz rolled her eyes. "Is this the bit where you tell me about your childhood and how you had to make your own entertainment."

"How old do you think I am? I'm not Victorian."

"What's the game?"
"Monkey Tennis?"
"What in all my days is Monkey Tennis?"
"You've seen Alan Partridge."
"No."
"You know of Alan Partridge."
"Yes."
"Well in one episode he's so desperate to get back on TV he comes up with all these awful ideas for TV shows, one of which is called Monkey Tennis."
"So what's the game?"
"We take it in turns inventing really bad TV shows."
"Sounds interesting. I'll go first." Tannaz thought for a moment, studying the interior of the cab, hoping inspiration would jump out at her. There wasn't much to see. "I can't think of anything."
"Okay," said Savage. "I've got one. A TV cop show, like *Miami Vice* but it's set in the Austrian Alps called *Edel Vice*."
Tannaz didn't react, didn't laugh, just looked straight ahead through the windscreen.
Savage continued, "You know, like 'Edelweiss' from the *Sound of Music* but the *weiss* bit is spelt..."
"Yeah, it's alright, I get it."
Savage sounded disappointed. "I thought that was a good one."
"Yeah, it is. I'm just thinking." Tannaz went quiet then said, "Hey, in one episode, they could hunt down a murderer from Switzerland called the Toblerone killer who bludgeons victims to death with large bars of triangular chocolate."
Savage laughed. "That's genius. We should send that idea to the BBC. Oh, I've got a tagline for the show: 'Von Trapping the bad guys'."
Tannaz sniggered. "Hey, I got one. What about a game show called *Running in Slippers*, you know the ones that always slip off your feet. That would be a laugh."
"That's a good one. Actually, that's given me another idea. What about *Drag Race*, where drag queens have running races in full get up, stilettos and everything."

"Er *Drag Race* is already a thing."

"What? Really? How come I haven't seen it?"

"Dunno, I guess you're not their demographic."

A noise came from behind the van. Not nice noises, but the noises of men. Men who'd been spending the whole day drinking. As they came round the front of the van, Savage counted four men attempting and failing to walk in a straight line, their words slurring.

"And they're certainly not the Balham demographic," said Savage. "They look up to no good."

The four men crossed the road. Apart from wobbling off course now and again, they headed for the house of Vikram Murthy. One of them carried a plastic bag by his side. In the dim light, Savage recognised the unmistakable ape-like gait of a south London thug who always seemed to cross his path. That walk. Hunched over as if the thickness of his skull was so dense it threatened to topple him forward. Shoulders as wide as a bridge and IQ as small as a gnat's. Tendency for violence, always bubbling below the surface.

Minchie.

CHAPTER 12

"Is that who I think it is?" asked Tannaz.

"Yep," said Savage. "That's definitely Minchie. And wherever Minchie is you can be sure there's trouble."

As Minchie approached the front door of Vikram Murthy's house, he pulled something out of the bag he carried, then tossed the bag aside.

Savage got out of the car and crossed the road towards the four men. Tannaz followed.

The plastic bag Minchie had discarded floated lazily in the air. Savage scooped it up in his hand and stuffed it in his pocket. Up ahead, the four men had assembled outside Vikram Murthy's front door, giggling drunkenly, swaying like reeds in the wind. In his hand, Minchie held a can of some sort. It didn't take long for them to realise what it was. They heard the tell-tale click-clack of a car-spray paint can being shaken. In a second, Minchie had bent down and sprayed something across Vikram Murthy's UPVC front door.

The men stood back, admiring Minchie's handiwork, chuckling loudly like naughty school boys.

"Minchie!" shouted Savage. "What are you doing?"

Minchie and the other three men spun round, the hilarity fleeing from their dumb faces, replaced by mean stares. They were all similarly dressed. Bland casual jackets, training shoes and jeans, T-shirts underneath, two of them were wearing Fred Perry polo shirts. They all had short cropped hair, three of them with far too much gel on top, making their heads look sticky. Minchie still kept his dry and natural. All four men stood head and shoulders above Savage.

Two eyes, as hard and as cold as ball-bearings, peered out from beneath Minchie's vast and bony brow. His eyes rapidly filled with terror when he saw who addressed him; a strange, uncustomary look for someone with such a hard exterior.

He dropped the can on the ground, guiltily. "Savage," he said in a small voice.

The other three men did a double take. Who was this little, balding man who'd put the fear of God into hard-as-nails Minchie?

Savage stood before them, Tannaz by his side. "Last I heard you were living in Southampton, Minchie," said Savage.

"H-how did you know about that?" said Minchie.

Savage took a step forward. "Oh, I make it my business to know." He didn't really. He just said it because he knew it would give this horrible racist, woman-beating thug the willies.

Minchie straightened up, tried to look more dignified in front of his mates. "Well, I'm here now."

"I can see that." Savage peered around Minchie's considerable girth and read the writing sprayed on Vikram Murthy's door: *Peedo*. Minchie's spelling hadn't improved since they last met. "Put an 's' on the front of that," said Savage, "and you've got 'Speedo'. Are you trying to out this guy as a paedophile or a wearer of skimpy swimwear?"

A guy on the left took a step forward putting his body between Minchie and Savage. He prodded Savage in the chest with his index finger. "Listen here, mate. You don't want to mess with us. What we're doing is a public service." His breath stank of cheap, stale beer. "Guy who lives here, Victor..."

"Vikram," Tannaz corrected.

"Murphy..."

"Murthy," Tannaz corrected again.

"... He's a dirty paedophile and we're just letting all the nice people here know that. Lots of kids in this neighbourhood and they should know a kiddie fiddler's living here."

"How do you know he's a paedophile?" asked Tannaz.

"We just know, alright."

"Hey," said Minchie, regaining some of his confidence, probably after his dense brain had caught up and remembered that there were four of them and just one of Savage, not counting Tannaz, as he would never consider a female a threat. "Is Murthy a friend of yours?"

Savage was about to say no then he thought, what the hell. "Yes, he's a good friend of ours."

The guy standing in front of him started with the chest prodding again. Stabbing Savage with the tip of his forefinger in time with every word. "If you're a paedo like him, you'll get what's coming to you."

On the last prod, Savage snatched the guy's finger and twisted it away, yanking it down hard. "I really wish you wouldn't do that."

The guy had no choice but to follow body mechanics, retreating from the burning pain, bending over in a humiliating submissive sideways bow.

The fear returned to Minchie's eyes. The same couldn't be said for the other two. The one nearest Tannaz went for Savage. She stuck out her foot and tripped him up. Being inebriated, he went over like a sack of potatoes, his face slamming against the ground, knocking himself out. The remaining thug, who was about to engage Savage, now turned his attention on Tannaz.

"Bitch," he said.

"You got that right, bedwetter."

He fired a jab at her head. Nothing special. A simple straight punch, but plenty powerful. Tannaz caught his fist easily. As she did, she took a step back, and kept stepping back, pulling the guy's fist with her. The forward momentum from the punch meant the guy had no choice but to go with it, throwing him off balance. As he went down, Tannaz gripped his fist hard with both her hands, bending it back towards him. Wrists weren't designed to bend backwards, no matter how strong they were. They were always the weak link. A link Tannaz was on the verge of snapping. The guy yelped in pain and had to go down on his knees, as if he were praying, to prevent his bones breaking. She raised her boot to stamp on his head.

"No, please!" he shouted. "I didn't mean it."

Tannaz laughed. "You are the worst thug I've ever met. Wasn't anyone better available?" She lowered her boot to the ground without striking him, but didn't relinquish her grip, keeping him at bay.

Minchie looked around at the carnage. His backup lying broken on the floor. He did the one smart thing he could do, and ran off.

"Bye Minchie!" shouted Savage. "Good catching up."

"What is the deal with that guy?" asked Tannaz. "He's terrified of you."

"Can you let go now," said the guy on the ground, his hand bent over at an awkward angle. "My wrist really hurts."

Tannaz ignored him.

"Oh nothing," Savage replied, answering Tannaz's question. "I left him locked in an abandoned warehouse once. Think it scarred him for life. Actually, I have no idea how he got out. Should've asked him before he shot off." Savage turned to the three remaining thugs. "As for you three. I don't want to see you around here again. Otherwise, next time, me and Tannaz won't go so easy on you. Life-changing injuries and all that. Now scuttle off."

Savage and Tannaz let go of the men they were holding onto. The pair of them immediately hoisted their unconscious mate upright.

He came around, groggily. "Did we win?" he said, dreamily.

Supporting him between the two of them, they shuffled off out of the cul-de-sac and disappeared.

The front door of Vikram Murthy's house opened. He stood in the doorway clutching his hands together. "Thank you for standing up to those bullies. I saw everything through the security camera."

"Don't mention it," said Savage. "I'm John and this is Tannaz."

Vikram stepped out to shake Savage and Tannaz by the hand. "They come around here all the time, shouting abuse, accusing me of all sorts of terrible things. My neighbours don't talk to me anymore."

"Do you have any soapy water?" said Savage, pointing at the misspelt graffiti. "Best to scrub it off before it dries. Otherwise you'll need a solvent to clean it off."

Vikram turned around, seeing the graffiti for the first time. The angle of his security camera clearly hadn't caught what they'd scrawled over the door. "You've got to be kidding me!" he shouted. "Those assholes, why are they doing this?"

"Vikram," said Savage. "Get me a bowl of hot soapy water and a scourer. It'll come off, no problem."

"Yes, right." He disappeared back into his house, returning with a bucket of suds and a handful of brand-new scourers still wrapped in plastic of various shapes and sizes. "I usually keep several grades of scourer, I didn't know which one would be best."

Savage selected one. "This will do fine." Savage took the bucket, dipped the scourer in it and set about cleaning off the mess on the door. The fact that it hadn't dried and that it had been sprayed onto plastic meant the paint slid off easily. In seconds it was gone. "There," said Savage, handing him back the bucket and sourer. "Good as new."

"Thank you, I am in your debt. Please come in. Let me make you a drink."

Tannaz and Savage followed him into a spartan, white cube of a hallway. A tall table sat opposite the front door, a vase placed on top of it, holding a single-stem white orchid, a long mirror above it. Each item had been arranged with laser-point accuracy so they all lined up. The white floor was spotless and gleaming. Tannaz and Savage instinctively slipped their shoes off. "Please, come into the kitchen," Vikram said.

The kitchen was a triumph of clinical minimalism. White, of course, an island in the middle topped with pale stone, with slick, shiny white cupboards below and a pristine white sink above. A single stainless-steel swan-neck tap curved over it. Placed on one side of the island stood three sleek white stools, arranged perfectly in line with identical gaps between. Savage could see no cooker or food cupboards. He guessed they were hidden behind secret walls to keep up the strict commitment to minimalism. The only object on show, sitting on its own white plinth, was a mighty Gaggia coffee machine, like a full-on Italian restaurant would have. A neat line of upturned white espresso cups perched on the top.

Tannaz nearly had a seizure when she saw it. "Whoa, nice coffee machine."

"Would you like one?"

"Hell, yeah," said Tannaz.

"And for you, John?"

"Just tea for me. White, no sugar."

Vikram busied himself, popping open invisible cupboards with a push of his hand. Savage got the briefest glimpse of a cupboard full of products that had been arranged with military precision. There was no kettle in the kitchen. Vikram just twisted a separate knob on the beautiful swan-neck tap, and out poured a stream of boiling water.

"Wow, boiling water on tap, eh?" said Savage. "I could do with one of those."

"Actually, I keep it just below boiling. Better for the tea. If the water's boiling it will scald the leaves. Ruin the flavour."

Tannaz tutted. "Didn't you know that, Savage? Everyone knows that. Savage thinks he's the expert on tea."

"Oh, really," said Vikram enthusiastically. "Where do you buy your blends from?"

"A little local place round the corner from me in Peckham."

"Ah, good to support independent outlets," said Vikram.

Savage didn't tell him that by small and local he meant Tesco Express. Vikram was an out-and-out connoisseur. Had to have the real authentic version of everything, and would probably trek across London just to buy a certain type of bread because of the artisan flour they used. Savage could overlook all that, especially as Vikram made tea the proper way in a teapot, and not with teabags, but loose leaves, like Savage's nan used to make. Vikram couldn't be all bad, surely.

When he'd made their drinks, they sat at the island sipping them. Vikram had water from a glass bottle that looked expensive, poured into a tumbler that had, no doubt, been imported from the finest glassmakers in Italy.

Tannaz groaned in ecstasy. "That is the most delicious coffee I've ever tasted."

"Roasted this morning," said Vikram. "I get it from a coffee roaster in Balham."

"Savage, you have to try this."

"I'm fine, thanks. This tea's amazing. Where's it from? Don't tell me you had it flown in from India this morning?"

"No, but it is from a single origin, shuffled by hand to improve oxidation."

"I've never had hand-shuffled tea before."

Tannaz downed her espresso.

"You want another?" Vikram asked.

Tannaz nodded rather too enthusiastically. Vikram set to work on his impressive coffee machine, pulling levers and making it hiss as if it were some Victorian steam contraption; all the while he wiped the machine down, cleaning away the merest hint of a stray drop. At last he handed Tannaz another cup of perfectly prepared espresso.

"Would you mind if I ask an awkward question?" said Vikram.

"Not at all," said Savage.

"Why were you outside my house earlier?"

CHAPTER 13

Savage came clean and told Vikram about Callum going missing along with three other children, and how they'd discovered that Vikram's physio work had connected all four missing children.

Vikram sighed, shook his head. "I'm terribly sorry that your neighbour's son has gone missing. Truly I am. But I've already been through this with the police."

"You have?" said Savage.

"Yes, they came here, at the end of May. Questioned me about the missing children. Obviously not Callum, he wasn't missing then, but three others were."

Tannaz and Savage looked at each other. So they hadn't stumbled on some incredible breakthrough. The police had already discovered the sports connection, identified Vikram, got here first and ruled him out.

Vikram continued, "All the children are members of different sports clubs that I donate my time to, as a physio. See, I trained as a physiotherapist until I switched careers. But I didn't want my skills to go to waste, so I offer my services voluntarily for youth teams across south London. The missing children just happen to be members of sports clubs that I donate my time to. Purely coincidental. The police thought I had something to do with it. Two detectives turned up to question me."

"Can you remember their names?"

"One was called Sutcliffe, I think. Real bully. Old-school. Accused me on the spot, said they had evidence I had abducted the children. Tried to get me to confess. Can't remember the other one. Female detective. Young, blonde, pretty. A bit nicer than her boss."

"So what happened?" asked Tannaz.

"I had a cast-iron alibi. Two of the children who went missing, Sally something..."

"Sally Woodrow," said Tannaz.

"That's the one. And Olive Foley I think the other's name was. One disappeared on May sixth and the other on May twenty-second. I was out of the country on both days. I sometimes work in Amsterdam, place called Van Rote Analytics. Showed Sutcliffe my tickets, receipts for the flights, taxis and trams. I'm freelance so I keep everything for tax. He even checked the company's security logs. Knew my alibi was watertight. Guy looked ready to throttle me. Thought he'd got his man, see. He looked like he would explode."

Savage didn't need to imagine. He could see Sutcliffe's face clear as day. Veins popping out on his forehead one by one as another lead, perhaps his one and only lead, turned to dust.

"What is it you do exactly?" asked Tannaz.

Vikram brightened up. "Let me show you."

They followed Vikram out of the kitchen into his office, another spartan room, that looked simple yet probably cost him an arm and a leg. White again with hidden cupboards along one wall to camouflage any clutter, although Savage couldn't imagine anything was cluttered in Vikram's life. A large rectangular desk made of a single piece of polished oak stretched across the width of the room. Placed perfectly in the middle were two large desktop Apple Macs and in the centre of them an Apple MacBook Air, sleek and silver. Savage couldn't see any cables. Vikram probably found them offensive to his sense of perfection and had them chased into the desk and under the floor.

Savage nudged Tannaz. "How come your office doesn't look like this?"

Tannaz's office in her flat was the antithesis of Vikram's. Crooked utilitarian metal shelving stacked with bits of old PCs and components. Not a spare area of useable space. Leads snaking off into every corner and the continual hum of electricity mixing with the stench of spent cigarettes lying in ashtrays in desperate need of emptying. And not an Apple product in sight. Savage knew they weren't her cup of tea. She once called them overpriced computers for technology fascists. Although, Savage was sure price had nothing to do with it. Tannaz didn't like being told by a corporate giant what she could and couldn't have in her hardware. She preferred building her own machines from the motherboard up, specced to her own preferences. Big, hefty weapons for virtual combat. Not pretty, but effective.

Vikram sat on a well-designed black office chair that made an expensive sigh as it took his weight, the sound of premium hydraulics.

After clicking the mouse pad on the MacBook all three desktop screens came to life, showing a paused video image of a BMX rider in mid-air over a painfully high double jump. "This is my current project, a professional BMXer from California. His coach sends me footage of him training on a track every day. This is the latest one. Cameras are placed at key points around the track, close to each obstacle."

Vikram hit play and the footage burst into life. The guy on the BMX landed the jump with buttery smoothness, then continued flying round the track as if his bike were part of him, taking jumps so high that Savage would have trouble walking over them, let alone riding over them. Some of the jumps on the track were arranged in clusters of two, three and even four. The rider leapt each set at once, always landing just beyond the apex of the last jump with impeccable timing.

"Looks good, huh?" said Vikram, pausing it again.

"That guy's got some skills," Tannaz remarked.

"Let's have a closer look at that last jump." Vikram opened another screen. "I'd been working on this one before you got here." The screen showed a paused, close-up image of the same rider about to land his bike, except it was covered in annotations, angles and movement vectors with stats all down the side. The footage shunted forward frame by frame, the calculations on screen constantly changing. "There's the first mistake." Vikram pointed to the back wheel and a vector with measurements that Savage didn't understand. "Regular video wouldn't pick this up but this software does. Can you see that his back wheel shifts to one side on landing?"

"I'll take your word for it," said Savage.

"And that's a problem because..." said Tannaz.

"If his bike's moving sideways on landing, he's losing speed. Even if it's a hundredth of a second, over multiple jumps that soon adds up. It's a bad habit he's got into. Obviously, his coach can't see this when he's riding but the computer can."

"Jeez," said Tannaz. "I didn't realise BMX racing was so competitive."

"Every sport is competitive," Vikram explained. "This guy's got big sponsors pouring money into him. They want him to win. It's the same everywhere. All the athletes I work with, whether they're tennis players or BMXers, swimmers, they all want to squeeze more efficiency out of their performance."

"This is really cool software," said Tannaz. "Apart from the fact that it's on a Mac."

Vikram smiled. "You're a PC fan I take it."

"Damn right. It's the only way to fly."

"We'll have to agree to differ."

"As long as you agree that PCs are better." She winked at him.

Savage's tone become more serious. "Vikram, those guys who hassled you tonight. How did they know about your connection with the junior sports clubs? I mean, we only found it because we knew of the missing kids already, and Tannaz here is a bit of a whizz at searching the Internet. The missing kids are not public knowledge. How did they know?"

"That, I can't tell you. I have no idea. They think I touch kids up because I do a bit of kids' physio at the weekend. It's ludicrous. The parents are always there with me when I do it. They can see everything I do. There are no private treatment rooms. I just do it on the sidelines at a match or by the side of the pool. Loosen up a few pulled muscles, that's all. Maybe the police told them."

"No chance," said Savage. "I tried to get some information out of Sutcliffe about Callum's disappearance. He was tight-lipped, almost wanted to arrest me for asking."

Vikram thought for a moment, searching his mind for clues. "One thing I do know. There's a whole gang of them. You know, these so-called paedophile hunters."

"Really?" said Tannaz.

"Yes, that was only a handful. Sometimes there's dozens of them out there."

"Have you reported them to the police?"

"Of course. Someone came out and took a statement. Never heard anything again. Then when Sutcliffe showed up I told him about them. He didn't seem to be interested."

"Police are underfunded and overworked," Savage said. "And Sutcliffe's too focused on catching the guy who's taken these kids to be interested. It's not his lookout so he's not bothered. Thing is, we recognised one of the guys who was hassling you tonight. Stupid brute called Minchie. We can get some answers out of him. I'd like to know how they know about the missing kids. It's not been made public, so where are they getting their information from?"

"First we have to track down Minchie," said Tannaz.

Vikram shut down his array of computers. "I can help you there. They all meet in a pub called the Bexhill Arms in Elephant and Castle. I've heard them mention it after they've finished hurling abuse at me. That's where they go afterwards for a celebratory drink. There's something else you need to know. They're organised and large. Those guys tonight were just dumb foot soldiers. They're led by a guy called Carl Cooper. I've seen him outside my house once or twice, stirring up trouble. If anyone knows anything, it's going to be him."

"Well, I think we need to pay this Carl Cooper a visit. Get some answers out of him, and see if we can get them off your back."

"That is very brave and kind of you, but I don't think that's such a good idea. You wouldn't want to make an enemy of him."

Savage placed a reassuring hand on Vikram's shoulder. "Don't worry. Me and Tannaz can be very persuasive. We'll go there right now. Bexhill Arms, you say; Elephant and Castle?"

Savage Children

"Yes. Please be careful." Vikram got up to show them out. As they reached the hall, he said, "Wait, I must give you something." He disappeared into the kitchen briefly and returned with two bulging, large, brown paper bags. He thrust one into Tannaz's hands and the other into Savage's. "Hand-shuffled tea for you," he said to Savage. "And freshly roasted coffee beans for Tannaz."

"Wow, thank you Vikram," Savage replied.

"Oh, I can't accept these," Tannaz said. "I don't even have a coffee grinder."

Vikram vanished into the kitchen and returned with a shiny electric coffee grinder. "Please take mine. I was going to get a new one anyway."

Tannaz took the slick silver device in her hands. "No, I can't. This looks brand new." Like everything Vikram owned, it was premium and expensive, built from stainless steel and not a mark on it. She handed it back to him.

Vikram pushed it back towards her. "Please, I insist. I am in your debt."

"Oh, well, I'll take it. But only because I feel sorry about you being an Apple user."

Vikram smiled. "Now, please be careful with Carl Cooper."

"Don't worry, Vikram. And thanks again for the tea," John said.

They headed back to Savage's flat briefly so Tannaz could get onto her laptop and do a bit of hacking. She checked out Vikram's alibi, getting into the passenger lists for both his flights to Amsterdam. Both times Vikram's name showed up. He was out of the country for two of the children's abductions. A cast-iron alibi if ever there was one. The police had already cleared him, but Savage had wanted to be sure.

"Right," he said. "Now we know Vikram's totally innocent, I think we need to find out about this Carl Cooper, then pay him a visit, see how he's connected with all this."

The Bexhill Arms was an estate pub; a concrete shoebox with a flat roof. The type of place where if you walk in and you're not a local, it will often result in patrons of said pub descending into an uncomfortable, if not downright threatening, silence, with every head swivelling towards you, drinks paused, raised halfway between table and mouth. The single-storey building looked like an impoverished youth club, cages on the windows and one for the main entrance, thankfully open to welcome weary travellers in. To the right of the entrance a disgruntled local villain had sprayed, *The Colemans are grasses*. No effort had been made to clean it off or cover it up, leading the casual observer to conclude that maybe the Colemans were indeed grasses.

Attempts had been made to give the building a traditional pub-like appearance. It had a hanging pub sign outside. How it had survived was anyone's guess. A chalkboard on the wall advertised two deals. The first was for home-cooked food. Probably bought in bulk then nuked in an industrial-strength microwave. Below this, another line of text advertised a special deal. Tannaz read it out loud as they sat across the road, observing the pub from the relative safety of the VW Caddy.

"Breakfast and a beer, only five pounds, served daily from seven thirty a.m. That's even too early for me. Who'd be drinking at seven thirty in the morning?"

"You know, get a quick one in before work," Savage replied.

"I can't think of anything more depressing than starting your day in that dump with a pint of high-strength, low-quality lager and a full-fat fry up."

"Don't knock it. These flat-roofed pubs are a dying breed," said Savage, almost fondly.

"That's like saying you really miss the days of cholera."

"Just reminds me of my youth that's all."

"Is that where your dad took you up the pub, bought you a lemonade and made you sit outside while he got smashed?"

"Not at all. My dad never drank. His father, my grandad, was a drunk, you see. Used to go out, get plastered then come home and hit my grandmother around. Made my dad teetotal. Didn't want to be an asshole like his father. So I was very lucky in that respect. In this country, coming home from the pub and knocking your wife and kids about is a bit of a national pastime. You growing up in Iran without alcohol did have its advantages."

Tannaz shook her head. "No, the women just get stoned to death instead. So why are you so nostalgic about dumps like this?"

"Well, let's just say, our local flat-roofed pub in Camberwell used to turn a blind eye to a spot of under-age drinking. Come on, let's pay this Carl Cooper and his cronies a visit."

They left the van, and entered the Bexhill Arms. The first thing that confronted them in the entrance lobby was huge flag covering an entire wall.

"Uh-oh, that's not a good sign," said Savage.

CHAPTER 14

THE GIANT FLAG WAS NAILED to the wall, presumably to stop it from being stolen. The English flag, St George's Cross. A simple heraldic design. White background with a red cross, sported by bloodthirsty crusaders on their way to liberate the holy land by slaughtering infidels and anyone who happened to be in their way, even if they were fellow Christians. In fact, the holy land did not really need liberating at the time, as Jews, Muslims and Christians were living in Jerusalem in relative peace and harmony. The crusaders' violent interruption unwittingly kick-started a blood feud between Muslims and Christians, which has survived to this day, reaching even this scruffy corner of London.

Two inner doors separated the pub from the lobby. Beyond them they could hear a lively buzz. A little bit too lively for a Sunday evening. Loud banter, glasses clinking and fruit machines trilling. Savage gently pushed one of the doors open to get a look at what they faced inside. More English flags hanging from every available wall space. A completely white clientele, mostly male, knocking back pint after cheap pint. The atmosphere appeared jovial. Savage knew that could change at any minute.

"You sure you want to go in there?" asked Savage. "Maybe it'd be better if I went in alone."

"Forget that," said Tannaz. "I'm not afraid of a bunch of white supremacists."

"There's an awful lot of them."

"Well, then you'll need all the backup you can get. Anyway, are they really going to pick on a war hero, an ex-captain in the SAS, veteran of the gulf war?"

"Probably not," said Savage. "Okay, let's do this. Ever seen *An American Werewolf in London*?"

"Nope," she replied.

"Classic horror film. There's a scene where two American hitchhikers enter a local pub called the Slaughtered Lamb. Everyone stops talking and stares at them. There's a cameo of a very young Rik Mayall."

"I don't know who that is."

"Sorry, I'm digressing. Just be prepared for some you're-not-from-around-here type stares, okay."

"Okay."

"And remind me to lend you *An American Werewolf in London*."

"It's okay. I'll just download it."

"And pay for it of course."

"Of course." Tannaz gave him a can-we-just-get-on-with-it stare.

Savage pushed open one of the double doors as quietly and uneventfully as he could, and slipped in, followed by Tannaz. Despite the low-key entrance, as predicted, the entire pub went mute, save for the fruit machine tweeting and whistling.

"Told you," Savage whispered.

As they sauntered slowly to the bar, dozens of eyes followed them, the aggressive silence pressing onto them from every angle. They made it to the bar and leant against its sticky edge keeping their backs to the rest of the pub. The bar hadn't been wiped down for a good while. Puddles of stale beer lay along its length. Savage eyed up the options for beverages. They had one lager on tap, Stella Artois, also known as the wife beater because of its high alcohol content and because it inevitably led to aggressive behaviour. An obvious choice of beer in one sense but also an ironic one in another, seeing how this was a fiercely patriotic pub and Stella Artois was from Belgium.

The silence continued all around them, increasing in intensity. The sound of nothing had never been so intimidating. Any minute now, thought Savage, a small posse of locals would surround them and Savage would have to weigh up their fight-or-flight options, or lay out his British Army credentials hoping that would appease them.

That never got to happen.

A clatter of glasses smashing to the floor came from further down the bar, and there was the ridiculous sight of Minchie standing over a tin tray that had clearly slipped out of his hands, spilling beer and shards of glass everywhere. His big dumb face had clocked Savage, causing his little mishap. His mouth hung open, eyes wide, fixed on Savage and Tannaz.

"Minchie, what the hell are you doing?" said a guy in a thick cockney accent sitting at a table nearby. About eight other men sat around the table with him, looking at Minchie disapprovingly.

"Sorry, Carl," said Minchie. Ignoring the mess on the floor he darted over to the table, and slid into an empty chair, hunkered down, never taking his eyes off Savage, like a child in an exam worried that the teacher had caught him cheating.

The barman came out with a dustpan and brush and began sweeping up the mess. "Don't worry, Carl. I've got this."

"Thanks, Todd," said Carl. The rest of the pub went back to its conversations, but a few suspicious eyes kept darting over at the two strangers.

Tannaz and Savage took the opportunity to sidle further down the bar, closer to where Minchie sat with this Carl. He seemed to be leading the discussion, holding court with the undivided attention of all the men at the table.

So this was the notorious Carl Cooper. He was small with a wide, red-lipped mouth and large, dark eyes, set in a perpetual rapey stare. His hair, clearly dyed, was solid black and neatly parted, giving him the overall appearance of a creepy old-fashioned ventriloquist's dummy, not helped by his pallor of a sickly Victorian child. The men certainly seemed scared of him, or at least deferential, despite his diminutive size; the way their bodies angled towards him and how they nodded at the end of every one of his sentences.

Minchie kept looking at Savage, not saying anything.

As they edged closer, Savage tried to pick up what the men were discussing. Not right-wing politics, as he first suspected, but one of the five default topics that men usually talk about when a bunch of them get together. The five Fs as Savage called them: football, fighting, films, females or food. In this case it was food. The mild conversation seemed at odds with the men's hard exteriors.

"Course," said Carl, sagely. "The king of crumbles has to be rhubarb, no contest."

"Then apple crumble," someone ventured.

"Then apple," Carl conceded. "Close second."

"I like pear crumble," said Minchie.

No one said anything. They looked at Carl for their stance on this matter.

"Pear?" said Carl, screwing up his face. "What are you, gay or something? No one eats pear crumble." The other men all jeered at Minchie now that Carl's position on the issue had been made clear. "What's up with you? You've been acting weird all night."

Minchie's eyes darted across to Savage and Tannaz.

"What are you scared of, an old man and his mail-order bride?"

"She's not my wife, or my girlfriend," said Savage.

Minchie leant across and whispered something in Carl's ear. Carl's expression changed, lightening instantly. A welcoming smile. Minchie obviously hadn't mentioned anything about him and his mates getting a beating at the hands of Savage and Tannaz earlier that evening. From what Savage could tell, the other three who had been outside Vikram's house didn't appear to be here. Wouldn't want to show up at the pub with bruised faces and egos, then have to explain that this was the result of a beating at the hands of an older man and an immigrant girl.

"Come and join us," said Carl. "Pull up a chair. War heroes are welcome here, especially ones from the SAS and the Gulf War."

Tannaz and Savage sat down. "I'm not a hero. This is Tannaz and I'm John, by the way."

"Don't be modest," said Carl. "You should be proud of your service to this country. Fighting oppressive regimes." He flicked a disapproving look in Tannaz's direction. "Let me get you a drink. Todd," he shouted to the barman, who stopped serving someone and came out from behind the bar quick as a flash. "Todd, get my new friends here a drink. What would you like?"

"Bottle of pale ale, please," said Savage.

"Whisky," said Tannaz.

"And a pint of Stella for me," Carl added.

Minchie went to put in his order but Carl closed him down.

"Nothing for you, Minchie. You've had enough already, dropping that tray of drinks all over the floor." Minchie sulked back into his chair. The barman left and returned with their drinks. Savage sipped his slowly, as did Tannaz, both wanting to stay sober but without offending their host.

"Minchie tells me you're a bit of a real-life action hero," Carl remarked.

"Yeah, he's like Jason Bourne," said Minchie, brightening up.

"Ever noticed all the action heroes' initials are J.B.," Carl said. Everyone nodded in agreement, except Tannaz and Savage.

"S'right," said one guy. "Jack Bauer."

"James Bond," said another.

"Maybe there's something in that," said Carl. "It could be a sign."

"The Jonas Brothers," Minchie proposed.

"Jonas Brothers aren't action heroes," Carl snarled.

"Maybe that's what they want you to think," said Minchie, trying to regain some credibility in the conversation. All the men snorted dismissively.

A heated discussion broke out, debating the merits of various names in popular culture with the initials J.B.

Savage quickly summed up the men around him. When they weren't discussing dessert, they were reading world-order conspiracies into everything. Seeing patterns where there weren't any. Imagining dangers that didn't exist except in their heads. Where everything, no matter how small, meant something huge and crucial. Always rounded down to the lowest common denominator—that their way of life was being threatened and eroded.

"Everyone shut up," said Carl. "I wish I'd never mentioned the J.B. thing. You sound ridiculous." The men seemed to shrink in their seats a little. He turned to Savage, calmed himself down and rolled his eyes, as if to say, I'm with these idiots, then smiled. "So, John, what brings you to our neck of the woods?"

"Is it true you lead a gang of paedophile hunters?" Savage asked, getting straight to the point.

Carl's grin dropped a little but not completely. "Yep, that's right. Our group's called St George Is Cross."

"St George's Cross?" Tannaz clarified.

Carl shook his head. "No. Not St George's Cross. It's Saint. George. Is. Cross. As is in St George is angry. St George Is Cross. It's a play on words."

Savage could now see why Tannaz cringed whenever he made a pun or a bit of word play. He was getting a dose of his own phonetic medicine. St George Is Cross was one of the worst names he'd ever heard of for an alt-right group, for any group for that matter.

"Why is St George Cross?" he asked.

Carl cleared his throat, as if he were about to address an alt-right convention. "Because, if he were alive today, St George would be cross. Cross at what's happening to this country. Angry at these middle-eastern paedophile gangs coming over here grooming young girls for sex."

"You know there are tons of white paedophiles that do that too," said Tannaz.

"And that St George is originally from the middle east," Savage added. "So you're kind of on to a loser on both fronts there."

"What?" said Carl.

"St George was Turkish, I believe," said Savage. "Born in Cappadocia. Died in Palestine in the fourth century if I remember rightly. And he definitely wasn't a knight, certainly not a crusader. First Crusades didn't happen until six hundred years later. Probably a soldier in the Roman Army. And at that time, girls in Rome got married off as young as twelve, and they had no say in it, so I doubt St George would be cross."

"How do you know that?"

"Oh, it's this really cool thing called reading," Savage replied.

"Read it in a book about ancient Rome. Reading's really useful. Helps you separate what's fact from nonsense."

Carl forced out a mock laugh. "You're so naïve. Believe everything you read, do yer? That's a load of liberal propaganda, mate."

"No, I don't think so. It was written by a history professor so I'm guessing she's got her facts straight. Otherwise, she wouldn't last very long in the history game. Facts are important when it comes to history."

"When it comes to everything," Tannaz added.

Carl leant forward. "They're pushing an agenda on you. And you don't even know it."

"Who is and what agenda?" asked Savage.

"The soft white liberals. Making you believe we should go easy on these immigrants, present company accepted." He flashed his creepy smile at Tannaz. She sent a scowl back in his direction.

"I don't think we should go easy on anyone who abducts young girls for sex," said Savage. "Lock 'em up and throw away the key, I say."

Minchie squirmed in his seat. Savage guessed that Minchie had failed to inform Carl that he used to be part of a group who kidnapped women and sent them abroad. Savage held his tongue, for now. That information might be handy as a bargaining chip to use against Minchie.

Savage continued, "What I do have a problem with is when you blame something like that on a single race. Your motivation isn't the protection of young girls, or you'd hunt down all paedophiles, whether they were white, black, yellow or brown. Your motivation is attacking a particular group. Blaming the whole problem on them. Creating racial stereotypes."

"I'm not a racist," said Carl. "Ask anyone in here."

Savage couldn't think of a group of less reliable witnesses than the clientele of this pub. "Why do you and your gang keep hassling Vikram Murthy?" he asked.

"He touches kids," Carl immediately replied.

"That's because he's a part-time physio," said Tannaz. "It kind of goes with the job."

Savage Children

Carl took a large, slow slug of his beer. He put it down, positioning it carefully on a beer mat. "You remember that physio in the states, Larry Nasser. Got convicted for sexually abusing young gymnasts? What colour was he?"

"You have to be kidding me?" said Tannaz. "You're telling me that you're targeting Vikram, purely because he has the same skin colour and does the same job as some asshole in America who fiddled with young girls. That's the very definition of racism."

"I'm not a racist."

"Listen," said Tannaz. "If I say I don't hate cats, then I pick up a cat and throw it in a bin. It's pretty clear what I think of cats."

"I prefer dogs," said Minchie. Everyone ignored him.

Savage got up. Immediately several men around the pub also stood, fearing Savage was about to start something with Carl. Savage held his hands up, palms out, to show he meant no aggression. "I think we're done here, Tannaz."

Tannaz got to her feet too. "Yep, it's pretty clear Carl doesn't know anything. And by that, he *really* doesn't know anything."

"I agree." Savage turned his attention on Carl. "I'd like you to stay away from Vikram Murthy. Unless you have some proper evidence he's abusing kids, in which case, take it to the police."

Carl waved a hand at the men standing around. Simultaneously, they all sat down. "Police won't do anything. They're part of the liberal agenda."

"Alright," said Savage. "Then come to me. Show me your evidence and we'll confront him together, but until then, we'd politely ask you leave the poor guy alone. It's not a very nice thing to do to a person."

"You're just a couple of snowflakes, ain't ya?" said Carl. "Coming in here all passive-aggressive."

"We can do aggressive-aggressive if you like," said Tannaz.

"You watch your step out there," said Carl. "St George Is Cross is a big organisation. A network of people just like me. Ordinary people. Van drivers, taxi drivers, postmen, factory workers, brickies and plasterers. All fed up with what going on around them. We're an army. Spread all over London. Ready to mobilise at a moment's notice."

Savage became ponderous. "What's the collective noun for a group of racists."

"We're not racists, we're patriots."

Savage continued. "You know, you have a pod of dolphins, a murder of crows, a—"

"An embarrassment of racists," Tannaz offered.

"That's it," Savage chuckled. "An embarrassment of racists."

Carl's brow folded in the middle. "You don't want to make enemies of us. You rock up to my pub—"

Tannaz cut him off. "No one says *rock up* any more."

"And I've never rocked up to anything in my life," Savage added.

Carl's eyes became more cold and rapey than already had been. "Listen. The only reason I'm letting you walk out that door with both legs intact is because of your service to this country…"

Savage leant over the table. "Listen, I didn't risk my ass fighting in the desert so you and your White Power Rangers can fulfil your racist fantasies."

"I'm not a racist."

"He's not," said Minchie. "I remember him saying he liked Denzel Washington."

"That's right," said Carl. "I like Denzel Washington."

"Yeah," said Minchie. "You said he was a talented black bastard."

Carl shot him a bullet-hard stare. "Shut up, Minchie." He turned his attention back to Savage. "You and your Arab bitch better leave while you still can."

"Persian bitch," Tannaz corrected.

"I don't care. But I will give you two a bit of advice. Don't ever show your faces around here again. You ain't welcome."

"Hmm," said Savage. "Let me think about that. Drinking in a depressing flat-roof pub with a Tesco Value Range Tommy Robinson. Not my idea of a good night out. I think you're pretty safe on that score. But thanks for the beer."

Tannaz and Savage made a swift exit before Carl changed his

mind and set his right-wing weapon dogs on them. Outside the pub, they jumped into Savage's van, which thankfully hadn't been vandalised or broken into, a miracle in this part of London. Savage started the engine and pointed it back towards Camberwell.

The mood inside the vehicle turned glum. Their one and only lead had evaporated. Vikram knew nothing, and Carl Cooper knew even less. St George Is Cross had no idea about the children's disappearances. It was nothing more than mindless racism aimed at a guy who happened to donate his time to doing physio for youth sports teams, which, coincidentally, all four kids were members of. Savage didn't believe in coincidences, but this time he had to concede that this was all it was. If St George Is Cross knew about the kids being abducted, they'd be doing more than spray-painting slurs on Vikram's front door.

Savage begun to understand how Sutcliffe felt. They were only a day or two into their investigation and nothing usable had surfaced. Sutcliffe had had weeks of this. No wonder the guy looked ready to pop. He wasn't even sure whether their visit to Carl Cooper and his cronies had done any good for Vikram Murthy, or if they'd exacerbated the situation, putting an even bigger target on his back.

CHAPTER 15

As they drove back across London, Savage finally succumbed and let Tannaz use his phone, seeing as hers was dead, and Tannaz without an electrical device in her hand was like Wolverine without his claws.

Tannaz thumbed away on the screen. "How can Carl Cooper base his actions on such flimsy evidence?"

"I'd say flimsy's an understatement," Savage added. "Carl Cooper has no evidence against Vikram, and possibly none of the other people he's targeted."

"True. And he certainly knows nothing about Callum and the other disappearances, which puts us back to square one. Thing is, I don't think Carl Cooper cares about catching paedophiles. I think it's about him."

"What do you mean?"

"This is just a guess, well, an educated guess. But looking at his social-media posts he wants to be famous. Make a name for himself. And like most people who want fame, he's also a talentless prick. So the only way he can get noticed is by being controversial because he can't do anything else."

"Stir up trouble. Like Katie Hopkins. Eventually get his face on TV, is that his angle?"

"That's what my gut's telling me. The guy's got a massive ego. He dyes his hair that ridiculous solid black colour because he's vain. And to fuel his media posts he needs people to blame so he can swoop in and be the everyday hero. There are tons of posts of videos of him standing outside suspected paedophiles' houses shouting abuse at them. One of them is Vikram's. He's building a following, judging by all the comments below."

"Can you get Vikram's video removed?"

"I could but there'd be no point. They'll just pop up somewhere else. I might be able to hide them, so they think the post is still there, but no one else will be able to see it. It'll have to wait until we get home."

They drove in silence for some time until Tannaz said, "So what do we do now?"

Savage inhaled deeply. "We've got no more leads. Only thing left is to go see the Red Crew gang in the park tomorrow. See if they've heard anything. That's if the park isn't still cordoned off with police."

Tannaz swore. "This detective stuff is hard work."

"Yep. If it were easy there'd be fewer criminals on the street."

It was after eleven when they pulled up outside Savage's flat and walked up to his front door. His security light flicked on.

"You want to grab your stuff so I can drop you back home?" asked Savage.

"Nah. Waste of time. My gear's all set up. I'll stay here if that's okay. Pull an all-nighter, go online and do some digging. We can't rely on the Red Crew having information for us. We need something else."

"I'll put the kettle on, then."

Just at that moment, Frank's door opened and Julie appeared. She closed it softly behind her.

"Julie," said Savage. "How are you?"

In the harsh artificial light her features looked puffy, as if she'd been in a fight. Her forehead was creased with worry lines and her eyes laced with bloodshot capillaries. "I want to crawl into bed and never wake up, not unless I can have Callum back."

Savage gripped her arm in a bid to offer some comfort. "Any word from the police?"

"Just the family liaison officer checking in. Oh, and Sutcliffe called earlier but had nothing to say really. Just a courtesy call."

That was an oxymoron, thought Savage. There was nothing courteous about that man.

"What about you? Any luck?" she asked.

"Er, we're following up a few leads," he replied. This was the same line that Sutcliffe was giving her, and now so was he. This poor woman was in the lowest circle of hell and all she'd been offered were policing clichés.

"Thank you, John. Thank you, Tannaz. I really appreciate you looking." Julie looked ready to cry.

Savage quickly changed the subject. "How about a nice cup of tea?"

"No. Actually I wanted to ask Tannaz something. Can I have a cigarette?"

Tannaz patted the pockets of her jacket. "I'm all out. But I can nip to the 24-hour convenience store. Get some more."

"No, that's fine," said Julie. "It's serendipity. I quit years ago. I don't want to start again."

"If ever there was a reason to start smoking, this would be it," said Tannaz. "You stay here, I'll get us some. Any particular brand?"

"No, just something with plenty of nicotine."

Tannaz jogged off down the road, leaving Savage and Julie standing uncomfortably on the step outside his front door.

"Are you sure I can't make you a cup of tea?" It was all Savage had to offer. Tea and sympathy. No use at all.

"No," she said. "I've drunk so much tea in the last seven hours my bladder's as big as a Zeppelin." She sat down on Savage's front step, her whole body deflating, as if someone had vacuumed the air out of her. "Is it okay if I just sit here? I just wanted to get out of Frank's flat, it reminds me of Callum."

"Of course," said Savage. So Julie and Savage simply sat there staring out into the darkness. Her mouth hung open, the mental exhaustion unbearable. The woman just wanted to be numb for a while, to go into neutral. To have a break from feeling all the pain and stress.

"You know what keeps hitting me around the head like a bloody trip hammer?" said Julie. "If we'd got here on time on Friday, Callum would still be with us."

It was the same conversation he'd had with Celia. The if-only-I'd-done-this scenario. A completely natural, yet extremely unhelpful, unjustified thought process that only led to a downward spiral of self-shaming.

Savage offered the same advice he'd offered Celia. "Julie, you didn't know this would happen. No one did."

"Yep, I know. I've been through that argument in my head, over and over. And I still feel absolutely terrible."

Savage didn't know what to say. He knew what Julie was like. She was a workaholic, and practically lived at the office.

"She's in denial," said Jeff Perkins, the voice in Savage's head. *"And she'll pay for it later."*

Not now, Jeff.

"See, you can't ignore feelings like that. Can't deny them. They'll only come back ten times worse."

How do you know that?

"Why, me, of course. I'm the result of all your denial. All that crap in your head. All those murders you committed."

It was war.

"Still murder, just government-sanctioned murder. Anyway, all that pain and guilt and remorse you hid away was feeding me. Making me stronger. Like that muppet plant thing in Little Shop of Horrors. *You were feeding me, Seymour. Feeding me corpses in a metaphysical sense. And I grew and I grew and grew, until I grew big enough to be the voice in your head."*

I wouldn't say grew. I'd say you festered like a boil. A septic boil. And every time you speak it's like a load of pus running out.

"Call it what you like. But here's something that will chill you to the bone. I'm still growing."

Good for you, Jeff.

"You're not taking this seriously, Savage. I'm growing bigger and stronger every day. Getting more powerful. Soon I'll rule your head completely. Then I'll be in charge and you'll be the voice in my head. Growing smaller and smaller all the time."

Yeah? Well you still don't seem too powerful when Tannaz is around. She's your kryptonite.

"She is."

I'm glad you're finally admitting it.

"Don't get too smug, Savage. There'll be a day when she isn't around. And on that day your head will be under new management. Me. She won't hang around with you forever. All good things come to an end. It's a ticking time bomb. Then we'll have some fun. Or maybe you could keep her locked somewhere in a little dungeon, like this child abductor has done to these kids. That's if they're even alive."

Shut up, Jeff. Jeff...?

Jeff had become quiet and Savage saw the reason. Under the yellow cone of streetlamp light he could see Jeff's kryptonite marching up the road, a lit cigarette dangling lazily from her mouth. Tannaz.

When she reached Savage and Julie, Tannaz delved into the pocket of her biker jacket and pulled out four different brands of cigarettes. She fanned them out in front of Julie like a conjuror with playing cards. "I got four choices of strength. Low, medium, strong and French."

The smallest of smirks crossed Julie's face, possibly the only time that had happened in the last twenty-four hours. "That's very kind of you," said Julie, selecting a packet of Rothman's. "Let me give you some money."

"Don't be daft," said Tannaz, "these are on me."

A small tear appeared at the corner of Julie's eye. A tiny act of kindness, bringing her emotions to the surface once more. "Thank you," she said, dabbing her cheek with her cuff. She fumbled with the packet, desperate to get a cigarette out, her shaking hands not making it easy for her. Once the cigarette was in her mouth, Tannaz lit it for her. Julie drew a deep, long drag, and blew out a whole lungful of smoke. The nicotine sent a shiver through her body as it hit her bloodstream. Her eyelids went heavy momentarily. "Not used to it," she said, swaying slightly.

Savage Children

Tannaz sparked up another cigarette for herself and smoked it down to the tip. Then ground out the butt under her foot.

Julie turned to John and said, "Would you mind if I sit here alone and just smoked?"

"Not at all," said Savage. "Come on, Tannaz. We've got work to do."

"Thank you," Julie replied.

Tannaz pushed her lighter and the packet of cigarettes into Julie's hand. "Just in case you run out. And if you need anyone to talk to, just knock on Savage's door. I'll be up all night."

"You don't have to do that," said Julie.

"It's okay," said Savage. "Tannaz is a night owl."

"That's very kind of you," Julie said for the second time.

"Don't worry," Savage said. "We'll find Callum."

Julie gave a weak smile, and was on the verge of crying again. They left her alone and went inside, despite all Savage's instincts saying otherwise. He wanted to stay with her and try to be of comfort, to put an arm around her shoulders and tell her everything would be okay. But he knew from personal experience that everyone dealt with loss in their own particular way. Some wanted to shout and scream and punch out, and he was sure she'd had her fill of punching and shouting at Frank. Others wanted their friends and family with them at all times, never wanting to be left alone. And there were some, like Julie at that moment, who just wanted solitude, perhaps to give them time to process and analyse. To try and make sense of what had happened, seeking out a solution, even if there wasn't one. Like grasping at the air.

Savage woke on Monday morning, went straight to the kitchen as he always did, and put the kettle on to make the *golden cup*. That was Savage's name for the first cup of tea of the day. The best one of the day. For there was nothing that compared to waking up with a parched, bird cage of a mouth and having it quenched with strong, hot tea. Although, this morning's first cup wouldn't be so golden, even though he was using the delicious tea leaves Vikram had given him, as Callum was still missing. And neither they nor the police had any clues.

While he waited for the tea to brew, he spied a mountain of cigarette butts in an ashtray outside on his patio. Evidence of Tannaz fuelling her night work with nicotine. He'd left her to it at around four in the morning, while she was still going strong, eyes intense, fixed on her multiple computer screens, fingers frantic as if she were attempting to shut down a nuclear powerplant, stopping it from going into meltdown.

He popped his head around the lounge door to see if she wanted coffee. Tannaz's head was slumped on the table, her lustrous black locks spilled over the keyboard like squid-ink fusilli pasta. Deep snores emanated from her, as she slept in the awkward position. He desperately wanted to lift her head and slide a cushion under it, but that would risk waking her. He gently closed the door and left her to it.

By lunchtime Tannaz was up but her mood was down. Very down. Her dark-brown eyes had somehow become darker, a permanent scowl had set in and those broad red lips had become tight and thin. Tannaz didn't handle failure well. Not that they were failing. An investigation was a slow process. Sometimes glacial. It was nothing like her world of hacking. Tannaz was used to creating solutions where there weren't any, exploiting loopholes, getting in through back doors. And if there weren't any back doors, she'd just create them, using her smarts to hack away until she got what, or more precisely, *where* she wanted to be. Savage had nothing but respect for her intelligence and her never-ending drive—Tannaz the Tenacious as he liked to call her, as if she were a female warrior from the land of Dorne. She certainly looked like one. But in this situation there was nothing to hack away at. No firewalls to get around, no security to breach. No zeroes and ones she could weaponise. Callum had disappeared into thin air. She had nothing to attack. Nothing to strike out against. At least she hadn't thrown any hardware across the room. Although, the day was still young.

Savage Children

Savage put a steaming cup of fresh ground coffee in her hands. She downed it in one.

"Want another?" asked Savage.

Tannaz nodded.

The second cup took two gulps to drain. By the third, Tannaz had slowed down to a more pedestrian pace, her mood marginally better.

"How did it go last night after I turned in?" Savage braced himself, expecting a venomous reply. It didn't come. Tannaz merely slumped, defeated.

"Didn't get anywhere. Dead end after dead end. Then I Just kept re-watching the footage of Callum going into the park, hoping something would leap out. A big zilch on that front."

"How about Roberts' texts and emails. Anything new?"

"Nothing. Apart from Sutcliffe sending her sexist messages, telling her she'd be better off raising kids than being a detective."

"How does she put up with that guy?" asked Savage.

"Beats me. He'd get a punch in his groin if he was my boss."

"Guy feels threatened," said Savage. "That's what it is. Smart, young woman like Roberts. He's frightened she's going to make him look bad. No better way to push the buttons of an old misogynist git."

"Yeah, well the git should retire. Get out of the way."

"Don't hold your breath." Savage took a sip of tea and then said, "Well, only thing left is to go find the Red Crew and pray they've got something for us."

After one more coffee and another tea, Savage made Tannaz eat something. The girl seemed to live off caffeine and cigarettes, fuelled by stimulants. When he'd made her finish the last crumb of her toast, they traipsed up to the park, half expecting the entrance to be blocked with caution tape and guarded by a uniformed police officer. No caution tape to be seen and no uniformed officers.

"Police must have got everything they needed," said Savage.

"Which I'm guessing is nothing," Tannaz added. "Nothing much to see except dog-ends and dog turds."

As they entered the park through the stench of the alleyway, just as before, they saw that a large gang of mean-looking, hoodie-clad youths had gathered around the one and only usable park bench.

But it wasn't the Red Crew.

CHAPTER 16

Like the Red Crew, this gang was a large group of about ten or twelve guys in their late teens, maybe early twenties. Savage guessed this must be the Mojos, Red Crew's arch-rivals. Had the Red Crew been ousted from their scrap of a park? It certainly looked that way, judging by how this new gang strutted around, cocksure of themselves.

Savage watched as the gang formed a semi-circle around a much younger boy, possibly only twelve or thirteen years of age. The kid looked terrified, eyes as big as saucers, hands shaking, lips quivering. Tannaz and Savage edged closer until they were within earshot.

"I didn't mean to lose it, Shankster. I swear," the young boy said, breathlessly, his voice wobbling all over the place. "Some guy robbed me."

The one called Shankster stepped forward, looking down on the boy with hateful eyes. He wore a large black puffer jacket, hood hanging out the back of it and expensive white Nike trainers. "We gave you one job to do. And you ballsed it up," he snarled. "Lost our gear. Well, now you owe us, big time. And you'll have to work to pay it back. Including the train fare. Else I will literally cut you into a billion pieces."

Now Savage should've have tried to win the trust of this new gang, just like he had with the Red Crew. Been respectful, deferential to them as rightful overlords of the park. To keep them onside with the aim of teasing information out of them, to see if they'd heard anything or knew anything or if he could recruit them to find out. That had to go out the window for now. The young boy was in trouble, about to become in this gang's debt, possibly for the rest of his short life.

Savage spoke up. "Let me, guess." The assembled mob swung round. Ugly stares flying at him and Tannaz.

"Walk away now, fool," said Shankster.

"I'm not talking to you," said Savage. Moving closer to the group, he looked at the young boy. "Let me guess. You had to deliver some drugs out of town. Somewhere rural or maybe coastal. I've read about it. Called 'going country'. Recruit a young kid to deliver drugs out in the sticks to avoid suspicion. Less risk of stop and search. Then you stepped off the train in Hicksville and got mugged. Rucksack full of drugs taken, worth hundreds, maybe thousands of quid. That what happened?"

The boy just stood there, frozen by fear. Nervous hands by his side.

"I'll take that as a yes," said Savage. "So you travelled somewhere you've never been before, and some random guy targets you in broad daylight. Must've been his lucky day. I mean, what are the odds of that happening?"

Tannaz's thumbs buzzed across the screen of her phone, feeding numbers into her calculator app, working out the odds from the ground up. "Chance of getting mugged in a rural UK town, zero point eight seven percent," she said.

"Wow," said Savage. "Less than one percent. That's really, really unlucky or... Wait a minute." Savage adopted a Victorian sleuth-like tone. "Hold on, what if it was planned? A set up? Gang member follows you up there. One you've never met before. Jumps you after you've left the train station. You lose the drugs and now you owe them, have to pay it all back. Yet they still have the drugs. What a fiendish plan."

"And you have to work for free," Tannaz added. "Indefinitely."

The young boy's face changed. Realisation blinking on like a faulty strip light, as he was presented with a new, more rational interpretation of his day's events. One that made a lot more sense.

Shankster shook his head slowly. "You don't know nothin', bruv. Got a wild imagination. Puttin' ideas in a young 'un's head."

Savage Children

Somehow his face had become meaner and more surly than before. "You better shut that mouth of yours."

"Or what?" said Savage.

Shankster laughed. "You know who we are?"

"The Mojos."

"S'right. Got a reputation, we have. 'specially me. I'm literally going to stab you, like, a million times." Shankster marched over to Savage, drew a knife from the back of his waistband, increased his pace and went to stab Savage in the gut.

Savage caught his knife hand by the wrist, twisted it outwards, putting pressure on the joint, but not enough to snap it and make him drop the knife. Just enough pain to lock his arm in place and hold him on pause so he couldn't move. Just grimace, face contorted in agony.

Savage spoke to the young kid directly. "Get out of here, kid. Don't worry, I'll make sure these clowns don't bother you again."

The kid sprinted out of the park.

Savage turned his attention to Shankster. "Comfortable? So first, where did you go wrong? Well, it all started when you said, *you were literally going to stab me a million times*. You couldn't have meant that literally, because that would take a whole lifetime. The way to use the word literally is when something is actually happening in real life. So for instance, if I said, you're literally in no position to make threats, that's literal because your predicament isn't a metaphor, it's really happening, see?"

"What?" said Shankster, breathlessly.

Savage twisted his wrist harder. Shankster cried out and the knife fell to the floor.

"Tannaz, could you hand me that knife."

She picked it up off the floor and gave it to Savage. He lifted the knife to eye level and examined it. "So I guess you're called Shankster because you carry a knife. Pity you don't know how to use it. Okay, everyone, let's examine where the knife-fighting bit went wrong."

Still holding Shankster by the wrist, his arm and body bent in an awkward and humiliating position, Savage held the knife out at arm's length, the same way Shankster had held it seconds ago. Savage addressed the rest of the gang as if he were teaching a class. They had no choice but to stand and listen while their leader was held hostage.

"Shankster here chose a classic forward knife grip, also known as the hammer. It's a good grip. Main advantage is the reach." Savage thrust the knife out several times to demonstrate, as if he were poking a fire. "Perfect if you don't want to get too close to your opponent. I can extend the knife out from my body a long way. However, if I do that, it also highlights its disadvantage. An outstretched arm is easy to grab by your enemy, as I've just demonstrated. I easily disarmed him."

A few reluctant heads nodded.

"And even if he manages to hold onto the knife, his weapon is out of action. Here, hold this." Savage put the knife back into Shankster's twisted hand. He just managed to hold onto it in a weak fist.

"Okay," said Savage. "He's still got the knife but his arm's out of action, so is the rest of his body, because there's nothing more painful than a wrist lock." Shankster groaned in agreement. "However, my right hand here is still free to use against him." Savage waved his right hand in the air. "Like so." Savage drew his arm back then rammed the heel of his hand into Shankster's nose, smashing it flat. He cried out. His eyes filled with water, nose ran with blood. Savage pointed to the watery eyes. "Now he can't see. And if he can't see, he can't fight. Which means I'm free to do what I like. I can punch him in the throat, elbow him in the temple. Gouge his eyes. He's basically at my mercy. So what have we learned today, guys?"

No one said anything.

"Anyone? Anyone? Anyone?"

"Don't play with knives," said Tannaz.

"Thank you. Especially if you don't know how to use them."

A tall guy with a baseball cap stepped out from the assembled gang and produced a knife of his own from his back pocket. He edged towards Savage, bravely or rather stupidly. Savage judged by the look on his face it was the latter.

Savage Children

"Really?" said Savage. "You really want to have a knife fight with me? After what I've just shown you."

"Damn right," the guy said, getting ever closer. He bounced on his heels a few times, limbering up.

Savage rolled his eyes. Snatched the knife clutched in Shankster's limp hand and threw it at the guy in the baseball cap. It whistled past his ear, less than an inch away.

Baseball Cap smiled. "You missed."

"Did I?"

A few heads swivelled round followed by gasps and the odd f-bomb. On the wall, far behind the them, someone had sprayed a yellow smiley face with a spliff hanging out of its mouth. Dead centre between the eyes, the knife had embedded itself in the wall, point first, the handle vibrating from side to side like a superfast metronome.

Eventually Baseball Cap slowly turned his head, looked at the wall and saw Savage's brutal accuracy. He turned back to face Savage, swallowing hard, his knife-hand shaking.

"You, in the baseball cap," said Savage. "Give me your knife."

Baseball Cap sheepishly dawdled towards him and held out the knife, sharp-end first.

"Other way around, dimwit."

He switched the knife round, offering Savage the handle. Savage took it and pulled Shankster close. He relinquished his grip on Shankster's wrist, switching to a neck hold. With his other hand, Savage put the blade to Shankster's smooth throat. The guy probably hadn't even started shaving yet. "Now we're going to have a little personality test," said Savage. "On a scale of one to ten, one being not at all, ten *literally* being the highest—see, I've used the word literally in its proper form again—how likely is it that I will use this knife to open up your neck?"

"Ten, ten," said Shankster desperately.

"... Is the right answer. Yes, I will drag this blade across your useless neck unless you answer my questions honestly."

"Okay, yeah. Anything."

"A kid called Callum Leighton disappeared from this park on

Friday afternoon. He's about the same age as that other boy you were trying to hoodwink. Did you have anything to do with Callum's disappearance?"

"No, no, no way."

Savage tightened the blade against Shankster's neck, took a tiny nick out of his skin. "Were you using him as a drug mule, making him go country?"

"No. I swear. I don't know the kid."

"I think you're lying."

"No, please. I swear."

"He comes up here all the time. Your predecessors, the Red Crew, knew him. So how come you don't?"

"Red Crew has held this park for ages," Shankster gasped.

"They said they kicked you out a week ago. Sounds like this park keeps changing hands on a regular basis."

"Listen, we don't recruit kids from no park. Just do business here."

"So you recruit your kids elsewhere? On the estates?"

"Yeah."

"Setting them up. Trapping them into working for you like a slave. I really think I'd be doing society a favour by putting an end to you right now."

"No, please. I'll stop. I swear."

"You know," said Savage, thoughtfully. "I swore I'd stop hurting people a long time ago. Gives me awful mental-health problems. But here I am. Still hurting people."

"Don't kill me. Please."

Savage tightened the pressure on the knife, drawing more blood. "Tannaz, show Shankster the footage of Callum going into the park." She got out her phone, cued up the footage and held it in front of Shankster's eyes. He blinked rapidly, clearing the blurriness then squinted at the scene in front of him. "Know him?"

"I don't know him. I swear."

Savage said, "Now show him the mystery gang going into the park and the guy in the red Adidas top."

She scrolled forward on her phone and held the phone up to Shankster's face once more.

"What about these guys?" Savage asked.

With the knife held firmly to his neck, Shankster managed a miniscule shake of the head. "Don't know them, neither."

"Positive?"

"I swear, man."

"Tannaz, show the others."

She approached the gang. They gathered round and watched the footage. "Tell me who they are," said Tannaz. "If you're lying, Shankster gets his windpipe cut, and possibly a few of you too."

There were rapid and desperate shakes of the head.

"Never seen them round here," one of them said. "We know all the guys in the neighbourhood. They ain't from around here. I swear."

Savage inhaled deeply, then exhaled slowly. "Okay, Shankster, that creates a problem because we hired the Red Crew to find out who they were, and find anyone who knew anything about Callum. Keep their ears to the ground. But now you've pushed them out of the picture. I've lost my investment. So in the same way you made that kid pay you back, you need to pay me back. So now you and your gang have got the job."

Shankster nodded imperceptibly, not wanting the knife to dig into his throat any deeper.

"Your gang works for me now. Understand? They're going to be my eyes and ears from now on."

"Okay," Shankster croaked.

"If you refuse, we'll have another knife fight. Actually, won't be much of a fight. You won't see it coming. One second your neck will be intact, the next it will be cut in half. You'll watch your lifeblood pouring out of you. You'll put your hands up to try and stop the blood but it will just keep pouring like a burst water main. Same will happen if you try recruiting any more kids to go country. Do you understand?"

"I understand."

Savage released his grip around Shankster's neck and gave him a thumping great shove. He just managed to stop himself tumbling over and landing face flat on the ground in front of his mates.

Tannaz and Savage left the park, Savage pausing momentarily to pull the knife he'd thrown out of the graffiti-sprayed wall. He threw both knives down the first drain he came to.

Tannaz went to speak.

"Yeah, I know what you're going to say," said Savage. "'Teach me how to throw a knife like that.' I will, I promise. It's just the list of things I need to teach you keeps getting longer. Not that I mind, by the way. It just might take a while to get round to it."

"No," Tannaz replied. "Well, yes. I would like you to teach me that. But I was going to say, next time we hire a gang to be informers it'd be better if we got one or two phone numbers off them. So we can stay in touch. We should've done that with the Red Crew. Now they're out of the picture, we have no way of getting in contact with them. Same thing could happen with the Mojos. We can't rely on them being up the park."

"You're right. That would have been a good idea. We could go back."

"Nah, that would kind of ruin the effect we just created."

"Yeah, it wouldn't look good would it? *Oh by the way, I know I nearly just cut your throat but could we swap contact details? Hey, how about we friend each other on Facebook.*"

Tannaz screwed her nose up. "Facebook? I doubt any of them use Facebook. Maybe their mums do."

"Well, InstaSnapGram or whatever it's called. What is the cool social-media platform to be on these days for young people?"

"Dunno. Even I'm too old. It changes. New ones coming out all the time."

As they walked down the street, back to Savage's house, coming in the other direction, hurrying towards them came Celia. Beyond, parked outside of Frank's flat was a car Savage recognised. Sutcliffe's sedan was sandwiched between two police patrol cars.

When Celia reached them, struggling for breath, Savage asked, "Celia, what's happened? Have the police found Callum?"

"No," said Celia. "They've come for you."

CHAPTER 17

As Savage approached his flat with Tannaz and Celia, the car doors of all three police vehicles swung open. Sutcliffe, his usual, miserable self, dressed in the same ugly waterproof jacket he'd worn when Savage had first encountered him, got out first, followed by DI Roberts. Her expression was bland and unreadable. Two uniformed police officers got out of each patrol car, making six police officers in total. They were clearly expecting trouble.

"Mr Savage," said Sutcliffe. "We'd like to ask you a few questions."

"That's a lot of people to ask a few questions," Savage replied.

Sutcliffe gave a fleeting smile. "As your lady friend said, you're a highly experienced special forces operative. Can't take chances."

Celia spoke up. "John's not a threat. He's trying to help us find Callum."

"A well-meaning amateur who's getting in the way of us doing our jobs," Sutcliffe corrected. "We just want to ask some questions."

Savage could sense Tannaz coiling, getting ready to pounce and give the horrible copper a very large piece of her brilliant mind. He put a steadying hand on her arm. Smiled brightly at Sutcliffe. "It's okay, this well-meaning amateur is happy to answer all your questions, I promise. Shall we?"

Savage led the small entourage of coppers up to his front door, followed by Tannaz. Just as they were about to go in, Sutcliffe turned and held up his hand. "Not you, Miss Darvish. We want to talk to Mr Savage alone."

Tannaz threw Sutcliffe a hand-grenade of a look. Celia stepped beside Tannaz and hooked her arm around hers. "Come on, love. I'll make you a nice cup of coffee next door."

"You can see your mail-order girlfriend later," said Sutcliffe to Savage.

He ignored the gibe and said, "Was it cold in the ground when they dug you up this morning?"

Before Sutcliffe could think of an equally suitable rebuttal, Roberts spoke. "Let's just get on with it shall we? See if we can help find Callum." She showed great restraint and integrity, reminding the two old servicemen of what was important, while they were about to start butting heads and have a slanging match.

"Quite right," Savage replied. He opened his front door and showed them into the lounge, four uniformed and two plain-clothes officers sat down, taking up every inch of sofa space. He offered them tea. They all declined. Savage perched on an arm of a chair. One of the uniforms stood up so Savage could take a seat.

Sutcliffe got straight down to it. "How would you describe your relationship with your neighbour, Frank Leighton?"

"Average," said Savage without pausing for thought.

"Really? You think you have an average relationship with your neighbour?"

"Yes," Savage replied.

"That's not the way he sees it."

Savage didn't reply. Didn't fill the silence that Sutcliffe left.

"I said that's not the way he sees it," Sutcliffe repeated.

Savage stared back blankly.

Sutcliffe smiled. "Listen, Mr Savage. I'm guessing you've been trained to resist interrogation, have been taught techniques for not revealing secrets, techniques you're probably using now, but that's not what this is about. It's merely an exchange of information to help us find Callum. So I'd like you to answer my last question."

"It wasn't a question," Savage replied. "I said I'd be happy to answer all your questions. You made a statement, *that's not the way he sees it*. Ask me a question and I'll be happy to answer. Or would you like me to help you form your sentences into questions?"

Sutcliffe was about to chastise Savage for being facetious but

Savage Children

Roberts got in before him, keeping the conversation civil. "Did you put out Frank Leighton's bonfire on Friday afternoon without his permission?" Roberts asked.

"Yes."

"That doesn't sound like an 'average' thing to do," said Sutcliffe making air quotes.

Savage hated air quotes. Savage hated people who made them even more.

"Technically, he was breaking the law," Savage replied. "Local by-law states bonfires are only to be lit after six p.m. Obviously you already know that being a policeman."

Sutcliffe eyes narrowed. "You could've called on him, asked him politely to put it out."

Savage didn't say anything.

"Well?" said Sutcliffe.

"You made another statement. Why don't you rephrase it as a question?"

"We get the feeling you don't like your neighbour very much. Is that correct?" asked Roberts.

"No, we get on like a house on fire, or a bonfire on fire. Or not on fire, if it's before six p.m."

"Why did you put out his bonfire?" asked Roberts.

"Can I just ask what this has to do with finding Callum?" Savage said.

"We're just trying to build up a picture," said Roberts. "A picture of the events that took place on Friday afternoon before Callum was reported missing. Standard procedure, as you well understand. Frank, Julie and Celia have given us their version, we'd like to know yours. An altercation took place and we'd like to know why."

"Okay, fair enough," said Savage. "I don't like smoke. Reminds me of the battlefield. Things burning. Don't like the memories."

"Ah," said Sutcliffe, sagely. "So you've been traumatised by it."

"I don't know anyone who hasn't."

Sutcliffe steepled his hands pompously. "So you have issues. Perhaps, mental-health issues?"

There was no point lying. They'd obviously done their homework and found out Savage had been to a counsellor.

"I've seen a counsellor, yes."

"Can you tell us what you talked about?" Roberts asked gently.

"No. It's private, confidential."

"Do you have flashbacks? Uncomfortable episodes?" asked Sutcliffe.

Savage shook his head. "It's more to do with losing my wife and daughter, if you must know." It was at least half the truth.

"Do you hear voices?" asked Sutcliffe.

"*Yes, yes he does,*" Jeff Perkins suddenly piped up from within Savage's brain. "*That's me they're talking about. Me, Savage. Don't deny it.*"

"No," said Savage. "I don't hear voices."

"*Oh, you bitch,*" said Jeff.

Sutcliffe lent forward. "See, my worry with you, Mr Savage, is that I wonder that you might like fighting."

Savage sat there nonplussed for a second or two, then burst out laughing. Big, fat belly laughs. Uncontrollable. Tears streaming from his eyes. When he'd regained some composure he said, "Wow. Nothing gets past you, does it? You're like some kind of super-cop. How did you work that out? I'm ex-SAS, went to the first Gulf War and hunted down Serbian war criminals, and you think I might like fighting. I hate to shock you, but it is kind of in the job description for being in the army. I mean, if I was dropped into a warzone and I didn't like fighting, I'd be a pretty useless soldier, and rubbish at defending the realm. But to be more precise, we call it controlled violence or management of violence. That is, the use of force against an enemy to suppress or neutralise a threat. It's not going round randomly punching people."

"*Yep, and Savage loves it. Gets off on it, he does,*" said Jeff.

"So they have to be asking for it, do they?" Sutcliffe asked.

"When you say *they*, I presume you mean the enemy? Yes, the enemy are asking for it when they invade another country or start the genocide of the local population. That's when we step in and stop them."

Savage Children

"Is Frank your enemy?" Sutcliffe asked, completely missing the point, almost certainly on purpose. Savage knew where this was going. Sutcliffe's interview technique was obvious. Questions so leading he might as well have put a ring in Savage's nose, hitched a rope to it and dragged him to the conclusion. Sutcliffe's simplistic theory probably ran along the lines of: Savage didn't like Frank, therefore, Savage had taken Callum to spite him. Clumsy but it made sense up to a point, until you factored in all the other children who had disappeared. Why would Savage have taken them? One thing he was sure of, Sutcliffe didn't have anything on Savage. He was desperate. Fishing around for a perpetrator. He needed a suspect with a motive, and he needed one fast, even if that motive was as flimsy as tissue paper.

"Enemy is far too strong a word," Savage replied. "More like mildly irritating. Like getting soap in your eye."

"*I'm the real enemy,*" said Jeff. "*Tell them about me. Go on.*"

"Would you say you're close to Callum?" Roberts asked.

Savage noticed Sutcliffe shot her a disapproving look. She'd changed the line of questioning. Switching from Callum's disappearance as a reprisal for Savage not getting on with his father, to a straightforward one of Savage did it because he had a thing for Callum. Her questioning was as bad as Sutcliffe's. Unless this was their plan. Keep changing tack to throw Savage off. Either way, it wasn't going to work.

"What?"

"I understand you let Callum use your garden to play football in," said Sutcliffe.

"You know I do," Savage replied.

"Just answer the question," Sutcliffe snapped.

Roberts interrupted. "Sir, we need to remember this is a chat, not a formal police interview..."

"Be quiet, Roberts," Sutcliffe barked. "Answer the question. Does Callum play in your garden?"

"Yes, he does."

Sutcliffe gave a creepy, sickly smile. "Rather odd, don't you think? Letting a neighbour's son play in your garden when he has a perfectly good one of his own."

"I told you before, Frank's garden is a tip. A death trap."

"Mr Savage," said Roberts. "We're just trying to establish why you would allow a young boy into your garden on his own."

"Unless you had a thing for him," Sutcliffe added.

Savage stared directly into Sutcliffe's burned-out and bloodshot eyes. "Yes, I have a thing, it's called being a responsible adult. Callum often comes home from school to find himself locked out. Sitting on the doorstep. Would you rather I left a ten-year-old boy to wander around alone in south London or should I be a good neighbour and invite him in, make him a sandwich and a cup of tea and have a kickabout with him?"

Sutcliffe smiled, smugly, perhaps sensing he had Savage on the ropes. "Bit creepy, isn't it? Man your age with a young boy."

"Don't forget the mail-order wife," said Savage. "Listen, Frank isn't a good father. He's irresponsible and a slob. He lets Callum go up that park where the local gangs hang out. Gangs that carry knives and enlist young kids to transport drugs out of town. That is not a good place for Callum to be, so I figure every time he's here's with me, he's not up that park and at risk of getting into gang culture or being stabbed."

Sutcliffe stared at Savage unblinking, then said, "May I use your bathroom please?"

"Sure," said Savage. "It's out in the hallway, under the stairs near the front door."

Sutcliffe got up and left. Barely seconds later he came back in the room and said, "John Savage, I am arresting you for the kidnapping of Callum Leighton."

CHAPTER 18

SAVAGE STOOD BOLT UPRIGHT. The four uniforms did the same, clearly thinking Savage might make a run for it or resist arrest or maybe hit their stupid boss. "What?" said Savage.

Sutcliffe spoke calmly, "I said, I'm arresting you for—"

"Yes, I heard that bit. Why are you arresting me?" Savage sneaked a glance at Roberts. She looked as shocked as he felt.

Sutcliffe's smile became intolerably smug. "On my way back from the bathroom I noticed you had a ball in your garden. One from the last world cup. Very distinctive design. We have CCTV footage of Callum entering the park on Friday afternoon carrying the very same ball under his arm before he disappeared. The ball was never recovered, and now I find it's lying in your garden."

"I doubt you could see the garden from out in the hallway," said Savage. "Unless you've been snooping around."

"What is that ball doing in your garden?" asked Sutcliffe.

"I have one idea," said Savage. "Maybe a burned-out copper, who's desperate for a conviction, planted it there, so he could arrest someone, anyone. Just to keep his superiors off his back."

"Really? So I entered your flat with a pumped-up football under my jacket, then tossed it in your garden on my way to the bathroom."

"Nah," said Savage. "Even you're not that stupid. You probably asked someone else to do it. Maybe some lowlife who owes you one."

Sutcliffe laughed. "I really did expect more from you, Mr Savage, especially being ex-SAS. Seems like you're just a shell-shocked soldier with a vivid imagination. Well, this isn't TV and you're arrested. Handcuff him and read him his rights." Sutcliffe turned to Roberts. "Put your gloves on and get that football in an evidence bag." Roberts did as she was told.

Once they had the football bagged up, they led Savage out of his house, so all could see. Friends and neighbours. A police technique for bringing shame on the suspect, no doubt. Soften them up for questioning down the station. Savage wasn't bothered. Compared to being held in an Iraqi prison this was like a spa day.

Before they got to the patrol car, Tannaz burst out of Frank's flat, quickly followed by Julie and Celia. Frank appeared in the doorway and leant against the frame, arms folded, a slight kink of a smile on one side of his mouth. The sight of his arch enemy being arrested was Christmas, birthday and bar mitzvah all rolled into one.

"Hey," Tannaz snarled. "DCI Shitcliffe, let him go."

"Please," said Julie. "John had nothing to do with this, he's been looking for Callum non-stop."

"That's right," Celia added. "You've got the wrong man."

"We'll be the judge of that," Sutcliffe said. "This is a police matter. Please go back inside."

"It's okay," said Savage. "These simple folk are helping us with our enquiries."

"That's enough," said Sutcliffe. He opened the squad-car door and plunged Savage's head down to stopping him banging it on the door frame.

"You really are the biggest prick I've ever met," said Tannaz.

"Tannaz," Savage called out from inside the squad car. "It's fine, go back inside." One thing he didn't want was for her to get arrested as well.

"That's right, Miss Darvish," Sutcliffe said. "Listen to your boyfriend. One more outburst like that and I'll arrest you too."

Julie gently clasped Tannaz's arm and guided her back into the flat. Tannaz glanced over her shoulder as all three police cars pulled away from the kerb. From the side window of the patrol car, Savage gave her a reassuring wink.

Savage was enjoying himself. Sort of. Maybe "enjoy" was too strong a word. "Curiously fascinated" would be more accurate. He'd never been arrested before. Even when he was a young tearaway, hanging out on the streets of Camberwell and Peckham looking for trouble, he'd never had a brush with the law. Sure, he'd done plenty of bad things that would merit arrest, but it had never happened. Even back then he'd shown the raw skills needed for eluding the enemy, even if it was the local bobbies who weren't particularly bright or fit. The only thing that marred this new experience for Savage was that every minute he was locked in here was a minute he wasn't out there looking for Callum.

Sutcliffe had nothing, apart from a plastic football that matched the one under Callum's arm in the CCTV footage. How it got into Savage's garden was a mystery. It was almost certainly a plant. Initially Savage had suspected Sutcliffe. He wouldn't have done it himself, of course, he'd have got someone else to do it. Probably not another copper. Possibly some poor unfortunate who Sutcliffe could apply pressure on to do it or else face arrest. That was Savage's first conclusion. Although, something about Sutcliffe told Savage that he didn't seem the type. He was from the era when planting evidence was the norm, sure enough. But something about Sutcliffe's character didn't fit with that behaviour. He was a proud old copper and that pride wouldn't have allowed him to do such a thing. He thought he was better than all these young up-and-comers. He would have wanted a clean conviction. One that he'd got using his own deductive powers, not cheap, dirty tricks. Yes, he was desperate, eager to have someone in custody, but not if it meant breaking the rules. Plus, he had Roberts to contend with. The young female detective seemed a by-the-book type of copper. She would've smelt a rat. And possibly dobbed him in. So if it wasn't Sutcliffe, who was it that wanted Savage to take the fall? And who could've planted a ball in his garden so easily?

It didn't take too much deductive reasoning.

Frank.

He certainly had the motivation. He hated Savage. And planting the ball was as simple as going down the market, buying a cheap knockoff world-cup football and tossing it over the hedge. And the guy had looked pretty pleased with himself when Savage had been arrested, though that could just be down to simply enjoying Savage's misfortune. One thing was for sure, Savage would be having words with him. But one step at a time. He had to get out of here first.

Savage clasped his hands behind his head and leant back in his chair, looking around the bland, uninteresting, windowless interview room. A chipped painted metal table was in front of him, the top covered in hardwearing fake-wood veneer, supporting a digital recording device, capturing audio and video. His eyes finally alighted on Sutcliffe's worn-out face.

"I'm sorry, what did you say?" Savage asked.

"I said where were you at around four p.m. last Friday? That's June 7th." It was the hundredth time Sutcliffe had asked him this.

"I told you. At home waiting for a delivery. Check with the phone company, you'll find my phone was at home with me at the time."

"That check takes a while," said Roberts.

Not if you're Tannaz it doesn't, Savage thought.

"Well, you better get started," Savage replied. "I mean, you'd look really stupid if you charged me and then the phone company triangulated my phone's position and placed it at my home. You'd have wasted days while the real culprit is still out there."

"The position of a phone doesn't necessarily prove you were at home," said Roberts. "You could have left it there. Then gone and abducted Callum."

Sutcliffe's grin grew wider, creating a matrix of crow's feet and ancient laughter lines. "She's right, Mr Savage. We have the football in your garden, currently with forensics, and you have no one to corroborate your whereabouts at the time of Callum's disappearance. Definite grounds for charging you."

Savage Children

Savage had had enough now. Time to bring out the big guns.

"When was the last time Callum was seen?" asked Savage.

"We have CCTV footage of him going into the entrance to the park at 4.11 p.m. CCTV doesn't lie. You can see him going in as plain as day."

"And at around about the same time I was at home."

"Yes, but you can't prove that."

"I signed for a delivery at, let me think, just after four p.m. Had to sign for it on one of those handheld devices. Records the exact time the parcel was handed over—had to scrawl my signature on the screen. Then they send you an email confirming your parcel has been delivered, bit over the top if you ask me, but good for proving exactly when and where you were. If you give me my phone back, I can show you. My usual delivery driver's called Lev. Nice Polish guy. We talk about punk music. You should get in touch. I mean, logistics these days, is all tracked and logged, down to the second. Very hard to fake that. Give him a call. Ask him to send you his electronic data. Oh, he's also a good old-fashioned witness too, will back up that I was at home."

Sutcliffe's face dropped. The skin went all saggy and hangdog. Apart from his eyes that looked like two volcanoes.

"Doesn't mean anything," he said. "You could've signed for the parcel then went up the park and abducted Callum." Now the guy really was struggling. Clutching at straws with two fat, clumsy fists.

"That's true," said Savage. "It definitely puts me at home at around four p.m. but then I suppose I could've legged it up to the park and snatched Callum. But you just told me you have CCTV footage of Callum going into the park."

"That's right."

"Then surely you'd have footage of me going in after him, then leaving with him. I mean, that park's only got one way in and one way out. Unless I flew over the walls or walked through them."

"You could've abducted him after that," said Sutcliffe. "Waited for him to leave the park. Bundled him into that little van of yours right outside his front door. Drove him someplace else. You paedophiles like panel vans don't you?"

Savage feigned hurt. Made them think they were getting to him. In a humble voice he said, "Can I just ask one small question?"

"Of course," said Sutcliffe.

"When Callum came back out of the park, which way did he turn?"

Neither Roberts nor Sutcliffe said anything.

Savage continued his humble-pie routine. "Look, I really want to clear myself. It's true I do have a van. And, yes, it was parked outside my flat on Friday afternoon. So, I could see how you could think that I bundled Callum into it before he had a chance to reach his front door. But if I did that, it would mean Callum left the park and made a right turn out of the alley to come home, back down my road. CCTV would have seen him turning right when he left the park. So I was just wondering which way he turned when he came out of the park, right or left?"

Savage knew he had them. They didn't know which way Callum had turned because the CCTV footage never caught him coming out.

Sutcliffe and Roberts remained silent.

Savage stared at them both, eyes flitting from one to the other, neither of them knowing how to answer the question. It was the main element of the case that didn't make any sense. It had them baffled.

"Sorry, do you want me to repeat the question?"

"Let's move on, shall we," said Sutcliffe, changing the subject. "We do have footage of you going in the park later on, Mr Savage."

"Yep, with Celia. Is that what you're referring to?"

"Yes. Care to tell us what you were doing there?"

Savaged sighed. "You know what we were doing if you've already spoken to Celia. We were looking for Callum. Went to fetch him because his mum was having him for the weekend. She stayed behind to get his things ready because Frank's too lazy. Tell me, in this CCTV footage of me and Celia, did you see us leaving the park?"

"Yes," said Roberts.

"Good. Did you see Callum leave the park?" Savage wasn't going to let up. He'd push them on this, keep digging the knife in until they let him go.

The pair of them went quiet again.

"A simple yes or no answer will suffice."

"We ask the questions, Mr Savage," Sutcliffe reminded him. "There are elements of an investigation we like to keep to ourselves."

"But surely it's an important piece of the puzzle," Savage replied. "I mean, I'm just a well-meaning amateur, but knowing whether he turned left or right when he left the park would give some clue as to which direction he went. Was he alone? Who left after him? Surely if you think it's me, I must be in the footage leaving with Callum before I went up there with Celia. Unless you think Celia and I abducted him together when we went in there to look for him. In which case you'd have footage of the three of us leaving the park."

"As I said before, Mr Savage, we're asking the questions."

"But you're accusing me of abducting him. I mean, can I see the footage, check the evidence for myself? Just to make sure I didn't block it all out in my head, seeing as how you think I'm a traumatised soldier."

Sutcliffe shook his head. "No, no way."

"Why not?"

"It's not public CCTV. Private camera. Police eyes only."

"Is it the camera on the warehouse? I'm sure if I ask them nicely, they'd let me have a look at the footage. See what's what."

"That footage is now police evidence."

Savage leant forward, as if he were the one conducting the interview. "Really? You're being very protective over that footage. Now if I were a copper, I'd say you're both acting very suspiciously. You sound like you're hiding something you don't want me to see. Thing is, if this goes to trial, you'd have to disclose the footage anyway. Well before it went to court. What's in that footage that you don't want me to see?" Savage knew very well what it was. Callum had gone in and not come out.

"Again, Mr Savage. We're interviewing you. Not the other way round."

"So am I free to go then? If not, you have to charge me."

Both detectives went quiet again.

Savage glared at Sutcliffe. "There's a missing kid out there, and you're in here questioning me when you know I was nowhere near that park. You're wasting everyone's time. All you're worried about is convicting someone. Anyone. Doesn't matter if they did it or not. You just want someone to pin it on. You're such a cliché, Sutcliffe. Meanwhile Callum's out there, alone, scared. And you're sitting in here playing good cop, dumb cop. And yes, Sutcliffe, you're the dumb cop in this scenario."

"That's enough, Mr Savage," said Sutcliffe. "I'm terminating the interview and you're going back to the cells. We'll resume this in the morning."

"You've got to be kidding me. Keeping me in overnight. For what? Because of a football in my garden? Or is it because I'm pointing out the holes in your case? Roberts, do you agree with this?"

Roberts went to speak but Sutcliffe cut her off, calling time on the interview. A fleeting sneer passed across Roberts' lips as she was silenced. Sutcliffe got up and knocked on the door, Roberts reluctantly followed him. As they left, three uniforms came in to lead Savage back to his cell.

He could've resisted, easily taken out the three uniforms. Savage didn't want to do that. These guys were just doing their jobs. Plus, Sutcliffe would've loved that. Would've played right into his hands, given him ammunition for charging him. Savage would be compliant. For now.

CHAPTER 19

Rhianna Pullman did not want to draw. She sat with her arms firmly folded across her chest, bottom lip protruding defiantly. In the darkened room, a single desktop lamp illuminated the paper and pencils arranged neatly in front of her, ready to let her imagination flow. Unlike most children, Rhianna Pullman did not like drawing or colouring in, not with pencils, that was so lame. It was boring and dull. Rhianna Pullman liked devices. In particular, iPads. Whenever she got bored or misbehaved, she got the latest iPad shoved under her nose to fiddle with, and maybe order herself some new clothes from an online fashion retailer, Mum's credit card details already saved. Once she'd overheard her mum say, *Anything to keep her quiet.* And Rhianna had exploited that slip of the tongue ever since.

"Draw me a picture," said the Archangel. "A beautiful picture of you soaring among the clouds as an angel. Do it for Mummy and Daddy. Make them proud. You want to make them proud, don't you? See what a great artist you are. Do the best work you possibly can. Better than anything you've ever done."

Rhianna shrugged and tightened her folded arms rebelliously.

"I want you to draw me a picture of an angel," the Archangel spoke with more insistence, edging each word with fury.

"Nope," said Rhianna, with a single shake of the head. She wasn't frightened, even if she was being held in a small, damp, darkened room by a stranger. "Not going to."

"I'll give you another lolly."

As if by magic, a sugary lolly with a small top and a flat plastic stem appeared over her shoulder.

"Urgh, they're gross," said Rhianna, recoiling. "What am I, seven and poor? I usually have ice cream from Spoons Gelateria. It's proper Italian. It's amazing. Made the same day. I have as much as I want, and I don't get fat. Mum says I have her metabolism. Fat-burning genes like her. She's always been a size eight. Says her friends hate her for it, even though they don't say it to her face. They have muffin tops they can't get rid of, but my mum can eat what she likes. They have to have personal trainers, because Mum says they have no self-control. Mum has a personal trainer, but she says she doesn't really need him because she says she's already naturally hot. She sees him a lot. He comes round our house to train her. We have a home gym. He's always coming round when Dad's at work. That's when I get my iPad to play with in my room, not a load of stupid paper and pencils. And definitely not yucky lollipops."

Archangel's voice rose in volume, terror creeping into the end of every word. "You will draw for me. Or you will never see your parents again."

"I'm not frightened of you. Dad told me not to be frightened of anyone. Fear is weakness, he says. He works on the stock exchange. He earns loads of money. I bet he earns more money than you. I can tell because your clothes are cheap. Was it one of those buy-one-get-one-free offers? My dad has his clothes made for him, his work clothes, that is. When my dad's not working, he does MMA. That stands for Mixed Martial Arts. He let me see one of his fights on video. He smashed a guy's cheek bone by hitting him again and again with his elbow." Rhianna swivelled round in her seat to look at Archangel. "That's what he's going to do to you. And you won't wake up. You'll be alive, just not awake. That's what he did to this guy and now he has to have a machine to keep him alive, and a tube that feeds him. So I'm not frightened and I'm not drawing a stupid picture for you." She turned back to face away from him. Arms still crossed.

Archangel took a step back and sucked in a deep breath.

"How would you like a new iPad?"

CHAPTER 20

Savage was back in the interview room again, early Tuesday morning. They'd taken him straight there for questioning. He hadn't had any breakfast and, more importantly, he hadn't had any tea. No golden cup for him, and that had put him in a foul mood. Spending a night in a cell also hadn't made him any friendlier towards Sutcliffe, plus, he'd had Jeff Perkins in his head on and off all night, laughing at him for getting arrested and, of course, loving the delicious irony of Savage getting blamed for something he didn't even do. In the end, Savage had tuned Jeff out as background noise, but not giving a man a cup of tea in the morning, well that was unforgivable, even if it was tea made in a police station vending machine.

The whole thing was a waste of time. Savage knew Sutcliffe knew this, yet he would still pursue Savage as his one and only suspect. Didn't matter if he didn't have enough evidence, a jury could decide that later. All he was worried about was having a suspect in police custody. Make it look like the investigation was progressing. In fact, it had stalled weeks ago and was now rolling backwards with the handbrake off.

"Good morning, Mr Savage," Sutcliffe said. "Are you ready to make a confession?"

Savage noticed the detective had a Morse code of egg-yolk stains down his tie. Had he done this on purpose, to rub it in that he had had breakfast and Savage had not, or was the frazzled copper just sloppy?

"Have you got the logistics from Lev the delivery driver?" asked Savage.

"We're waiting on them."

Sutcliffe was lying. Getting that information would be simple. Sure, might have taken an hour or two at the most. They'd had all the time they needed since the last interview. By now Sutcliffe would've checked out the data from Lev's handheld device. Confirmed his delivery time at Savage's flat, putting Savage in the clear. Sutcliffe had obviously decided to ignore that evidence as it didn't fit with his narrative of the afternoon's events. But when had that ever stopped a police investigation? "I wouldn't pin your hopes on those logistics," said Sutcliffe. "Just means you signed for something at your house, doesn't mean you then didn't go on to snatch Callum at the park afterwards."

"Big Harry Potter fan, are you?" Savage asked.

"What?"

"Harry Potter, you must be a fan. A huge fan. Almost believe it's real. Bit of magical thinking."

"Where are you going with this?"

"You must think I had a Deathly Hallows invisibility cloak, which I used to sneak up to the park so I could snatch Callum, slip him under the cloak so I could get him out again without CCTV recording it. Or maybe it was a broomstick. Flew in, flew out again. Or maybe I did a shrinking spell, *Reducio*."

"I have no idea what you're talking about. Watch a lot of children's films do you?"

"I tell you, what I would like to watch is that CCTV footage. You know, the one you won't let me see."

Savage was also itching to ask him about all the other children who had gone missing. If Savage had taken Callum, then surely he must have taken Leo Bright, Olive Foley and Sally Woodrow. How was Sutcliffe reconciling this? But it would be suicide if Savage revealed he had knowledge about the other missing children. He would have to explain how he came by the information. It was not public knowledge yet. Sutcliffe had so far managed to fob off the press. How long this would last was anyone's guess. It was only a matter of time before the story of the Archangel and the missing children were all over the newspapers and the TV. Media would have a field day. If Sutcliffe felt under pressure now, once the story was out there, he'd be hounded day and night.

For the moment, Savage would have to keep it to himself that he knew about the other children. Otherwise, it would make him look like even more of a suspect, and once they started looking into Tannaz's background, they'd put two and two together and realise she'd hacked the information. She'd be hauled in as well. Savage wasn't bothered about himself, but he did care greatly about what would happen to her. He'd keep a lid on it for now.

But surely Sutcliffe would have to start questioning him about the other missing children at some point. When would the DCI start laying large-format photos in front of him of each missing child, mainly to gauge his reaction? *Do you recognise these three children?* That's what Sutcliffe should have been asking Savage. But it would present an uncomfortable dilemma for Sutcliffe. He'd have to have evidence that Savage was in the vicinity for all four abductions. A tall order, even for Sutcliffe, who wasn't averse to bending the truth into giant pretzel shapes. It was clear Sutcliffe was ignoring the other children on purpose. If he could just pin Callum's disappearance on Savage, he could charge him and get him into court. Let a jury decide the rest. That would get the pressure off him for a bit. He could tell his superiors he had someone. They wouldn't have enough evidence, of course, and the case would be thrown out. Sutcliffe knew this and either didn't care or was just using Savage's arrest to buy himself some time, to tread water. Make himself look good. Boost that fragile ego of his.

DI Roberts popped her head round the door. "Can I have a quick word, Sir?"

Sutcliffe frowned, got up and left the room. When he returned, DI Roberts joined him. Her cheeks were flushed as if they had been scalded with hot water. She wouldn't look at Savage. Just stared away at a slight angle as if something nasty on the floor held her attention.

Sutcliffe continued to witter on. Savage ignored him, more interested in Roberts and what had gone down outside the interview room between her and her superior. She looked ready to explode.

They'd had an exchange. A passionate exchange by the looks of it. Roberts had clearly lost to the stubborn old fool of a DCI.

"Sir, can I have another word with you outside?" Roberts' voice was flat and calm like the water behind a dam—before it bursts.

Sutcliffe sighed haughtily. "Is it absolutely necessary?"

"Extremely," Roberts replied.

Once again, the pair got up and left, leaving Savage alone.

This time when the door opened, only Roberts returned. There was no sign of Sutcliffe. "You're free to go, Mr Savage. Thank you for helping us with our enquiries."

"At last, someone with some sense."

"Your things will be returned to you at the custody desk."

"Very kind of you."

Roberts gave a weak smile. "One thing DCI Sutcliffe and I do agree on is you not getting involved in solving this case. It's better if the public stay out of police matters. But if there is any information you come by, it would be better if you tell us."

"That's a contradiction, isn't it?" said Savage. "On the one hand you're telling me to back off, but on the other you're saying, if I find information I must come forward. Which is it?"

"Withholding information is a criminal offence, as is vigilantism. However, they're two different things. All I'm asking is you tell me anything you know, and refrain from taking matters into your own hands."

Savage mustered as much sincerity as he could. "Like you, I haven't found any clue to who took Callum. Believe me, if I find anything, you'll be the first to know."

"Make sure I am, Mr Savage." It sounded like an innocent, throw-away comment, but the subtext was clear: don't trust Sutcliffe. Only trust me. Talk to me first. Savage understood perfectly well. Sutcliffe was unreliable. Not in the bent-copper kind of way, more the arresting-anyone-in-sight-without-a-shred-of-evidence kind of way. Anyone could see that. "You still have my card?" she asked.

"I do indeed, and I'll put it to good use." Correction, they already were putting it to good use. "One more thing, how did you get Sutcliffe to change his mind about me?"

"I didn't. Something else did. Good morning, Mr Savage, and have a good day."

Outside the station, Savage was about to pull out his mobile and call Tannaz to ask her to come and pick him up. He didn't need to. There, parked by the kerb, was his little white VW Caddy with Tannaz leaning against the side of the bonnet, holding a Styrofoam cup and puffing on a cigarette.

Savage hurried towards her. "Is that what I think it is?"

"One cup of lukewarm tea." She held it out to him as he approached. "It's gone a bit cold. Sorry. I thought you'd be out earlier."

"Don't care." Savage took the lid off the cup and took several big gulps. "Even cold tea is better than no tea. Hey, how did you know they'd let me go?"

"Let's discuss it in the car."

They got in and Tannaz drove them back to his flat, while Savage slurped contentedly.

"I intercepted a text on Roberts' phone this morning," said Tannaz. "Preliminary results of a lab test of another angel drawing. There was another abduction over the weekend. Girl called Rhianna Pullman reported missing late Sunday afternoon. Drawing showed up at her parents' this morning. It all happened while you were in custody. Perfect alibi. Nothing stronger. They had to let you go."

"Jeez," said Savage. "Another kid taken. That's bad. Really bad. This guy needs to be stopped."

"Damn right. So you see, I knew you'd be getting out as soon as they knew this. Just took a bit longer than I thought."

"You have Sutcliffe to thank for that. I get the impression he didn't want to let me go, despite the cast-iron alibi."

"Why do you say that?"

"Sutcliffe and Roberts had an argument. I didn't see it or hear it, but guessing by Roberts' face when she came back in the interview room she lost."

"So how come you're out?"

"Roberts called him into the corridor again. I don't know what she said to make him change his mind. Guy seems to be allergic to logic. Whatever she said, she got him to see sense."

"You were locked up while another abduction took place. What other conclusion could he have come to?"

"Yeah, but this is Sutcliffe we're talking about."

"The guy's a liability. So what's next?"

"Next, I have a rather large bone to pick with Frank. I think he set me up."

Savage stood on Frank's doorstep. He'd asked Tannaz to go inside his flat; he wanted to talk to Frank alone. Julie answered the door. Two tired eyes stared back at him. Her hair looked limp and lifeless. A person in desperate need of a good night's sleep. He knew that would never happen. Not until Callum was safely back home. She managed a feeble smile at the sight of Savage.

"John, are you okay? What happened?" she asked.

"I'm fine. Just some questioning."

"But they kept you overnight."

"Honestly, everything's fine. Is Frank in?"

"Yes..."

"I need to speak to him alone."

"Yes, I'll go get him." Julie disappeared down the hallway. A second later Frank appeared at the door. Savage couldn't tell whether he too was suffering from sleepless nights because he looked his usual dishevelled self. Joggers, T-shirt and dressing gown. At least he didn't have an Xbox controller in his hand. Although he wouldn't have been surprised if Frank had a clear conscience about completing a few levels even though his son was missing.

"Savage," Frank said.

"Surprised to see me?"

"Not really." Frank pushed his hands deep into the pockets of his stained dressing gown.

"You sound surprised."

"I'd rather not see you at all if that were possible."

"Now that I do believe," said Savage. "Probably prefer it if I was still behind bars."

"Best place for you."

"Is that why you planted a ball in my back garden?"

Frank's mouth hung open. "What?"

"That's why the police arrested me. Callum went up the park with a football under his arm. It was caught on CCTV, remember?"

Frank thought for a moment, processing the information.

"You remember your son, don't you?" said Savage. "Blond hair. Nice kid. Hard-working. Takes after his mum, luckily."

"Shut up, Savage. I'm signed off sick."

"Don't care. Your son had a ball under his arm when he went up the park. It mysteriously wound up in my garden or one that looks exactly like it. Know anything about that?"

"I've got no idea what you're talking about."

Savage took a step closer. "I think you do. I think you put it there, tossed it over the fence. Nice bit of evidence for the coppers to find."

Frank retreated into his hallway. "You're insane."

"Yep, totally insane. So just a small warning for you. Do that again and you'll see how truly insane I am."

"What, are you going to go all SAS on me? Ex-war veteran attacks neighbour. I can see the headlines now."

"I bet you can," said Savage. "In fact, I think this is the reason you're doing all this. Sell your story to the papers, get a nice fat payout, fuel your slobbish lifestyle."

"You don't know anything, Savage."

"See, I'm going to be watching you now, closer than ever before. Maybe *you* abducted Callum. Made him disappear."

Frank's face darkened. "Why the hell would I do that?"

"You're a scrounger, Frank. You want people to give you money for nothing. And nothing makes people dip their hand in their pockets like an appeal. *Let's raise money for the family of missing Callum Leighton.*" Frank went to shut the door. Savage shoved it back open. "Did you make Callum disappear so you could cash in? A bit of sympathy finance?"

"How dare you. What do you think I am? I love my son. And I haven't been anywhere near the media or the press. You know that I haven't. Do you see any press out here? I don't want them parasites hassling me. This is killing me, Savage, killing me, it is." Frank was shouting now. "And you stand here accusing me of abducting my own son for money."

Tears appeared in both Frank's eyes. Julie appeared behind him.

"What's going on?" she asked.

"Savage here is accusing me of abducting my own son."

"What?" Julie snapped.

"It's true," said Frank. "Said I was doing it for the money."

"John, how could you say that? Me and Frank don't get on, I'll grant you. But he'd never do that to his own son. It's a terrible thing to say."

Savage shook his head. He went to speak, to tell them about the football in the garden. How he thought Frank had planted it there to get him arrested. Right at that moment, it sounded like a weak story. Childish. Just like Sutcliffe, he had no evidence. He was no better than the burnt-out DCI trying to pin evidence on someone just because he wanted someone to blame.

"I think you should go," said Julie.

Savage turned tail and went back into his flat.

"*That went well, Savage,*" said Jeff Perkins. In his head he could hear Jeff slow clapping.

CHAPTER 21

The new evidence from the last abduction hadn't helped any. The last text Tannaz intercepted from the lab to Roberts stated that rather than a coloured-pencil drawing, this angel picture had been a computer printout, drawn with fingertips on a touch screen, created on a tablet, almost certainly on an iPad with something like the Apple Pages app.

"Surely, that's a good thing," said Savage. "Can't you trace anyone who's downloaded that app recently?"

Tannaz shook her head. "No way. Pages app comes preloaded on most Apple iPhones and iPads. Everyone's got it. Millions of people, probably."

"What's the significance of the computer printout? Why has the Archangel suddenly switched to digital? Does it mean anything?" asked Savage.

"Who knows? Ran out of paper. Could be anything. Maybe one of the kids tried to stab him with a pencil."

"What about this Rhianna Pullman?"

"Rich kid from Dulwich. Dad works in the City. Mum's a lady that lunches. If I didn't know better, they'd be the perfect candidates for a ransom."

Savage pulled up a mental image of a map of London; the four previous abductions' locations forming the distorted parallelogram. Dulwich was just inside of it. Archangel was sticking to his area of operations.

"Ransoms aren't what this is about," said Savage. "I'm actually starting to think Archangel is a classic serial killer. I mean serial abductor—we don't know if he's killed anyone yet. But he's staying within a region, not travelling out of it. Not yet anyway. This would lead me to believe these kids have a connection. We had a sports connection with the other four kids. Anything there?"

"None at all. Rhianna's the last kid to be picked for sports, according to school records. Bit of a mouth on her too."

"Maybe we were right first time. Maybe it is as straightforward as a serial killer with some sort of creative angle. Or what about religion?"

"Not with Rhianna. Her family are about as materialistic and tacky as they come. All jet skis and Champagne bars."

"Okay, so art it is then."

"But apart from Callum, weren't all the other kids rubbish at art?"

"I know. That's all we've got at the moment."

"What should I be looking for?"

"Let's start with teachers. Try cross-referencing art teachers and supply teachers. See if any have crossed paths with all five victims. Maybe this Archangel taught at all their schools."

"Savage, won't the police have already tried this?"

Savage frowned, then sighed. "Yep, definitely. They'd have pursued all these lines of enquiry, I'm sure."

"And they've come up with nothing."

Savage blew out through his mouth in resignation. "Could be a total waste of time. And they've been on this for over a month with all their tech guys."

"Yeah, but their tech guys aren't as hot as me."

"True."

"Let me see what I can find. They may have missed something."

Five hours later, Tannaz slammed the lid of her laptop. Savage was just about to place a cup of black coffee next to it and narrowly missed a spillage.

"Nothing," she said. "No connections to do with art—art teachers, art therapists, art competitions, art exhibitions, nothing arty whatsoever."

"Okay, good."

"Good?"

"We can rule that out. Next, we should concentrate on this guy doing it as some sort of artistic expression. You know, sees taking kids as an artistic project for himself."

"How will we do that?"

"I've got no idea."

Tannaz took a large slug of coffee. Her phoned pinged. She checked it. "Another intercepted text to Roberts from Sutcliffe. Guy's got it in for you, alright. He sent a text to Roberts, saying he's still not convinced about you, even though you were in custody when Rhianna Pullman got snatched. Demanded Roberts do a search of all the ANPR cameras to locate your VW Caddy at the time of all the other disappearances."

"Really?"

Her phone pinged again. "Don't worry. Roberts just replied. Said she already had that information and sent it to him."

"That guy's losing it."

Tannaz laughed. "She's texted him back the details of where your van was when each child went missing. Apparently, your VW was miles away in a B&Q car park when Leo Bright disappeared. Parked outside a café ten miles away when Olive Foley disappeared. And best or worst of all, spent three hours parked in a garden centre when Sally Woodrow was abducted. Three hours? How can you spend three hours in a garden centre?"

"Well, let me tell you. Garden centres have got it sussed. Lots of stuff for the home and you can get a great roast dinner there, and they serve a good cup of tea."

"Savage, is that all your life consists of, home improvement and drinking tea?"

"Pretty much, yeah. And the odd second-hand record store."

Tannaz laughed again.

"What's so funny?"

"It's just odd, that's all. Ex-SAS, trained killer hanging out at garden centres with all the other retirees, buying compost and trellis."

"Don't knock garden centres. Bet you've never been to one."

"Nope, don't intend to either. They have nothing I need in my life right now."

Savage got up. "Come on, grab your laptop. We're heading to my favourite garden centre. Change of scenery. We'll work offsite today."

"Oh, no. I'm good thanks."

"Don't worry. They have Wi-Fi."

"Nah. It's really not my thing."

"Not cool enough for you. Gardening's the new black, don't you know."

"Shut up."

"Come on. Grab your stuff."

This wasn't really about giving Tannaz a new retail experience. He really wanted to get away from the flat. Leave behind the argument he'd had with Frank. Savage had stepped over the line with that one. Maybe Frank had planted the ball in his garden. Maybe he hadn't. But accusing him of abducting his own child was going one step too far. Frank was a bad father, an idiot and a layabout, but even that was beneath him. Savage should go round and apologise. It would have been the right thing to do. Not just yet. He'd wait until things had calmed down. Right now, he wanted to put some distance between himself and his neighbour, and a garden centre café seemed the perfect place.

The VW came to halt on the gravel car park. They were lucky to find a space.

"It's packed," said Tannaz.

"Told you it's the new black."

The pair of them entered Goodwell's Garden Centre on the edge of Camberwell and immediately headed for the Gardener's Rest Café. Savage secured his place in the queue for hot drinks but when he turned around Tannaz was not with him. A quick survey of the store and he spotted her stuck by the entrance, fascinated by a display of water features, all trickling away. He went over and joined her.

"This is nice," said Tannaz. Nice was not a word Tannaz used. Ever. Her attention had been held by a compact wall-mounted water feature, shaped like a shield with a lion's head at the top. Water gently poured out of its mouth into a collecting basin at the bottom where it made a pleasing babble. The whole thing was made of moulded terracotta. "It's very calming," Tannaz said dreamily.

Savage looked at Tannaz curiously. They'd only been in the garden centre a minute or two and the place had already worked its magic on her. "Are you feeling okay?"

"Yeah, fine. I mean, I don't have a garden but could I put this on a wall inside my flat?"

"Don't see why not," said Savage. "I could fit it for you."

Tannaz wheeled round on him. "Who says I can't fit it myself?" she snapped. The old Tannaz was back. Savage was pleased to see her.

"Quite right. Sorry, didn't mean to be condescending."

She smiled. "That's fine. You could help me. I'll get a trolley and grab one of these. Then we'll go to the café."

That was wishful thinking. It took them over forty minutes to get to the café. Tannaz kept stopping at various aisles to fill the trolley with more items for her gardenless flat. She picked out three potted plants, vases, a potpourri holder and a packet of potpourri to fill it with, a little stone Buddha, plus the terracotta water feature. On the way, she got into a discussion with a woman about the best plant compost to use for house plants.

She shoved Savage on the arm. "Why didn't you tell me about this place? It's amazing. Such cool stuff."

Savage smiled smugly. "Ah, you're one of us now."

"Damn right. I've always thought my flat was dreary. Too much technology. Not enough living things. Needs a bit of natural colour."

"And a water feature."

Tannaz left her laden trolley outside the café, and sat at a nearby table so she could keep a beady eye on it. Savage went and got them drinks. A pot of tea for him and a pot of coffee for her, plus two large slices of Victoria sponge. Tannaz took a bite and gulped some coffee and started setting up her laptop. "I am definitely coming back here again. I just wish I had a garden."

"You could always get some window boxes."

"That's a great idea! Where are the window boxes?" Tannaz got up, ready to go on a mission.

"Let's get them on the way out, shall we? Do a bit of work first."

She sat back down again. "Yes, right. We'll do that later and—" She stopped mid-sentence.

"What is it?"

She pointed at the myriad of CCTV cameras up in the vaulted roof, pointed down at them. "Seriously, do people steal from garden centres?"

"I guess people steal from everywhere."

"But, I mean, a garden centre. The clientele are so... genteel."

"We're not."

"Yeah, but we're the exception. And I mean, you can't exactly sell this stuff down the pub. Who's going to buy it?"

"True. I don't know. Can't say I've given it much thought."

Tannaz continued gazing up at all the cameras. "Still can't figure out the CCTV footage with Callum disappearing. I've watched it hundreds of times and still don't get it. The only thing I can think of was that the abductor had somehow deleted himself and Callum from the footage, so there's no sign of them leaving."

"I thought your video-expert friend said the footage hadn't been tampered with."

"He did, but it's the only explanation that makes any sense."

"What about getting a second opinion?" Savage asked.

"I don't know any other video experts, well, not any I'd trust to keep their mouths shut over illegally obtained CCTV footage."

"What about Vikram Murthy?"

Tannaz scratched her head. "He's certainly got the skills. Do you think he'd be comfortable analysing hacked footage? He seems kinda straight. Anal. But in a good way."

"Well, he does owe us one," said Savage.

"Then, let's give it a go. Got nothing to lose."

"It's the only way to be sure," Savage raised his eyebrows in expectation.

"What?"

"Classic film line from..."

Savage Children

"I'm not playing this game. Come on, Savage, you've been really good recently. No more movie quotes, you know it annoys me."

"It's from *Aliens*. Wanna know who says it?"

Tannaz's eyes clouded over with boredom. "Not particularly."

"Corporal Hicks played by Michael Biehn, who was also in the first and best *Terminator* movie."

"Actually, Ellen Ripley says it first, played by the great Sigourney Weaver."

Savage nearly fell off his chair. "Hey, what? Hold on. Really? How do you know?"

"And actually, the first *Terminator* film is not considered the best. Similar to *Aliens*, it's one of those very rare cinematic occasions where the sequel is considered superior to the original."

Savage felt his whole world shift. "What's going on? Where's all this coming from? How do you know this?"

"Been swotting up. You must know by now how competitive I am. Hate losing and that includes having discussions about movies, so I've been studying."

Savage went to speak. Tannaz held up a hand to silence him.

"And, yes. I did just win that last discussion."

Savage was about to protest or at least find out about Tannaz's newly acquired movie knowledge when her phone pinged. "Hold on," she said. "Another intercepted text from Roberts."

"What does it say? Anything useful?"

"Vikram will have to wait. Your Polish delivery driver, Lev. Sutcliffe's arrested him."

CHAPTER 22

They left Tannaz's trolley full of garden products stranded in an aisle of hose-pipe attachments and made straight for Savage's van. Savage started it up and headed for the police station where he'd been held.

"Why the hell have they arrested Lev?" asked Tannaz, her laptop resting on her knees.

"My fault. Should've seen this coming. Lev was my alibi, sort of. He delivered a package to me around the same time CCTV caught Callum going into the park. The data from his handheld device got me off the hook. Had to sign for the package. But it's also made him a suspect. Puts him near the scene of the crime. Just down the road in fact."

"Do you know the registration number of his van?" Tannaz tapped away furiously on her laptop.

"What are you doing?"

"His van will have a tracker."

"What about his handheld device, could you hack that."

"His vehicle tracker will be easier."

Savage gave her Lev's registration number. An old habit from the SAS; memorising vehicle numbers and any information that could be useful. She began her hack, pulling up the data of the vehicle's whereabouts over the past couple of weeks.

"Er, Savage," she said. "You're not going to like this. Lev's van was in the vicinity of all four abductions on the days they occurred."

"That's impossible." Savage swung the van over and pulled in at the kerb, killing the engine.

Tannaz angled the laptop so he could see. "This is the day Leo

Bright went missing." A network of streets appeared with a continuous squiggle all over it like a ball of tangled wool, representing the route Lev's van took on that day, making his deliveries. "He stopped in the next street alongside the park where Leo Bright was snatched." Tannaz pulled up another page. "This is the day Olive Foley disappeared. His van passed by the park, see?" Savage could see it all too well. She switched to another screen, showing his route for the day Sally Woodrow disappeared, followed by Rhianna Pullman. Both times his van was in the neighbourhood, just streets away."

Savage sat back in his seat and took in a deep breath. "I don't believe it. Not Lev. He's a good guy."

"Sorry, Savage. But I think this time, Sutcliffe has something."

"This can't be right. I'm sure of it."

"The data doesn't lie, Savage."

"Could a hacker like you have changed the information. Made it look like he's guilty."

"Yeah, anything's possible."

"Can you check?"

"Of course. It will take some time though." Tannaz resumed typing on her laptop.

"How long?"

"Depends how good the hacker is. If they're as good as me there's a chance I won't find anything. If they're sloppy, maybe a day or two. Savage, there's no guarantee I'll find anything."

Savage stared out the window, the shock still hard to bear, like being doused with ice water. Savage thought he could read people. Thought he could sniff out a rat just by talking to them. Lev had been his friend. He enjoyed his company. Savage liked people who liked the same music as he did. Maybe that was the problem. It distracted him from detecting that Lev was no good. A child abductor. Prowling the streets for someone to snatch. Come to think of it, it made sense. A delivery driver with a big panel van to throw kids in the back. He could go anywhere, pull up anywhere and no one would bat an eyelid. The perfect set up for an opportunist. Except his vehicle tracker had betrayed him. Put him at or near the scene of every abduction.

Savage sat bolt upright. Something didn't make sense. Even the most stupid delivery driver would know that their every move was being recorded, tracked and monitored. Incriminating evidence of the highest quality.

"Pull up a random day on Lev's vehicle tracker," Savage said. "Any day in the last week or so."

Tannaz tapped away. Pulled up a screen from a Wednesday, two weeks ago.

Tannaz and Savage peered at the screen. "There," said Savage. "Lev passes by the park where Olive Foley was taken in Forest Hill. Pull up another screen. Any day at random."

Tannaz obliged. They both stared at the black squiggle representing his route on the screen. "He's in Clapham, near the park where Leo Bright was abducted," said Tannaz.

"Do another one."

She pulled up a Monday from over a month ago. Lev's van had stopped to make a delivery on the same street where Rhianna Pullman was taken in Dulwich.

Tannaz kept opening screens and each time the result was the same. On any given day, Lev had passed by or stopped nearby the site of all four abductions to make a delivery.

"What does it mean?" Tannaz asked.

"He's just doing his job," said Savage. "His van's always going to be close to the parks where the kids were abducted because this is his patch, where he delivers. He drives his van from the delivery depot in Croydon loaded with parcels, then he drives around the same neighbourhoods every day. Doing hundreds of deliveries, criss-crossing this part of south London, sending him past all these locations. That's just a fact. Probability. Doesn't mean he snatched a bunch of kids. You could probably put in any location in our neck of the woods and find he passes by it every day, or at least near to it. Archangel's operating in an area of twelve square miles. Lev's is more like fifteen. Not that big a size difference. It's inevitable he'll be near to an abduction site on any given day."

Tannaz flicked through more screens on random days. "You're right. He comes near to my flat nearly every day of the week too."

Savage started the van, put it in gear and pulled into the traffic.

Fifteen minutes later they sat in the reception area of the police station. They had given their names to the desk officer and asked if they could speak to DI Roberts, claiming they had some information about an ongoing case. He put a call straight through to her. Two minutes later, Roberts stood in front of them dressed in another one of her bland, ill-fitting trouser suits.

"Mr Savage, Miss Darvish, would you like to follow me." She punched a code into a keypad beside a door next to the front desk and showed them into an interview room, similar to the one where Savage had been questioned. They all took a seat. "How can I help you?" Roberts asked.

"We heard that Lev, the delivery driver, had been arrested," said Savage.

"How did you know that?"

"Doesn't matter. Little bird told me. You've got the wrong man."

Roberts placed her palms on the table. "I'm afraid I'm not at liberty to discuss matters of this case with you."

"Okay," said Savage. "Well, I'll do the discussing for you. I'm guessing you, or more likely Sutcliffe, arrested Lev because he was near to the park when Callum disappeared."

"As I said I'm not at liberty—"

"Yeah, I know, you're not at liberty to discuss the case. So here's the thing. Lev comes up my road or a road near me almost every day. Peckham, Camberwell, Clapham, Dulwich, Denmark Hill, Forest Hill, Saint John's, Nunhead, Tooting Bec." Savage made sure he peppered all the locations of the abductions into his long list of neighbourhoods. "He's in this area of south London, day in day out, delivering packages. It's his patch."

"What's your point, Mr Savage?" asked Roberts.

Savage had to be careful. He had to hint that Lev was in the vicinity of all the abductions without actually revealing he knew about all the other abductions. "Lev is a delivery driver. A very hard-working delivery driver. Driving all over this part of south

London. Name a location and he'll be near it on any given day of the week. That's not evidence. That's just probability."

"I still don't know what your point is."

"You can't arrest someone just because they were near something when it happened," said Tannaz. "Especially if it's their job to be there."

Roberts stared at Tannaz with two cold, hard eyes. "Actually, we can. Lev Jankowski is a suspect for exactly that reason."

"So why haven't you arrested the local postman?" asked Tannaz.

Roberts didn't answer.

"What about the people who work in the petrol station behind the park?" said Tannaz. "They were nearby when it happened. You better haul them in too."

"Oh, don't forget all the thousands of people driving through Peckham and Camberwell at the time," Savage added. "All the commuters who regularly drive those routes. They're all suspects. Better start harvesting number plates from ANPR cameras. Going to take a long time to question them all. By your logic, anyone nearby is a suspect."

Roberts paused before she answered. "The evidence we have on Mr Lev Jankowski is a little more sophisticated than that, Mr Savage."

"But you're not at liberty to discuss matters of this case, yeah I get it."

"Good." Roberts got up. "Like I said, if you have any useful evidence or information, I'd be more than happy to hear it." She gestured to the door, signalling their meeting was over.

"But, according to you, you've got your man," said Savage. "What else is there to do? Unless, you don't think he did it and you're going along with Sutcliffe's hare-brained theory that Lev did it, when you know he didn't."

Roberts stared at Savage blankly. "Have a good afternoon, Mr Savage. You too, Miss Darvish." She opened the door for them. They got up and walked out.

"You can call me Tannaz. And I like your suit. Very roomy."

Roberts didn't answer. Just showed them to the front lobby of the station without saying a word.

Out in the car park Savage said, "Were you flirting with the young DI back there or trying to mock her?"

Tannaz shrugged. "Don't know. Bit of both. But she's not really my type."

"What's your type?"

"Well, being a hacker, definitely not anyone in law enforcement. Or anyone with a thing for trouser suits. She looks like a Tory candidate."

They got to the van, climbed in and drove out of the police station, headed back to Savage's flat.

"What are we going to do about Lev?" asked Tannaz. "Sutcliffe's going to pin this on him, isn't he?"

Savage shook his head. "Nah. He's got no evidence. Can't charge him for just being near a crime. It's not enough to get the Crown Prosecution interested. Sutcliffe knows that, but he can and will hold Lev for twenty-four hours, extend it for another twelve, and he can ask for even more if a magistrate grants it. There's plenty Sutcliffe can do in that time to fish around for a confession. He's an old-school copper. It won't be pretty."

"But Lev's innocent."

"Sutcliffe doesn't know that. Doesn't care. Needs a result and he'll work over whoever he's got in front of him. He'll get in Lev's head. Break him down. It'll traumatise the poor guy."

Tannaz's phoned pinged. Another intercepted text from Roberts' phone. Tannaz swore. "Sutcliffe says he wants to charge Lev for theft. There were items reported missing from his delivery depot a couple of weeks ago."

"Damn it," said Savage. "That means he can charge him. Keep hold of him. He's got Lev where he wants him. This is going to put him through hell. Especially when it gets released to the press. He'll be hounded. Lose his job. And there's nothing we can do to help him. Unless Archangel snatches another child while Lev's in custody. It'd exonerate him, same way it did me. But that means another child will have to be taken. Definitely what we don't want."

"There is one thing we can do. Catch this Archangel son of a bitch before another child goes missing."

"We'll go back to my flat, give Vikram a call and see if he's up for doing a little bit of CCTV video analysis for us."

As they turned into Savage's road, they could see a large gathering of people at the top of the street, spilling across the entire width. Savage's first thought was that the story of Archangel and the missing children had finally been leaked to the press, and that they were outside Frank's flat harassing him and Julie for a story, a comment or even a camera shot. Maybe Savage's idea that Frank just wanted to make some money out of this by selling his story wasn't as far-fetched as he thought. But as they neared the gathering it became clear this was not a bunch of story-hungry press hounds but something much worse.

It was an unruly rabble of mean, white, thuggish men chanting "Savage is a paedo" outside his front door.

Saint George Is Cross had shown up in force.

CHAPTER 23

Savage pulled up halfway down the road to assess the situation. He could clearly see Carl Cooper being filmed by a couple of his thugs on mobile phones. Savage couldn't hear him but he could see him ranting away, gesticulating wildly. Another one of his little films to post on his many social-media sites, no doubt, about how he was ridding the streets of paedophiles, not caring whether the people he was targeting were innocent or not.

The men around him were in a frenzied state. Excitable and full of adrenaline, they shuffled on their feet, unable to keep still, as if they'd had too much caffeine and Haribo. Faces pinched, eyes wide and alert. Chanting mindlessly.

"We need to get out of here," said Tannaz. "Come back when they're gone. Lost interest."

Savage knew people like this never lost interest. They'd stay, day and night, taking it in turns like shift workers to picket Savage's flat. Savage wasn't bothered. It was the effect it was having on his neighbours he was more worried about. Frank and Julie were on the edge already, waiting for some word about Callum. Last thing they needed were a bunch of racist paedophile hunters with misplaced ideals camping out en masse on their doorstep. They'd been through enough already. He had to deal with this.

"Tannaz, take the van back to yours, I'm going to confront them."

Tannaz scoffed. "On your own? No way."

"Tannaz. This is probably going to get nasty."

"Probably? I think it *will* get nasty. Then you'll need all the help you can get. But how are you going to fight over twenty men? Even with two of us, that's far too many."

"I have a plan."

"Want to share it?"

"Sure. Have you seen *300*?"

Tannaz rolled her eyes. "More movie references. I hope there's a point to this. Yes, I have seen it," she said wearily. "Guys in leather underpants. Lots of shouty acting."

"Well, it's not just an action flick. There's serious historical military strategy in there. Every army officer learns it. Three hundred Spartans plus about a thousand Greeks, grossly outnumbered by nearly two hundred thousand invading Persians."

"I was rooting for the Persians."

Savage smiled. "Wouldn't have expected anything less. Here's the lesson: How to hold off a superior attacking force when you don't have the numbers. Clever King Leonidas uses local geography against his enemy. Forces the Persian Army to fight in a bottle neck by confronting them in the narrow *Thermopylae* pass."

"Where their numbers count for nothing."

"Exactly. Nice bit of film quoting, by the way. Great line—where their numbers count for nothing."

"So what are we going to do?" asked Tannaz. "We haven't got a Thermopylae pass handy."

"Nope, but we have something very similar. Come on. Time to teach St George Is Cross a lesson in fighting."

"On one condition. I get to knock Carl Cooper out."

"Done."

Savage and Tannaz exited the car, walking purposefully up the road towards Savage's flat. As soon as the rabble caught sight of Savage, they surrounded him and Tannaz, jeering and calling him a paedophile, shouting disgraceful things in his face. The two guys filming Carl turned their phone cameras on them. Savage and Tannaz breezed through the lot of them as if they were going for a country stroll.

At his front gate, blocking their way, stood Carl Cooper, flanked by several heavies.

Savage feigned surprise. "Oh hi, Carl. Didn't notice you there. Fancy a cup of tea?"

"Nah," he sneered. "Don't drink tea with men who abduct children."

"Oh, okay. Maybe another time, then."

Carl Cooper held up his hand. "You need to answer some questions. We know the police arrested you but let you go because of lack of evidence."

Savage looked around the gathered mob, spotting Minchie skulking away at the back. "Oh yeah. Who told you that?"

Carl folded his arms defensively. "Not important. Tell us what you did with Callum."

"Didn't do anything with Callum," said Savage. "Been trying to help find him."

"Why did you abduct Callum? Where is he?"

"I wish I knew, then I could hand him back to his parents."

A few men behind shouted, "Paedophile! He should be locked up."

"Hear that?" said Carl. "Everyone thinks you're a paedo."

Savage shook his head. "No, just you and your White Power Rangers."

"I keep telling you, we're not racists."

The door to Frank's flat opened. Julie stood there, a face burning with anger. "Clear off, all of you. Don't you think we've been through enough already? Leave us alone. Or I'm calling the police."

"Yes, of course," said Carl. "We've nearly finished. We'll be leaving soon, won't we lads? Soon as we've got the truth out of Savage."

"Savage had nothing to do with it, you idiot," Julie shouted. "Now piss off." She slammed the door.

"Time to speed things up a bit," said Carl. Savage noticed the guys filming on their phones had now put them away.

Carl got closer to Savage, spoke quietly. "Tell us what you did with Callum or us decent folk will dispense a bit of street justice."

"Decent is a loose term," Savage replied.

"I know you're an SAS hero and all, but look around you. You're outnumbered. You'll get hurt. Hospitalised."

Savage shrugged. "Been hurt before. Used to it."

"And what about your little Paki Bitch?" Carl swung his hateful gaze on Tannaz.

"I keep telling you," Tannaz replied. "I'm a *Persian* bitch. If you're going to be racist, at least do it properly."

"She can take care of herself," said Savage.

"What, against twenty men?"

"Okay," said Savage. "So my two options are: tell you what I've done with Callum or face street justice at the hands of you and your thugs?"

"Correct."

Savage looked around at the gathered mob. "Well, I truly have no idea what's happened to Callum, so I think I'll have to pick door number two—street justice."

Carl didn't answer straight away, probably thinking that Savage would try and talk his way out of a serious beating. "Okay, but you're going to get hurt, really hurt."

"There's one condition," said Savage.

"What's that?"

Savage pointed at his next-door neighbour's flat. "Callum's parents are in there. I don't want to add to their trauma by having a brawl outside their house. So I suggest we quickly and quietly move this to the park at the end of the road. Leave these poor people in peace."

"Done," said Carl. He turned to his men and said, "We're doing this up the park."

They all cheered.

"Right, I'll lead the way," Savage said. "Follow me, chaps." He caught Tannaz's eye. Far from fearful, her eyes had a spark to them. The thought of draining all that anger and frustration pent up inside from their lack of progress suddenly energising her. Anyone else would've wanted to run a mile at the thought of facing a gang of racist hardmen, even with an ex-SAS soldier next to them. Not Tannaz.

As the rabble lumbered up the road, Savage glanced over his shoulder and saw that Carl was right behind them, followed by his

Savage Children

goons, leading the way, marching them into battle, and certain victory. A battle he couldn't possibly lose, surely.

They crossed the road and entered the alley between the two warehouses. The one and only entrance and exit to the park. The narrow lane formed by the two buildings was barely wide enough to allow Savage and Tannaz to walk side by side, shoulder to shoulder. It was a squash, but they just managed it; they had to, to ensure no member of Saint George Is Cross could get in front of them.

Savage chanced another look behind. All the men were walking single file, too big and meaty to fit two abreast, with absolutely no idea they were being led to the slaughter in south London's version of the Thermopylae pass. Not as dramatic or historical as the real one or the one in the movie. Just a grotty, seedy little alleyway. But it would function just the same. Only allowing them to fight one at a time. Their numbers would count for nothing. While Savage and Tannaz—being much, much smaller than their opponents—could stand shoulder to shoulder and take each man on, two against one.

Just before they reached the end of the alleyway, a metre or two shy of the park itself, Savage turned to Tannaz and said quietly, "This'll do."

Tannaz spun round in a tight arc, arms tucked into her body so she didn't bump into Savage. At the last second, she released her right arm into a hooking punch and hit Carl Cooper in the side of the jaw. That would have been enough to put him on the ground, but just to be on the safe side, she left-jabbed him hard on the nose.

Carl's eyes fluttered as he lost consciousness. His body started to crumple. Tannaz hit him with a double palm strike to his solar plexus sending him into the guy behind, hoping for a domino effect. Carl was too small and light, and the man behind too big for that to happen. But Carl's limp body did a good job of getting in the way.

The next guy in line had to step over Carl, and so eager was he to get into the fight and not caring in the slightest for his leader's wellbeing, he lost his footing and tripped, putting his head right in the firing line of Savage's left knee. Savage thrust it upwards, smashing it into the guy's nose, making his head snap back with the force of the strike. Savage then grabbed him by both ears and pulled his head down for a second knee to the face. The guy toppled to the floor, joining Carl, creating a small logjam of two bodies. A nice little speed bump for the idiots behind.

The next thug who stepped up was more nimble, and hopped over his two comrades. As he landed on the ground in front of them, Savage unleashed his favourite move and kicked him twice in the shin of his left leg. While he was busy dealing with the pain, Tannaz attacked him with her fists, a machine gun of blows to his face. He turned away from her flurry of punches only to meet a brutal right hook from Savage, taking him out of the game.

"Two always beats one," said Savage.

Now there were three bodies piled up.

The rabble surged forward, sending the next man in line colliding into the small collection of lifeless men on the ground, making him fall forward onto his front, exposing his back. Savage took him out of the fight with several elbow strikes between his shoulder blades.

Four bodies piled up.

Next guy up vaulted the pile, converting the move into a kick, which caught Tannaz on the side of her jaw. She gasped in shock. As he landed, he pulled back his fist to follow it up with a punch. Savage kicked him in the side of his knee, forcing his leg to kink awkwardly. Tannaz butted him on the nose, then kneed him in the groin.

Five bodies piled up.

"You good?" Savage asked.

"Never better." She rubbed her jaw and got back into a ready position. Two guys came at them at once, scrambling over the unconscious bodies together, eager to get into the fight. A bad move. They ended up wedging themselves against the wall, neither one of them able to throw a punch. Tannaz and Savage were unmerciful and pummelled them both in the face repeatedly with the heels of their hands.

Two more out of the game.

Another guy clambered over the human barricade and collided with Savage, knocking him backwards. Savage landed on his back, smacking his head on the ground. His opponent seized the advantage and tried to stomp on Savage's head. In his desperation to take Savage out, his arms waved around erratically, and his left arm hovered briefly in front of Tannaz's face. She didn't waste the opportunity and snatched his wrist, pulled his arm straight and then drove the heel of her other hand into his outstretched elbow, making it bend the wrong way. She heard the joint crack before the guy screamed. Still holding his wrist, she turned and slammed him into the wall, knocking him out.

Turning back to Savage, she held her hand out and hoisted him up from the ground.

"You okay?"

"Never better."

Bodies were mounting up now. The narrow gap almost impassable. Carl lay at the bottom. Weighed down by his own men.

But still they came.

Savage got a punch to the face, dazing him. He automatically took a step back, drawing his opponent in. The guy followed it up with a straight jab. Savage caught the guy's fist and slammed it against the wall. Still holding him by the hand, Savage spun the guy around and threw him over his shoulder onto the ground, following it up with a quick kick to his stomach, winding him. He glanced up to see someone had Tannaz by the hair. She whimpered in pain. But then her expression turned to one of rage. She reached behind and grabbed his manhood, squeezing hard. The howl that came from the guy was inhuman. He let go and she snapped her head back, butting him on the nose with the back of her skull. He collapsed like an empty sack.

Back at her side, Savage was ready to take on another assailant. It was a face he knew well, peering over the top of the dazed mass of bodies. "Oh hi, Minchie, come to join us?"

Minchie looked as if he needed the bathroom but couldn't go. An uncomfortable, constipated face. He wheeled around and shoved his way back out of the alley, shouldering past the other men. Following his lead, not helped by the sight of their beaten and bloody brethren, the remaining members of St George Is Cross lost their nerve and fled.

A few moans came from the pile of battered bodies. Carl lying at the bottom of them, mumbling something about calling his solicitor.

Savage examined his and Tannaz's handiwork. "Well, that is rather fortunate," he said.

"What's that?"

"I recognise these two." He pointed to one guy clutching his nose and coughing up blood, and another guy who had crawled out from the pile of bodies and was curled in a ball to contain the pain. "They were filming us earlier, when all the chanting was going on, probably to post on YouTube or Twitter."

"Well, that ain't going to happen." Tannaz reached into one of the guy's pockets and pulled out a large iPhone. He was in no state to stop her. "Oh, this is the new one, I think. Must've set you back a bit." She slammed it against the wall. Once, then twice. Then again for good measure. "Better take it back. Looks like the screen's cracked." She tossed it on the ground beside him and crushed it with her heel. Then moved over to the other guy and did exactly the same.

"Will you give me a hand with Carl Cooper?" asked Savage. "Get him to his feet."

Together they pulled Carl Cooper out from the bottom of the pile by his arms, his face all bloody, then stood him upright, supporting him by his shoulders. Carl muttered something about suing them. His head lolled around drunkenly.

Tannaz examined him, not quite sure what she was looking at. "What are we going to do with this piece of shit?"

"We need to revive him and get some answers, and some shit might just do the trick."

CHAPTER 24

Carl Cooper was dragged over to the park's one and only dog-poo bin, his limp feet scuffing along the dirty ground. The thing hadn't been emptied for weeks and overflowed with little black poo sacks. Several had dropped on the floor.

"Lift the lid up for me, will you," Savage said to Tannaz. She let go of Carl's shoulder and pulled the lid open. Savage unlocked his arm from around Carl and snatched a fistful of his hair, and shoved his head deep into the dense pile of poo bags.

Savage made a robotic voice like the ones you get on self-service tills at the supermarket. "Unexpected shithead in bagging area."

Carl coughed and came back to life, gagging uncontrollably. Savage pulled his head back up. Carl gasped desperately for fresh, unsullied air.

"You know, since I've been trying to find Callum," said Savage, "you and your White Power Rangers keep cropping up. At first, I just thought you were picking on people. Anyone with a connection to kids so you could accuse them of being child molesters, but now I'm thinking there might be more to St George Is Cross. Like you're something to do with him disappearing."

"We're doing a service for the community," Carl garbled.

"Do me a favour." Savage plunged Carl's head back into the bags. "What if St George Is Cross is a paedophile ring? What better way to distract attention away from yourselves than by pretending to be kiddie crusaders. Pointing the finger at others so you can hide your true nature." Savage lifted Carl's head back up.

Carl heaved dryly. He gulped several times, then managed to say, "I swear we just go after people who we think are dangerous."

"Rubbish," said Savage. "You're just doing this so you can make little videos for clicks and follows. Trying to build an online presence so you can be the next alt-right social-media star. The controversial Carl Cooper. Trying to make a name for himself so he can get a slot on a chat show. Let me tell you, I've dealt with the far-right before, and they didn't come off well."

"We're not alt-right or racist."

This time Tannaz grabbed a clump of Carl's hair and shoved his head in the bin. "Why did you target Savage?"

Carl mumbled something inaudible. She shoved his head deeper. "Why did you target Savage?"

Carl's arms began to flail as he began to suffocate, frantically trying to find somewhere to get a grip to force his head up to get air. Tannaz was too strong and pushed him down deeper.

"Okay, let him speak," said Savage.

They hoisted his head out. Carl drew air like a drowning man crossed with someone who had contracted stomach flu.

When his erratic gasps had calmed down, Carl said, "I swear we didn't target you. Your neighbour did."

"What?"

Carl took a gulp of air then said, "He messaged me on Twitter. Told me about your arrest. Asked me to come around and hassle you. I can show you." Carl Cooper delved into his pocket and pulled out his phone, flicked the screen a few times and showed Savage and Tannaz a direct message from @FrankLeighton1980. It read:

> *My son Callum went missing last Friday. I think I know who did it. My neighbour John Savage. Police arrested him but the bastard wriggled out of it. I knew he did it because he's always hanging round my son. Send your men round and shame him for what he's done.*

Tannaz took her phone out and took a shot of the message.

"So that's your evidence against me," said Savage. "A badly

written tweet from someone you don't know. That's all it takes to mobilise your White Power Rangers to go out and dispense justice."

"In my experience, there's no smoke without fire," Carl said.

"Have you heard of the Stasi?"

Carl shook his head. "Let me guess, this is where you tell me they're a Nazi organisation that killed hundreds of Jews or something."

"Opposite of Nazis. They were the communist secret police in East Germany. But they did kill lots of people. People were so frightened of them that they would become informers just to stop themselves from being hauled in and questioned. They'd make up stuff about their neighbours to keep the heat off themselves. Thousands of innocent people disappeared during the Stasi's reign of terror. At one point they had a quarter of a million informants all spying for them. Ready to point the finger at their neighbours."

"But we're not like that," said Carl.

"That's exactly what you're like," said Tannaz. "On a smaller scale. You've just taken the word of an informant, you haven't checked any facts, or got any evidence. Have you? Then you've used intimidation and bullying to force a response out of someone. You picked on the wrong people. Got your asses kicked."

"We're doing a public service," Carl said, pompously.

Tannaz swung a punch, landing it right in the centre of Carl's mouth. Now he had a bloody mouth to match his bloody nose.

"I came to this country to get away from pricks like you," she said. She prepared to follow it up with a kick. Carl cowered on the ground. Savage held her back.

He knelt down next to Carl and spoke calmly. "Okay, I'll make this really simple for you. You will now go back to your men and tell them Saint George Is Cross has disbanded. That you'd got it wrong, made a mistake. Going after people without any evidence is wrong. The bullyboy days of Saint George Is Cross are over. You can start doing something positive. Digging wells in Africa. Feeding homeless people. Pulling plastic bottles out of rivers. I don't care as long as it's something that's not fuelled by hate, because what you do just creates more hate. And the logical conclusion to that is we're all going to hate each other. And then where will we be?"

"And if I refuse."

"Well, then you'll put me in a rather difficult situation. I'd have to weigh up the cost of letting you live. See, you're just doing this to make yourself famous with your little social-media stunts, stirring up controversy because controversy gets noticed. Say something factual and nobody listens. Say something true and nobody listens. But say something outrageous and heads turn. It's the modern shortcut to fame and attention. Before you know it, *Question Time* is calling and so is *This Morning*. Not because you're smart or talented, but because your extreme ideas pull in viewers. And you'll be banking all those appearance fees, getting rich. But people watching won't realise that's why you're doing it. They'll believe your bullshit. Your hatred.

"Hatred is a virus. It spreads and infects others. Whole countries. Seen that in the Balkans. Neighbours who got along fine suddenly turning on each other because some right-wing power-hungry prick like you has told them they're the enemy. Then things get really nasty. Murder becomes normal. Genocide acceptable. And that's what you're peddling to make yourself famous. I don't want to see that happen in this country, which means *if* you carry on like this I will have to make you disappear. Do society a favour. Like going back in time to kill Hitler."

"Are you threatening me?" Carl croaked.

"Of course I am. Well done, you're catching on. I'll dust off my SAS kit. Come into your house at night..."

"We both will," said Tannaz.

"Yep, me and Tannaz will enter your house, watch over you while you sleep like a baby, then we'll snuff you out like a cheap scented candle. Look on the bright side, though, you won't even know about it."

"I have lots of men protecting me."

"Didn't do much good tonight, did they? Me and Tannaz weren't even trying. Just using our bare hands. Think what we're like when we're holding weapons. I've taught Tannaz everything I know. She's trained to SAS standards. We'll cut through your White Power Rangers like we're playing *Call of Duty*. Then we'll cut your throat. Think about it. Think if the price of fame is worth it. Have a good evening."

Savage and Tannaz left Carl Cooper to think, slumped against a poo bin, weighing up his options for the future. Almost certainly the first time a poo bin had been used for such contemplative thinking. They exited the park through the alleyway, sidestepping a few of Carl's goons still licking their wounds.

Back on Savage's street, Tannaz asked, "What are you going to do about Frank?"

"Nothing."

"Nothing!" Tannaz halted and rounded on him. "Savage, that ungrateful lazy urine stain set you up. Tipped off Carl and his men. Falsely accused you."

"Yeah, well I did kind of falsely accuse him of something."

"What?"

"I suggested that maybe he'd abducted Callum so he could sell his story to the papers, which I'm pretty sure he hasn't. Guy hasn't got enough brains for it. So we're sort of even."

"Even so. Accusing is one thing, but he tried to have you killed tonight."

"S'alright. I'm used to it." Savage smiled. "They keep trying. It's always the right-wing, though. They either want to hire me or kill me. Strange."

"Well, if you won't confront him I will. Got that screen shot of Carl's direct message. I'll rub his face in it. Show it to Julie. Show her what a bellend he is."

"I think she already knows that," said Savage, as they continued walking. "Besides, I really don't want to upset Julie any more than I have to. She's already going through hell. There's nothing to be gained by showing her that message. It'll just add to the pressure on her. Tip her over the edge. If she's not there already."

"I think you're being soft. Frank has to take some ownership of the mess he's caused tonight."

"Maybe. After this is all over, I'll confront him, but now's not the time. That little distraction at the park has cost us. We need to get back on track. Go see Vikram. Ask him if he'll give us his expert opinion on that footage of Callum.

"Okay, but I don't like it. Let's stop off at yours and I'll grab my laptop."

"Let's just hope Vikram Murthy is in the mood for bending a few rules. Because if he isn't, I have no idea what we're going to do next."

CHAPTER 25

NEXT DAY, THEY PHONED AHEAD to ask Vikram if it was okay to call round for his advice. He struck Savage as the kind of guy that didn't like spontaneity or people turning up unannounced without him first weighing up the pros and cons of such a visitation, probably on a spreadsheet or with an algorithm he'd designed. To give the guy credit, he sounded happy to hear from them. It was a good sign as they'd be needing his professional skills—free of charge.

Vikram swung open the door with a jolly smile on his face. "Please, come in my friends."

A waft of freshly ground coffee drifted out, making Savage feel hungry.

Tannaz groaned in ecstasy. "Is that your amazing coffee I can smell?"

Vikram's face dropped when he'd had a chance to take in their battered faces. "My friends, what happened to you?"

"Oh, nothing," said Savage. "Just had to set a few people straight about some things."

"I'd feel better with a cup of your amazing coffee in my hand," said Tannaz.

"Of course, right away." He led them into the kitchen and set to making the three of them premium hot beverages.

They sat in his kitchen, perched on his stools, sipping their drinks, looking at each other.

Savage broke the ice. "Vikram, we've come to ask a favour."

Vikram smiled broadly. "Of course, anything."

"Your video analytics. Does it stretch to CCTV?"

"I'm an expert in all types of video. Why do you ask?"

"We need you to analyse some CCTV footage for us, see if it's been manipulated. One of Tannaz's contacts has already checked it and says not, but we'd like a second opinion."

"Manipulated?"

Savage spoke quietly, as if they might be overheard. "Before you agree, I have to let you know that this footage wasn't, er, acquired with the legal permission of the people who owned it."

Vikram shook his head. "I'm sorry, John. I don't and will never get involved in anything illegal."

Savage went to speak but Tannaz held her hand up to stop him. "Vikram," she said. "It's not what you think. Remember we told you about Savage's neighbour's son, Callum, who went missing last Friday. Snatched from a park. Like the other children the police questioned you about."

'Of course, I remember," he said, sitting a little straighter.

"We've been trying to find them. The only evidence we have is some CCTV footage we found, taken by a camera mounted on a warehouse. When we watched the footage it didn't makes sense."

"In what way?" Vikram asked.

"Callum goes into the park but doesn't come out," said Savage.

"He got out another way," Vikram proposed. "Climbed over a wall. Got through a hole in a fence. There are many ways to evade CCTV. It's not foolproof."

"Not this time," Savage explained. "The park is like a prison exercise yard. Surrounded on three sides by buildings and on one side by a very high, spiked metal fence. There's no way in or out except past that one CCTV camera."

"This is very strange. Are you sure? There must be a rational explanation."

"Positive," said Tannaz. "And it gets weirder. But the following information I'm about to tell you isn't public knowledge. Police are keeping it under wraps and they can't know that we know. We can stop now if you want, if you're uncomfortable with this."

"I'd like to help if I can," Vikram answered. "A missing child is a terrible thing. Four missing children. Terrible for the parents. Please, go on."

"Another child has been abducted the same way, five in total now," said Tannaz. "Same pattern. They're caught on CCTV going into a park. Different parks each time. Then they never come out again."

"It's horrible."

"It gets worse," Savage added. "A day or two later, their parents receive a picture, drawn by the child. A picture of them as an angel."

Vikram's face became a mask of horror. "Really? That's vile. How could anyone do such a thing?"

"Police have a nickname for the abductor. The Archangel."

Vikram stood up, gulped down his coffee. "Show me the footage. Let's catch this bastard."

In Vikram's office he fired up his array of Apple screens. Tannaz took a seat beside him and placed her laptop on the desk. Savage sat on the other side of Vikram.

"Send me each video file, if you please," Vikram said.

Tannaz obliged. In the next minute, Vikram had each piece of footage spread out across two vast Apple screens, including the latest footage of Rhianna Pullman. Tannaz gave him the relevant time stamps and he watched each child enter their respective parks one after the other.

"Quality is awful," said Vikram.

"Is that a problem?" asked Savage.

"No, I can enhance the quality a bit."

But Vikram didn't move. Just sat and watched the footage again and again as God intended, in its original form with his bare eyes. No software, no analytics. No digital forensics.

"Er, when does the cool analytical stuff begin?" asked Tannaz impatiently.

Vikram pointed to his head. "This is the best analytical software we have. Our brains and eyes. Common sense. I'm just watching naturally. See if anything stands out as odd or peculiar. Shadows that are too long. Movement that isn't right. Anything that looks artificial."

"And does anything stand out?" asked Tannaz.

"Not yet."

Vikram did this over and over again, silently examining each film until he was satisfied he could see nothing untoward. "Okay, next stage. Let's enhance the footage."

Tannaz became animated. "Ah, now the cool shit begins. I wanna learn. Tell me everything."

Vikram put all the footage through several software tools. Like magic, the low-quality CCTV footage became a little cleaner and crisper.

"Wow, that makes a difference," said Savage.

"Now, again. We watch them one at a time. Look for anything odd. Anything unnatural. Even the best hoaxers make errors. Pay attention to shadows at the wrong angle, perspective lines."

They shared out the surveillance duties. Tannaz watched Olive Foley's and Sally Woodrow's footage, while Savage watched Leo Bright's. Vikram watched Callum's and Rhianna's footage then they swapped over. Checking, double-checking and rechecking each other's work. At the end, they'd watched each individual piece of enhanced footage five times. Nothing stood out as odd.

"I'll do a geometric analysis," Vikram said. "Just to be on the safe side."

"What's that?" asked Savage.

"Reflections," said Vikram. "We're lucky all the footage was taken outside. There's only one light source, the sun. All lines of reflection should intersect in the same place." Vikram punched a few buttons, the software got to work, pinging back the data in seconds. "Okay," he said. "They all check out. Sun's in the right position in all four of them. If these images have been manipulated, the reflections aren't going to reveal it. Okay, let's take it up another level. We'll look at the metadata of each file. This will reveal lots of interesting things. Like what camera the footage was captured on. And any software that's been recently used on the footage. It all leaves a trace, like a fingerprint. If it's editing software, then we know someone's modified something."

Vikram meticulously scanned each file, scrutinising every line of code, every forward slash and backslash. Tannaz never took her eyes off the screen either. This was her territory, what she excelled at.

They both looked at each other, disappointed. "I can't see anything," said Tannaz.

"Me neither," said Vikram.

They repeated the exercise with each file. Double- and triple-checked it, and came up with nothing.

Vikram pushed his fingers through his thick black hair. "Okay, not the end of the world just yet. Cameras vary in what data they choose to store. We might have been unlucky and these are old cameras so not the most sophisticated kit in the world."

"What's next?" asked Tannaz.

"We attack the footage at pixel level," Vikram explained. "If you want to remove a person or an object from a video it leaves a hole. You have to fill that hole with something. A clone of what's already there. Like taking a back pocket from a pair of jeans and sewing it onto the knee. It's called masking. This software can detect if even a single pixel has been moved."

Again, Vikram took keyframes and fed them into the software, analysing thousands of pixels at a time, testing them for manipulation. One by one, each frame came back negative. Each piece of footage intact. Vikram soldiered on. Opening more software packages, bringing up vast on-screen dashboards, clicking buttons and adjusting parameters, and analysing results and values. Savage had given up a long time ago trying to understand what he was doing. Tannaz was still in the game, that keen mind of hers soaking up everything, following what Vikram was doing. Neither of them looked happy.

This went on for hours, until Vikram finally admitted defeat. "I'm sorry," he said, "but I think your friend was right, Tannaz. I can't see any evidence of tampering."

"Really?" said Savage. "A dead end?"

Vikram smiled. "I didn't say it was a dead end. Just that I can't find evidence of manipulation."

"Isn't that the same thing?" said Tannaz.

"No. There is a possibility we may be looking at a next-level deepfake."

"What's a deepfake?" asked Savage.

Tannaz answered. "A deepfake is a piece of footage so good it's very hard to spot that it's been faked. The first deepfakes were so incredible everyone believed them. Plays on what we call 'Illusory truth'."

"Illusory truth?" asked Savage.

"Seeing is believing," said Tannaz. "We trust our eyes above everything else. If we can see it, we think it must be true."

"That's right," said Vikram. "We want to believe it's true, and ignore the other signals from our brain. Most deepfakes are of famous people. Head shots of them talking. Making them say outrageous things. People are wise to deepfakes now, and the analytical technology has caught up. Digital forensic tools anyone can use to spot them. Deepfakes are no longer, well, deep, they're just fakes. But there is a possibility that we're dealing with a guy who's moved everything on. He's no longer just manipulated footage of someone's face. This guy's created a way of erasing himself without a trace. A next-generation faker, I suppose you could call it. A fake that's so good it outsmarts all current analytical tools."

"How can you be sure, though?" Tannaz asked.

"I'm not," Vikram replied. "This is just a theory. When we were looking through the metadata, I noticed all the cameras that shot the footage are of the same quality. Lo-fi."

"So?" said Savage.

"To get an idea of why that's significant you have to know about the present state of CCTV. It's a big mess. Tons of different systems, different cameras, from different ages. It's a Frankenstein's monster held together with system patches and updates and compatibility workarounds. You've got old cameras, sometimes from as far back as the late nineties and the early noughties, mixed up with current tech. Narrow bandwidth cameras rubbing shoulders with the latest high-definition models. Gradually cameras are being upgraded and replaced but that takes time and money, especially if they are local-authority owned—they can't afford to update them all.

"Now, this guy has made sure that he's snatching kids only in areas where the cameras are old-school affairs, first-generation digital, low quality but hackable. If I wanted to create a program that would erase me from CCTV existence without a trace, that's exactly what I would do. Lo-fi cameras that produce poor detail images are far easier to edit than a pin-sharp advanced HD one. The footage from the park where Callum was taken, that camera is not as old as the other local-council cameras, but it's still over fifteen years old, and a domestic system at that. It's unsophisticated, just there as a deterrent really, can't do anything fancy. So while not as bad as the others it's still very hackable."

"Why doesn't he just snatch kids where there are no CCTV cameras?" asked Tannaz.

"In this city that's virtually impossible," Vikram replied. "Apart from Beijing, London has more cameras than any city in the world. Around half a million. Whatever you do, anywhere in London, a camera is going to catch you. So he's been smart and is confining his actions to areas where he can easily manipulate old cameras without raising any eyebrows. Delete himself and his victim from the frames."

"But why show his victims going in the park and not leaving? Why not just erase all trace of them?" asked Tannaz.

"Because of witnesses," said Savage. "Good old-fashioned flesh-and-blood witnesses. If someone saw Callum go into the park, but he didn't appear on the CCTV footage, police would know someone's mucked about with the CCTV. They'd question every video expert in London. Get alibis from them. Haul them in for questioning. But showing Callum and the others going into each park stops them pursuing that line of enquiry. Remember their tech guys have checked the footage like we've just done, found nothing wrong with it. They think the CCTV's working fine and don't look any further. It's very clever. Now they think they're dealing with a suspect who can do a disappearing act. They start looking for answers elsewhere. No wonder it's driving Sutcliffe insane."

"So, should we be looking for a video expert?" asked Tannaz.

"Well, I can't say for sure," said Vikram. "It's just a theory."

Savage stared at Vikram, concern on his face. "Oh, no. It's not a theory. It all makes sense."

"How so?" asked Tannaz.

"Because of you, Vikram."

Vikram looked worried. "Me? What do you mean?"

"At first I just thought it was a coincidence," said Savage, "and Tannaz knows how much I hate coincidences. But it's just occurred to me. I think this Archangel has tried to set you up. First four kids taken were all members of sports clubs where you donate your time. Archangel manipulates video, you work with video. It's no coincidence. He's tried to point the finger at you. Make you the prime suspect. He's targeted you. Targeted the kids you work with. Picked you because you're also a video expert, just in case the police cotton onto the CCTV manipulation thing."

Vikram went pale. "I feel sick. Why has this horrible bastard picked on me?"

"Do you know anyone who's got a grudge against you? Any enemies?"

"No, none."

"Then it's highly likely he's marked you out as his fall guy. Bit of insurance to keep the attention off him. Buy him plenty of time to fulfil his plans."

"Didn't work, though, did it?" said Tannaz. "Guy's not as smart as he thinks he is. You had an alibi. You were out of the country for two of the abductions. Didn't do his research. Got sloppy."

"See, the pattern of abductions makes sense," said Savage. "He tries to set you up, but when the police clear you, Archangel changes tack. He no longer needs to bother abducting sporty kids. Takes Rhianna Pullman."

"There's just one problem with that," said Vikram. "Police cleared me end of May. Callum went missing in June. Callum's also in a sports club I work with. Why would Archangel keep trying to frame me once the police had cleared me?"

"Maybe he didn't know you'd been cleared," Tannaz offered.

Savage shook his head. "A guy like Archangel would make it his business to know. But yeah, that doesn't make sense, why take another kid from a sports club when his scape goat is out of the picture. He doesn't need to keep up the pantomime anymore. Plus, it's an extra risk. Police would have learned the sports-club pattern by now."

"So where does that leave us?" Vikram asked.

The room descended into a puzzled silence.

Tannaz took a deep breath. "I've been dazzled by this Archangel. We all have. Police too. An evil genius who makes children disappear. It's a bit of misdirection. Smoke and mirrors. This guy who may or may not have perfected undetectable editing. He leaves no trace. How did he do it? He's got us chasing our tails. Who cares? So what? We don't understand it, doesn't matter. He's invented some fancy software. Woo-hoo. Feeling pleased with himself. Got us all running round in circles. However, to put his new, cutting-edge software into practice he still has to hack whichever video system he's targeting. He's just a dirty little hacker. Like me."

"How does this help us?" asked Savage.

"Data traffic," Tannaz replied. "Whenever you hack a system for whatever reason, data levels increase. Just because he's targeting a CCTV system, it's still a hack. And if there's a sudden unnatural spike in data traffic, you can bet your bottom dollar there's a hack going on."

Vikram brightened up. "She's right. His software may leave no trace, but data traffic would. More so with CCTV systems. They just look at the same thing every day. Data traffic is fairly constant, the second he hacks it, it'll show up like someone sending up a flare."

Tannaz got to work on her laptop. Had that look on her face. The look of a shark about to go in for the kill: cold, determined and deadly. She started hacking the local-authority CCTV systems for each park and the warehouse near where Callum had been taken.

"Can data traffic be faked? Could he have covered his tracks?" asked Savage.

"Oh, I bet he has," Tannaz answered. In a matter of minutes, she had the data-traffic levels on the day of each child's abduction, expressed as line graphs. They were all fairly similar. Roughly horizontal with a few jagged bumps and troughs, indicating a steady stream of data. Nothing dramatic. No spikes. No evidence a hack had taken place. "There, all nice and neat. Just as expected. No alarms and no surprises."

"*Ok Computer*," said Vikram. "Good album."

"Try telling that to Savage," said Tannaz, not looking up. "He only listens to The Jam."

"Who are The Jam?" asked Vikram.

Savage shot Vikram a deeply offended look. "*Who are The Jam?* Only the best band in the world."

"Oh wait," said Vikram. "Do they do ambient trip hop dub, because I think I saw them in Ibiza."

"No, this is proper music. Post punk, new wave mod."

"It's okay, Vikram," said Tannaz, typing away. "Savage thinks it's only music if it has electric guitars in it."

Savage sounded hurt. "That's not true. I like The Stranglers, they had a keyboard."

Tannaz glanced at him, shook her head disapprovingly, then went back to her screen, trying different ways to attack the data. She fired lines of code into each system. Still the graphs did not change. Sedate lines, showing nothing of any interest, exactly as expected.

"This is what he wants us to see," said Tannaz, hitting keys frantically. "Wants us to lose interest. Buy in to his little camouflage. *Nothing to see here, now move along.* Police techies have probably already been here. Had a look. Satisfied their curiosity, then left it alone. This Archangel has covered his tracks. Played the game. Well, he may be a hotshot when it comes to video manipulation, but when it comes to hacking, guy's out of his depth. Might be able to hide from the cops but he can't hide from me."

More furious typing followed. More lines of code. More swearing from Tannaz. The graphs on screen remained unchanged.

"Okay, let's try something else." Tannaz attempted to sound calm, but each word was forced through clenched teeth.

She hit the keys, her fingers blurring. Again, the graphs refused to give up any secrets.

Tannaz slammed her hands down on the keyboard.

Vikram jumped. Shock on his face, he looked at Savage.

"You get used to it after a while," said Savage.

"Bit of quiet please. Trying to work here." Tannaz resumed typing. A pattern began to emerge. She'd type. Expect a result. Nothing would happen. Then she'd smash her fists on the desk in frustration. She'd try something else. More anger. More bashing of Vikram's nice office furniture.

"Do you want to have a break, Tannaz?" asked Vikram. "I'll make you a coffee."

Tannaz sat mesmerised, not hearing him. As if she were channelling a spirit, her hands possessed as they danced across the keyboard. Again nothing. She would restart the process. A woman on a mission. She barely breathed, the initial anger gone, replaced by pure determination. Minutes turned into hours. Vikram and Savage sat and watched, unable to help. Tannaz, an unstoppable force, mouth set into a hard line, brow furrowed. Digitally, she was out to take this guy down and nothing would stop her.

She hit the return key.

Suddenly the graphs transformed.

Gone was the flat line of data traffic. Dominating each graph now was a huge spike like a steep-sided mountain peak. A massive unexplained increase in data traffic. Evidence of a hack.

Tannaz jumped to her feet.

Punched the air.

"Got you, you son of a bitch!"

CHAPTER 26

Tannaz stood hands on hips, chin jutting out like Superman. "Archangel, my ass," she said. "You are going down. We're coming for you."

Savage glanced down at her laptop screen. "Hold on a second." One of the graphs hadn't transformed. No spike, just the same horizontal jagged line. "That's Callum's camera. The data hasn't changed."

"That camera's not local authority," said Vikram. "Different system might need a different hack."

Tannaz ceased her celebrations and slotted herself back in front of her laptop again. "Let me try some more things."

"Don't need to," said Savage. "Four out of five is good enough for me. I think it's pretty obvious what this guy's up to. Good work, Tannaz. Archangel's a video expert. Vikram, we need a list of how many people are capable of doing this."

"There's probably only one person at the moment," said Vikram. "The software this Archangel has developed, it's a one-off. Unique. Ground-breaking."

"Okay," said Savage. "What about people who have the potential to do this?"

"It's in the thousands," Vikram replied. "In London, digital video editing is everywhere. Every Internet business, marketing agency and advertising and production company will have at least one or dozens of video experts depending on their size, even big corporations will have in-house editing teams and videographers. Social media demands a video presence. Not to mention the ones with set-ups in their bedrooms and all the special-effects people working in the film and TV industry. It's going to be a very long list."

"We should pass this information on to Roberts," said Tannaz. "Police have the manpower to go through them all. Get uniforms out there knocking on doors, drag them out and do interviews."

Savage shook his head. "That could take months. And there's no guarantee they'd actually catch this guy. Plus, if he gets wind of the police interrogating anyone with any video skills he's likely to get spooked and disappear. What's more, Sutcliffe thinks he's got his man. Lev's safely locked up. He'd never go for it. Doesn't want anything to get in the way of his conviction." Savage paused. Thought for a moment. "I might have a better idea. Vikram, is it possible to locate all these lo-fi first-generation digital CCTV cameras that are still knocking around?"

"Yes, definitely."

"How many are we talking about?" asked Tannaz.

"A hundred, five hundred. I couldn't say without some serious research."

"What about ones just trained on parks?" Savage asked.

"That's going to take the number down considerably. Again, I wouldn't like to hazard a guess. But it would be far more manageable. It would take some time to locate them all, what do you have in mind?"

"I noticed when comparing the time stamps on the videos to the time of the spike on the graphs, that Archangel is uploading his hack before he takes the kids. He has to. Can't do it afterwards. Because then there's a risk anyone monitoring those CCTV cameras will see him. So the software has to be uploaded just before he goes in, to mask what he's doing. Make it look like he was never there."

"That would make sense," said Vikram. "If his software clones video footage to block himself out, he'd need to upload it as close as possible to the point of abduction, so it matches. That way all the light levels and shadows would look the same."

"Yeah," Savage agreed. "I also can't imagine he abducts a child, then goes home afterwards and tries to edit himself out."

"Or he could have developed some sort of stealth software," Vikram proposed.

"But that's impossible," said Tannaz. "Are you saying he's invented some sort of Predator technology. Because that's just whack. Not possible."

Vikram dismissed her comment. "No, more likely it's a programme that rearranges pixels and puts them back together…"

"Guys, guys. Stop," Savage blurted. "We're falling into his trap. Getting hung up on how he's doing this. Doesn't matter. I don't care. Maybe it's a video genius or the Predator himself. It's not important. This is what's driving Sutcliffe mad. He can't figure it out. Neither can we. The conundrum he's left is working its magic. We're chasing our tails again. Like Tannaz said, we don't need to figure it out."

"So, what do you propose?" Vikram asked.

"We set a trap."

"What sort of trap?"

"We know the spike in data happens before he abducts the child. With his hack in place, he's shielded from view, so he never appears on CCTV entering the park and is not seen leaving with the child either."

"But how does he make the child invisible?" said Vikram.

"Don't know. Don't care," said Savage. "Again, doesn't matter. Let's just say it's a clever bit of new software and leave it at that. Here's how we catch him. We log the position of all the old first-gen digital cameras looking onto parks in that parallelogram area that Archangel's working in. Actually, we'll expand the area, make it bigger, by at least a few miles in each direction, just to be on the safe side. Vikram, that's your job."

"I can do that."

Savage turned to Tannaz. "Now. I'll need you to write some software that monitors the data traffic going to Vikram's list of camera locations. I need you to design it so that as soon as there's the smallest sniff of a spike in data traffic, an alarm goes off. Tells us which camera is being hacked. We head over to the park in question. Catch this bastard in the act."

Tannaz clapped her hands. "I love it. A digital tripwire." Her fingers started hitting the keyboards. "Writing it as we speak. This guy ain't going to know what's hit him."

Vikram looked doubtful.

"What's up?" Savage asked him.

"I hate to be negative."

"Vikram, if there are holes in the plan we need to know them now."

"It's a really good plan, John. Please forgive me."

"Vikram, just tell me."

"Well, from the moment his hack starts, I'm wondering how much of a window we'll have. Specifically, how long it takes him to get in the park, grab a child and get out again, undetected."

"I don't know," Savage replied. "Could be any time at all. Two minutes, ten minutes, twenty. Who knows?"

"Let's be conservative," said Vikram. "Say there's a twenty-minute window in which he uploads the hack, gets into the park, finds his victim and tries to abduct them. We're in Balham. Imagine an alarm goes off from a camera in say, Sydenham, over five miles away, maybe at the height of the rush hour. We'd never make it in time. Could take us forty-five minutes or an hour to get over there."

Tannaz stopped typing and looked up from her screen. "He's right. The area's already too big for us to cover as it is, and we've just increased the parameters. Fine, if we're close by, but if we have to trek across south London, he'll have been and gone before we even get there. And what if he decides on this next occasion to take his victim from way outside of the area he's been operating in? We're screwed."

Savage stood up. Rubbed his balding head. Paced the room a few times. "You're right. It won't work with just the three of us, even if we each camped out in different corners of south London, we couldn't cover the area he's working in. We'd need hundreds of people standing by at various locations, ready to drop everything and spring into action at a moment's notice. It's unrealistic. Unfeasible."

"We could always try Roberts," Tannaz ventured. "Ask the police for help."

"Even if we did and she believed us, which is highly unlikely, the police can't spare that many bodies. There just aren't enough coppers to do that. Police cuts and what have you. And even if there were, it'd be such an expensive operation. She'd never get the budget cleared."

Much sighing filled the room. Tannaz stopped typing and leant back in her chair. No point writing code for an early-warning system if they didn't have the people to implement it.

"We need an army of people," said Savage.

"Where are we going to get an army from?" asked Tannaz.

Savage stopped pacing, looked at them both as if he'd just remembered that he'd left the gas on. His face screwed up in pain. "Oh, no, no, no."

"What is it?" asked Tannaz.

Savage pushed out a large, unhappy breath of air. "There is a way to do this. But you're both going to hate it. I hate it, in fact."

Tannaz and Vikram looked at him expectantly.

"I know where we can get an army," said Savage. "Carl Cooper and St George Is Cross have the numbers we need."

Vikram shook his head.

Tannaz was more vocal, dropping f-bomb after f-bomb. "There is no way we're teaming up with that little racist prick and his White Power Rangers. That's like asking Bill Cosby to lead the Me Too movement. No way."

Savage sat back down again. "Think about it for a second. Who else has got that many spare bodies all sitting around London in flat-roof pubs doing nothing? You heard him that first time we met him. He said he had an army spread across the capital, ready to mobilise."

Tannaz looked doubtful. "He's probably exaggerating. Only about twenty showed up to fight us."

Savage countered. "That was because it's all he thought he'd need. Proved him wrong on that front."

"Wait a second," said Vikram. "Is that why your faces are all cut up? You had a fight with St George Is Cross?"

"Yep," said Tannaz, not hiding the triumph in her voice. "I knocked Carl Cooper on his alt-right ass."

Bewildered, Vikram said, "How did you manage to fight so many of them?"

"For once, Savage's poor taste in multiplex movies came in handy. We got all *300* on them."

"I don't understand," Vikram said.

"We lured them into a dark, narrow alley," said Savage.

Tannaz did her best, gruff King Leonidas impression. "Where their numbers count for nothing."

"They could only come at us one at a time," Savage added. "Two always beats one."

"Wow. I bet that felt good," said Vikram. "I'd love to see that little snake Cooper get a beating."

"It felt amazing," said Tannaz. "Trouble is, he's going to be in no mood to help us."

Savage had a twinkle in his eye and a mischievous smirk on his lips. "Oh, he will. I'll make sure of it. By the time I've finished with him he'll be begging to help us."

"What have you got in mind?" asked Tannaz.

He turned to Vikram. "Can I borrow something?"

CHAPTER 27

SAVAGE WRENCHED THE HANDBRAKE AS they stopped outside the Bexhill Arms. The place was still covered in England flags, still advertising beer and breakfast. A viper's nest of white racists.

Tannaz turned to Savage. "How are you going to stop Carl's men from lynching us the moment we walk in? We haven't got the benefit of a dark alley to fight them off."

"I have an idea," said Savage. "Let's go."

They exited the VW, Tannaz with her computer bag over one shoulder.

"Ready?" asked Savage.

"As I'll ever be," Tannaz replied.

They entered the lobby of the pub, the stale-beer-soaked carpet stench rising up to meet their nostrils. The pair pushed the inner doors open to a sight that was a carbon copy of the last time they were here. Even though it was Wednesday evening, the place was packed with white people, nearly all men, drinking and sneering at each other, their banter sounding like the buzz of angry bees. Carl Cooper in the centre of it all, holding court around a large wooden table, flanked by his thugs, still sporting black eyes, cut lips and bruised egos. Minchie sat with them, his face unmarked.

The room went silent.

Carl Cooper swore and stood up. A third of the men in the pub stood up with him, their fists clenched.

"You're barred from here," said the barman, pointing in Savage's direction.

"Oi," said Carl. "I say who's barred and who's not."

Savage Children

"Sorry, Carl." The barman shrank back.

"Any last words before my men beat the crap out of you?" asked Carl.

"Yes," said Savage. "I'd like to buy everyone a drink."

Carl laughed. "Ha. You think you can buy people's loyalty with the offer of a drink. You're sadly mistaken. This pub and everyone in it are loyal to me."

"How about two drinks then?" Savage offered.

Nobody moved.

"Alright," said Savage. "Three drinks for everyone."

Again, nobody moved. But a few lips were licked and bottoms fidgeted in their seats.

Carl looked around. Folded his arms and grinned smugly. "Nice try, Savage. Not going to work."

"Okay, then," said Savage. "Let me remind everyone. That's three, I'll repeat, three free drinks that you're turning down. Just think, three beers and not a penny to pay. Crisp ciders, ice-cold lagers, pale ales, tasty bitters. All free today." Savage was aware he sounded like the child catcher from *Chitty Chitty Bang Bang*. Tempting children with sweeties. As he surveyed the room, that wasn't far from the truth. People licked their lips and swallowed deeply. Looked down at their almost-empty pint glasses, then longingly at the bar.

There was the tiniest scrape of a chair from the corner of the pub. An elderly guy in a dirty white vest that hung on him like a baggy sail slowly got to his feet. The collective eyes of the pub all followed him, as he padded over to the bar like Scooby Doo, trying to be inconspicuous. When he got there, he said to the barman in a quiet voice. "I'll take three pints of Stella if that fella's paying."

The barman looked at Carl for approval. Carl shook his head.

Savage reiterated his offer. "Three pints. All on me." He pulled out a thick wedge of notes, went over and slapped them down on the bar, right under the barman's nose. "Payment in advance." He went back and joined Tannaz.

The barman eyed the stack of notes like forbidden fruit. This could be a lucrative evening.

Three teenage lads in baseball caps, who looked too young to be allowed in a pub, bounced their way over to the bar and put in drinks orders. Several more people got up and joined them. Then a stampede. Men, young and old, jostling to get their orders in. Under such consumer pressure and the thought of all that profit, the barman had no choice but to oblige, pulling pints as fast as his saggy tattooed arms could manage.

An odd-looking guy with comb-over hair and a portly build sidled up to Savage and asked in a conspiratorial voice. "In this deal for free drinks," he said in a surprisingly well-spoken accent, "could I substitute two of the three drinks for a meal of equal value."

"You certainly can," said Savage. "What are you thinking of having?"

"A nice plate of sausage and mash." The guy beamed. "Then my remaining free pint to wash it all down with."

"Be my guest," said Savage, gesturing to the bar. The guy smiled even wider and turned to join the thronging mass waiting to make an order.

Savage turned and looked at Carl, whose table was now empty, apart from Minchie and a couple of others. The rest had abandoned him for the promise of free booze.

"Sorry," said Savage. "What was that you were saying about loyalty?"

Carl's shoulders dropped. His bashed-up face remained defiant. "What do you want, Savage?" he asked, slumping into his chair.

They sat down in front of him. Tannaz unhitched her computer bag and laid it on the table.

"Got yourself a little computer, have you?" Carl said with a sneer. "Sure you know how to use it? Country you're from don't let you use computers. I bet you're not even allowed to leave the house, are you? Do you even know what the Internet is?"

Tannaz kept her cool. "How's that thick lip I gave you? What's it like being beaten up by a woman? Although, you might be one of them blokes that like that sort of thing."

Carl ignored them both. "What do you want, Savage?"

"I need your help."

Savage Children

Carl belly laughed. Minchie and the other two men joined in. Four thugs chuckling in unison. Carl leaned forward, tried his hardest to look threatening. Impossible when his thick bottom lip resembled a collagen implant that had gone wrong. "You've got a nerve," he said. "Your little stunt with the free beers may have distracted everyone, but when the booze runs out, they'll lay into you. Count on it."

"Barman!" shouted Savage. "Make it four drinks for everyone!"

The collective alcoholics at the bar and all around the pub, turned and cheered Savage.

"I can do this all night," said Savage. "See, you may think your men and the clientele of this pub are politically motivated but it's just like the Roman Empire. I've been reading about it. Bread and circuses, they call it. Give the masses what they want and their political ideology and ambitions get distracted by dangling food and entertainment in front of them, or in this case, free pints of Stella."

"What do you want?" Carl said, crestfallen.

"I told you, your help."

"I'm not helping a kiddie fiddler like you."

Savage sighed. "Carl, we've been through this already. You didn't come out of it too well. Actually, if you help us, you could possibly save the life of four children. Catch the guy who really took Callum Leighton. Think about it. St George Is Cross would be heroes. You'd be a hero. Catching a genuinely dangerous child abductor, not just someone you've picked on because of the colour of their skin."

"What are you talking about?" asked Carl, getting interested.

Savage outlined how Callum had gone missing, how kids were being taken. He explained about the CCTV and how Tannaz had written a programme that would alert them. "We need an army to cover an area of south London," said Savage. "An alert could go off anywhere, and with your large network, which I'm guessing is mostly made up of cab drivers, builders and white-van drivers, we could have someone there in minutes to stop him. A willing and able army to hunt this guy down. Not for us, but for Callum and those kids who have gone missing. There's still a chance we can get them back. They might still be alive. But we can only do it with your help."

Carl leaned back. "What colour is this guy?"

"We don't know," said Tannaz, "and it shouldn't matter. What about the kids? You should be thinking of them."

"Answer's still no." Carl leaned back smiling smugly, enjoying his little bit of control.

"You must be joking," said Tannaz. "There are kids out there in danger. More could be taken and you're refusing to help."

"That's right."

"Let me get this straight," said Savage. "Even though you, Carl Cooper, and your group have a chance to catch this guy, who has snatched four kids, you point blank refuse to help, even though you could possibly be instrumental in freeing these children and prevent more being taken, *and* putting a monster who abducts children behind bars."

Carl leant forward, slammed his palms down on the table, and with plenty of melodrama, as if he were making a statement in court said, "Yes, I Carl Cooper, of sound mind and body, and the rest of the members of St George Is Cross, refuse to help find these little brats. Because I don't care. You're right. I'm a racist and St George Is Cross is just a front to go after filthy immigrants coming into this country, threatening to destroy our way of life. I couldn't care less about kids. I just want people like her—" He pointed to Tannaz. "—out of Britain. Got it?"

"Yep, we got it alright," said Tannaz.

"Wow," said Savage. "So, you finally admit it. That's your agenda. Well, at least you're honest. But I guess that's the end of you and St George Is Cross."

"Oh, no it's not," said Carl, firmly. "We intend to go on and on. Fighting the cause. As long as it takes."

Savage looked confused. "But what happens when the public find out about why you're really doing this? I mean, you've just admitted it to us."

Carl laughed, falsely. "Oh, Savage. You're so naïve. No one's going to believe you. The word of a suspected paedo and his little brown sidekick."

"Oh no, they won't need to believe me. But they will believe you."

Tannaz reached into her computer bag, which didn't have a computer in it at all. She pulled out a small black rectangular device, revealing a tiny hole in the bag's side, about the size of a button. She placed the device in the middle of the table, on its end. It was a little bigger than a USB stick, thicker and longer, with a round aperture at the top.

"That," said Savage, "is a 1080P, HD spy camera."

Tannaz dug into her pocket and pulled out her smartphone. Hit a few buttons and turned the phone round so Carl could watch the play back. It was the bit where Carl said, "... Yes, I Carl Cooper, of sound mind and body, and the rest of the members of St George Is Cross, refuse to help find these little brats."

Carl watched open-mouthed for several seconds. He clamped his jaw shut, fixed Tannaz with a cold, stony-eyed stare. "You'll never get out of this pub alive with that footage."

"Too late, sweetheart. It's wireless. Been sent all over the place. I've learnt how to use email and everything." She fluttered her eyelids demurely.

"Remember, Carl," said Savage. "The Pentium is mightier than the sword. The footage is being stored on many different computers and servers. Nothing will happen to it as long as nothing happens to us. Oh, and unless you refuse to help us."

"Then it will go viral," said Tannaz. "And you know what that means?"

"Yeah," said Minchie, enthusiastically, as if he had his hand up in class. "It'll be on those YouTube clip shows of people falling into canals and dogs dancing."

"Shut up, Minchie," said Carl. He thought for a moment, chewed it over in his small monkey brain. Weighed up his options and kept coming to the same conclusion that they had him. He had no choice. "What do you need?"

Savage smiled. "We need all your contacts, right across London. Saint George Is Cross. All of them. I want you to brief them. Tell them that they need to be on high alert. Sometime in the next week or so they'll receive an automatic text telling them the location of a park in south London. Any member near to that park has to drop everything, go there and be on the lookout for someone possibly trying to abduct a child. Stop them, restrain them, but do not hurt them. I can't stress how important that is. Hold onto them until we get there. If this guy gets hurt, the kids that are missing may never be found, do you understand? If that happens then your little video goes viral, so make sure your members have that clear."

Carl nodded his head slowly.

"They need to be smart about this," said Tannaz. "Don't just grab a guy who's obviously walking his kids home from school. Also, the abducted child may have been given a lollipop."

"Lollipop?" asked Carl. "What, tempting them with sweets, really? That still works?"

"Not just any lollipop," Savage replied. "We think it's laced with fentanyl, the drug. That's how he makes them compliant. Keeps them calm and sleepy."

"Jeez, that is sick," said Carl, dropping some of his previous resistance to the idea of helping.

"See, it's a good thing we're doing here," said Tannaz, "catching this asshole."

Carl sighed. "Okay, I'll make sure my members get the message."

"Remember," said Savage. "Restrain the guy until we get there. No beating him unconscious." He stood up.

Tannaz joined him, retrieving the spy camera and putting it in her bag. "I want you to send me your contact list tonight. I've sent you an email you can reply to," she said.

"But I haven't given you my personal email address," said Carl. "It's private."

"Nothing's private, Carl." Tannaz flashed him a wicked smile. Then they left.

When they got back to Vikram's, Savage pulled out an empty pint glass from inside his jacket pocket and held it up by the bottom. "Vikram, do you have a resealable plastic bag?" he asked.

"Of course, I have several sizes."

"Thought you might, it's to put this pint glass in."

"Why have you been carrying a dirty pint glass in your pocket?" asked Tannaz.

"It's Carl Cooper's pint glass."

"Why are you carrying Carl Cooper's dirty pint glass in your pocket?"

Vikram held out a medium-sized plastic bag with a resealable strip. Savage popped the pint glass in and sealed it up. "It's a surprise."

"You're weird," said Tannaz. She rubbed her eyes, not in tiredness, more out of irritation. "Why do I feel like we've just used a sledgehammer to crack a nut."

"Or worse than that, Mjölnir to crack a nut," said Savage.

"Mjölnir? What's Mjölnir?" asked Tannaz.

"Thor's hammer," said Vikram.

Tannaz groaned. Now there were two of them hitting her with comic-book movie references. "I don't like this," she said. "We've unleashed a load of dumb alt-right wingers to catch a guy we've never seen. The odds of them restraining the right person are slim. Someone innocent's going to get hurt, I just know it."

"I know, I know," said Savage. "It's clumsy. But what else can we do? Who has that number of people on call at such short notice?"

"And who's prepared to do what we ask, thanks to that footage," Vikram added. "He's scared as hell we'll release it."

"I guess I don't like control slipping out of my hands." Tannaz patted her jacket, searching for cigarettes to smoke.

"All we can do now is hold our nerve," said Savage. "Wait and see what happens."

CHAPTER 28

TWO DAYS LATER, BOTH VIKRAM and Tannaz were getting antsy, not helped by the quantities of premium coffee she had poured down her throat and the fistfuls of M&Ms he kept pushing into his mouth. While waiting for Archangel to make his next move they'd triple- and quadruple-checked the software Tannaz had written, the early-warning system that would ping as soon as anyone tried to hack any first-generation camera overlooking a park entrance. Vikram had also done his fair share of checking, making sure he hadn't missed any CCTV location that might be a potential site for an abduction. And Carl Cooper had kept his word. Had sent over every contact in Saint George Is Cross, which now sat in a database ready for a pre-written text to be sent out, as soon as they could insert the location of Archangel's next abduction.

Tannaz returned from smoking outside into the temporary command centre they'd set up in Vikram's office, with Tannaz's laptops sprawled at one end of the table, along with a mass of snaking leads, blinking lights and humming fans. By contrast, Vikram's Apple Macs sat all in a neat, pristine, stainless-steel row, as if he'd used a spirit level to check they were in line.

"Anything?" she asked, sitting down in front of her screens.

Vikram slowly shook his head as he sat spinning from side to side in his overpriced office chair.

"This is doing my head in," she said.

"Relax. It's only been two days," said Savage. He sat in an easy chair in the corner, sipping his tea, taking his time with every mouthful. "We're in surveillance mode. Most important mode there is. Did I ever tell you the time I sat in a bush in the jungle for two weeks, observing the enemy..."

"Yes, you did," said Tannaz, sounding exhausted.

"I haven't heard it," Vikram said.

"Well..." said Savage.

Tannaz interrupted him. "Basically, he peed in his trousers for two weeks so they could keep an eye on the bad guys twenty-four hours a day."

"There's a bit more to it than that," said Savage.

Tannaz looked at him blankly. "Not really."

"Okay, yeah," Savage replied. "That's about it. But the point is we have to keep calm and stay positive that this will work. If we start losing faith then we may as well give up and say goodbye to all those kids and any hope of catching Archangel."

"I'm going to make more coffee," said Tannaz, standing up.

"That'll be your sixth cup today," said Vikram.

"Yeah and I'm just getting started. Stop caffeine-shaming me."

"I'm just saying you might want to cut down, it's not good for your heart."

"Oh yeah, and how many bags of M&Ms have you had today?"

Vikram went quiet.

"Hey," said Savage. "We're guests in Vikram's home. Take it easy."

"Fine, I'll back go to my flat. Set up there."

"I didn't mean to shame you," said Vikram. "Just looking out for a friend."

The pinched expression on Tannaz's face relaxed a little. "Sorry, I know you were. I didn't mean to be rude either."

"We have to stay positive," said Savage. "If we don't, things can spiral down. You can lose yourself to negativity in an instant. So drive out the doubt. There's no room for it. Why don't I make us some sandwiches?"

"Hey what about I order pizza?" said Vikram. "I know this great sourdough place that delivers."

"Savage doesn't like pizza," said Tannaz. "He calls it glorified cheese on toast."

"I think it's overpriced for what it is, that's all," Savage replied.

Tannaz shook her head disapprovingly. Scooped up her empty coffee cup and headed towards the door.

"One more thing, Tannaz," said Savage in a serious tone. "And this is important." She spun around to look at him, an angry but expectant look on her face, as if more life coaching were to follow. "Tea. Milk, no sugar," he said, holding his cup in the air and grinning.

Tannaz reluctantly took his cup. "How can you be so calm?"

"Would it help if I stomped around the room, getting irate?"

"I am not getting irate," said Tannaz.

"I didn't say you were."

Tannaz clinked the two cups together, holding them in her fist. "It's just this sitting and waiting is driving me nuts."

"This is the strategy we've chosen to follow. We need to all get behind it. As one. If you think there's a better one, we need to know."

"It's not that. I'm just saying we're sitting here while kids are missing. I just don't feel like we're doing anything. Staring at monitors, waiting for something to happen. When we could be out looking for Callum."

"What do you suggest?" asked Savage.

Tannaz shrugged.

"Okay," said Savage. "Stop thinking of it as doing nothing. You need to get that out of your head. This is surveillance. Wars are won with it. Lives saved. It's productive what we're doing here. And surveillance takes patience. Think of it as an investment. If we pull out now, we get nothing back."

"Yeah, I get that. But I feel like I should be doing something." Tannaz swung the cups around in her hand, gesticulating. Vikram followed their trajectory, worrying that a stray drip might fly off at any second.

"What do you suggest?" Savage asked again.

"Would you stop saying that?"

"Saying what?"

Savage Children

"*What do you suggest? What do you suggest? What do you suggest?*" she said, mocking Savage. "It's really patronising."

"I think I only said it twice."

"Well it sounded like more. I don't know what to say, I'm just voicing a feeling, that's all."

"I think you need to calm down."

"I am calm."

"Guys, please," said Vikram, pleadingly.

"You don't sound calm," said Savage.

"Believe me, this is me calm," said Tannaz, her jaws tight.

Vikram's voice increased in volume. "Guys!"

"Well, I hate to see you when you lose your temper," said Savage.

"You have seen me lose my temper." Tannaz's arms were windmilling now. The safety of Vikram's expensive cups in grave danger. "Do you see any laptops flying around the room?"

"Guys!" Vikram shouted. "We've got an alert."

In an instant Tannaz and Savage were by Vikram's side, staring at a pulsing red dot on a map of south London on one of his screens.

"It's Bellingham, Forster Memorial Park," Savage said.

Tannaz leapt up and was at one of her laptops in a millisecond. "Sending the location to everyone on Carl's list. Okay, the text has gone out. We've got you, Archangel. You nasty little prick. You're about to have one hell of a bad day."

"How far is Forster Memorial?" Vikram asked.

"About twenty minutes' drive," said Savage, grabbing his keys.

Vikram put on a headset with a microphone. "I'll tap into the traffic cameras. Find you the clearest route there."

"I'm coming with you," Tannaz said to Savage, getting to her feet.

"No, I need you here to help Vikram."

"But I want to kick this guy's ass when we find him."

"I know you do, but that's not the goal. I need you here, helping Vikram."

"But..."

Savage became more insistent. "Tannaz. No. Your skills are

unique. So are Vikram's. I need you to help each other. There's no time for debate. I have to go."

Tannaz conceded, grudgingly. This was about catching Archangel and finding the missing children. Not her getting the satisfaction of putting him in an arm lock. She sat back down at her laptops and computer screens.

Savage was just through the office door when Vikram shouted, "Wait!"

Savage popped his head back in. "What is it?"

"Another alert's appeared," said Vikram.

"Impossible," said Savage.

"Well, it's flashing," Tannaz added.

"Where is it?"

"Clapham."

"That's miles away."

"Could be a system update," said Tannaz. "Council could be uploading new software for the camera. That would increase data traffic, also trigger an alert."

Savage thought for a moment. "Send that location to Carl's men too. Just to be on the safe side."

"On it," said Tannaz.

Savage turned and left the room.

"Wait!" shouted Vikram. "Wait!"

Savage was back again. "What?"

"Another alert's popped up."

"You're joking." Savage was back by Vikram's side.

"And there's another one," said Tannaz.

"And another." Vikram pointed to his screen.

In the next five seconds the whole map of south London pulsated with red dots, like it had a chronic dose of the measles, as every camera on their list sent out an alert that it was being hacked.

"What the hell's happening?" said Savage.

"Maybe the local authority's doing a systemwide update," Vikram said.

"Or maybe he's on to us," Tannaz ventured.

"Could he have known?" asked Savage. "Did we somehow tip him off?"

Tannaz shook her head. "Don't see how. I didn't leave any tracks."

"Then he's being smart," said Savage. "Ultra-cautious. We only checked four cameras for evidence of hacking. We should've checked them all. I bet he sends the hack to every camera, as decoys, just in case anyone's watching."

Tannaz typed rapidly on her keyboard, pulling up historical data. "Damn it, you're right. We've been sloppy. All previous abductions, the hack was sent to every low-tech local-authority camera in south London. He's smarter than we gave him credit."

"What do we do?" asked Vikram.

"Nothing's changed," said Savage. "Except we'll have to send out all the locations to Carl's group and hope he has enough men to get someone to each location. There's a chance we can still catch this guy."

"There are over a hundred cameras," said Vikram.

"Better be quick, then. Otherwise he'll get away with it. Again."

CHAPTER 29

MINCHIE HAD JUST BEEN TO the barber. And now he was irritable. And when he got irritable, he got punchy. His neck was itchy because he had got his hair cut at the cheapest place he could find. This one did it for a fiver. And that's what he got. A five-pound haircut that did nothing for his ape-faced appearance. When the barber had asked him what he wanted, Minchie simply replied, "Don't make me look gay." The barber had obliged and gone almost down to the skin round the back and sides, leaving barely half an inch on top.

He looked tough alright, and slightly weird, seeing as he was walking along the pavement with one arm thrust down the back of his neck, trying to dislodge pesky hairs that were tormenting his thick skin because the barber didn't use a proper neck guard, just stuffed some kitchen roll round it. Now it felt as if someone had tipped iron fillings and asbestos down his back.

Minchie's phone pinged. An alert. One of the ones Carl had talked about after Savage left that night. He'd been really serious about it. Banged his fist on the pub table. *You get texted a location and you're nearby. You go to that location. Pronto. No excuses.* Then he'd said something about catching a kiddie fiddler, saving innocent kids. Minchie couldn't remember the rest of it.

Minchie didn't want to read the text. He didn't want to go on one of Carl's missions. Previous missions had been protesting outside a kebab shop because they were Turkish or shouting at the men working in the Halal butchers. He wanted to spend the rest of the afternoon drinking in a pub, sitting outside, ogling posh office girls leaving work, then lose a load of money on the fruit machine like

Savage Children

he always did. Then he'd get angry and get into a punch-up with someone. A perfect day.

Equally, he didn't want to incur the wrath of Carl Cooper. Not respond to the text and he'd risk being thrown out. And he liked being in Saint George Is Cross. Being part of something. A big extended family. He just didn't like the work involved.

Reluctantly, Minchie opened the text. Weird. It was a great big list of locations in south London. Minchie thought it'd be just one. Probably a mistake.

He scrolled through them. In his head he kept saying no to each one. Too far away. Too far away. So's that one. And that one. Nearing the end of the list he was hoping he could make it a clean sheet. Yeah, none of these locations were anywhere near him, he was nearly off the hook until he came to the third from the end. A long narrow strip of riverside green near St John's known as Brookmill Park. He'd just got his haircut on Brookmill Road. That was where he was. Right this minute. All he needed to do was cross the road and he'd be in the park.

Minchie hesitated. Apathy held him back. Did he really want to get involved? If he crossed that road, he might have to do something, and Minchie didn't like doing things. For anyone, apart from himself. It'd be so easy to just walk away, turn his back. Head in the other direction. But then he'd have to account for his whereabouts today. Make stuff up. Minchie wasn't good at making things up. Especially not in front of Carl. He'd have to think about what he was saying. Not blurt stuff out like he usually did. Minchie would stutter like an idiot. Say he was seeing his old nan in Brentwood. You don't have a nan in Brentwood, Carl would say. His mind would lock up like the back wheel of a bike tangled up with a mud guard, his brain skidding out of control. That settled it. He'd have to do something. Not out of concern for abducted children but because he couldn't take the heat of a Carl Cooper grilling.

Minchie crossed the road.

He replied to Carl's text as he crossed, informing him he was checking out the Brookmill Park location.

Sandwiched between the River Ravensbourne and a parallel

railway line on one side and Brookmill Road on the other, the park was a green serpent of land planted by the Victorians. A breathing space for the city, an ornamental oasis with towering trees and plenty of hidden corners for picnics and secret liaisons for lovers, or probable paedophiles.

In front of Minchie stood two grand entrance columns flanked by a pair of impressive wrought-iron black gates. A sign at the side informed visitors that they would be shut tight at sunset. In either direction a red brick wall topped with a high, spiked black fence encircled the park. Minchie noticed a rusty CCTV camera on a high metal pole pointed down at the entrance. He hesitated briefly, then entered the park, not noticing its landscaped beauty. All he saw was somewhere for dogs to do their business. A narrow tarmac path wound its way through the park. Minchie followed it, dawdled along, scanning the area for anyone who looked dodgy. Although, right at that moment, Minchie was probably the dodgiest-looking character in the park. In fact, he seemed to be the only one in the park. He continued walking and turned a corner by an old rugged oak tree. Up ahead, he could see a bearded hipster dad with a neat crop of facial foliage, coming the other way pushing a fancy pram. Not one of the modern ones that folded up like a Transformer, it was a retro *Call the Midwife* fifties-type pram that was becoming trendy with posh London twats. You had to be posh to own one because they didn't fold up and you needed a Range Rover to fit them in the back. The pram was huge, like a small boat on bicycle wheels. Minchie hated the guy already.

He remembered Carl's words, don't jump on the first guy you see. Especially not someone who's clearly with their own kids. Be smart. Look out for someone suspicious. This wanker's taking kids around the age of ten.

Minchie processed what he saw and compared it to what Carl had said. A guy with a pram wouldn't have a ten-year-old, even Minchie knew that. Prams were meant for babies. The single mum in the bedsit above Minchie's had a baby and she had a pram. She was always lugging it up the stairs whenever he was trying to get to his bedsit, huffing and puffing going one step at a time. Baby in one hand, pram in the other, struggling. Sweat forming on her brow, kid screaming the place down. Minchie would never help her. Never get involved. If he did it once he'd have to do it every time he saw her. Why didn't the stupid cow leave the pram in the hallway? He knew the answer to that. Because he would steal it and sell it on eBay. Although, Minchie had been banned from eBay after he'd sold a car that didn't exist. Well, if people were stupid enough to by cars without looking at them first, that wasn't his problem.

Yep, Minchie was confident he could strike this guy off his suspects list. As the hipster passed, Minchie clocked a sideway glance. The pram's hood was up and the cover was across, covering its entire length apart from a small gap. He couldn't see anything. Kid was probably asleep under there. "Afternoon," the guy said as he passed Minchie. Minchie mouthed the word *prick* under his breath. Guy should be at work, doing a job, not looking after kids. That was for the woman to do. Not that Minchie had a job, but he didn't have a kid either. But he knew what was what. Men should work and women should be at home with kids. Bet the guy cooks as well and watches subtitled movies. The only reason Minchie ever watched a subtitled movie was late at night when he was a teenager in the hope that some French bird would get her kit off.

Minchie looked up and down the park. There was no one else here. So that's that, he thought. He could go to the pub now with a clear conscience. He turned around and walked back the other way, promising to stop at the first boozer he came to where he'd order a pint and whisky chaser. Some booze would help numb that itchy neck of his.

Up ahead, the hipster dad neared the big iron gates at the exit to the park. That was when Minchie saw it. A small hand came out of the pram and dropped a lolly stick. Lolly stick. Hipster dad stopped momentarily to pick up the litter and slot it into the back of his jeans. The guy was one of them environmentalists. Minchie hated him even more now.

But something lit up in Minchie's tiny sixteen-bit brain. What was it? Lolly sticks. An image flashed into his head of the child catcher from *Chitty Chitty Bang Bang*. Savage had sounded like him back in the pub that night when he was trying to tempt everyone with free booze. He hated that film because of the child catcher, that guy was definitely a paedo. After seeing it on telly, the young Minchie had wet the bed for a month, getting a clip round the ear from his dad every time he woke up to sodden sheets. "What's wrong with you, you pansy?" his dad would say. Followed by another cuff to his head. Young Minchie was too scared to tell him that he'd had nightmares about the creepy, child-snatching character offering sweets to the pretty blond children. The memory made him sad for his childhood, remembering the deep-rooted fear of the film and the back of his father's hand. That overwhelming terror, tattooed on his brain. The painful memories of his dad slapping him. The pain that soon turned to deep buried anger. Up ahead he saw, not the hipster dad, but the child catcher. Then he remembered. Carl had said that this guy takes ten-year-olds, gives them lollies with drugs in them.

Minchie stomped up the path. He needed to get a look in that stupid oversized pram. Make sure the guy wasn't hiding a ten-year-old in there.

How would he get a look in the pram? Minchie hadn't figured that one out yet as he marched towards the guy. If Minchie had had more than half a brain, he would have known it was pretty easy to get a look at someone's child. You could subtly engage the proud parent, with a mixture of affectionate curiosity and flattery. *How old is she/he? You must be so proud. How are you finding parenthood? How does he/she sleep at night? I love your pram. I was thinking of getting one of those. Are they good?* He could've even gone as far as saying, *I've got two kids of my own, a girl and a boy. What've you got?* At which point the proud father might have offered Minchie a quick peek at the little one asleep.

But Minchie didn't do any of this.

Instead, he caught up with the dad and said, "Oi, mate. Let's have a look at your kid."

Quite rightly the hipster dad looked at him horrified, quickened his steps and said, "I'd rather not, he's sleeping." The guy sounded posh, educated. One of them sensitive types who beats himself up if he didn't separate his recycling.

"Go on," said Minchie, matching his pace. "Give us a look."

The hipster broke into a slow jog now. "I really have to go. Nice talking to you."

Minchie kept up, shoulder to shoulder. "I really need to see your kid. Or I'll get it in the neck from the guy in charge of this gang I belong to."

The hipster made quickly towards the park's entrance, but before he could fully escape, Minchie caught him up and rounded on him, in front of the pram, shunting it to a halt with a pair of thick, meaty hands.

"Hey," said Hipster Dad. "Get off."

Minchie could get in trouble for this, but he'd be in more trouble from Carl if he didn't check.

Hipster Dad tried to yank the pram back, snatching it from Minchie's grasp. No chance of that happening. Minchie's hands had a grip like King Kong's. He pulled the pram back towards him and grabbed a corner of the cover. It was held in place with press studs all along its edge. In one muscular jerk of his arm, Minchie ripped the cover back.

Curled up double inside the pram, squished into every corner like a hibernating hamster was a small, young boy who was at least nine or ten. His eyes were sleepy, barely open. His head slowly turned to look at Minchie. "I want my mummy," the young boy croaked.

Minchie had only gone and done it. He'd found the paedophile. He'd actually done something right. Saved a kid.

Before he had time for any more self-congratulation, a rage spread across Minchie like a flash flood in April. In his mind's eye, he saw the child catcher and his dad all rolled into one. Time to punch someone's light out with those big fists of his. And this time, he had a genuine reason for hitting someone. It wasn't one of his usual violent urges where he hit a random stranger.

Minchie pulled back his sizeable fist. But before he had a chance to launch an attack, he got it full in the face from a can of pepper spray from the child-abducting hipster.

Minchie rarely inhaled though his nose. He was your archetypal mouth breather, gob constantly hanging open in a dopey expression. The full force of pepper spray went down his throat into his lungs. In his ears. Up his nose. In his piggy little eyes. It was as if someone had stuck pins in them. Minchie gasped, struggled to breath, collapsed on the floor in a coughing fit. Turned over and spat phlegm everywhere, so hard he nearly threw up. The burning wouldn't stop. Just constant searing pain in his eyes and mouth.

Through small slit-like eyes drenched in tears, Minchie caught a glimpse of Hipster Dad running out of the park, pushing the pram in front of him.

Minchie's phone rang. He managed to answer it.

"Minchie. Anything?" asked Carl.

All Minchie could do was cry. "My eyes are hot."

"What's happened? Have you spotted anyone?"

"He's got a kid," Minchie sobbed. "Hipster with a pram. Leaving Brookmill Park. Tell Savage. He's got pepper spray. It's not like pepper. It's like someone's eaten vindaloo and shat in my eyes."

"Anything else?"

"Yeah, my neck's really itchy."

CHAPTER 30

There was a lull in traffic. Not that there were any sizeable lulls in London traffic. The place was jammed 24/7. This lull was barely perceptible, but Savage noticed it and was thankful. It was 4.20 p.m. and the school run had just ended; the rush-hour proper had not quite begun. Give it another ten minutes and it would be rammed with desperate people trying to be somewhere else.

On speaker phone in the van he had Vikram and Tannaz, continually feeding him instructions. Tannaz had hacked into all the available traffic cameras along the way and sent their video streams to Vikram to monitor and act as Savage's navigator, showing him the path of least resistance to Brookmill Park. Every second counted, since they'd first got the hurried call from Carl Cooper telling them that Minchie, of all people, had apprehended Archangel, only to be doused with pepper spray while Archangel made his escape. There was a chance that the dimwit had got it wrong and had merely stopped a father with a pram, out for a walk, who had quite rightly defended himself by squirting Minchie in the face with something noxious. Quite understandable. Minchie had that effect on people.

They hadn't been able to talk to Minchie directly to verify the facts. The big oaf was incapacitated. Still sitting in a heap on the pathway, presumably with pepper-spray-laced tears dropping from his eyes like hot ball bearings. Still, they had to go with his story. All they knew was that Archangel, if that was who Minchie had encountered, looked like a hipster and had been forced to exit the park pushing a pram through one of its four entrances that opened onto Brookmill Road. This posed a problem. The park was long and narrow, stretching nearly a kilometre, each of its entrances spaced equally along that length. There was no way of knowing which entrance he'd used. Hacking the park's CCTV was no help. Archangel had already uploaded his stealth software to take himself out of the picture. Once across the busy Brookmill Road, there were plenty of small insignificant residential side roads he could've slipped down. And side roads meant no CCTV. And even if there were cameras, the guy was smart. He'd hack the ones he could to mask himself and avoid the ones he couldn't.

Despite this, Tannaz had been busy hacking cameras in the area, just in case the guy made a mistake. Savage could hear Tannaz's furious typing and swearing in the background in a frantic attempt to detect the guy. She'd found nothing. They already knew he didn't make mistakes. Minchie had been a stroke of luck. In the right place at the right time, or wrong time, if you saw it through Minchie's weepy eyes. Still, they had to try. Savage was nearly there, approaching the outskirts of Brookmill Park.

"Take a left into Manor Avenue," said Vikram. "You should have a clear run to the end."

"Got it," said Savage. "Tannaz, any sign of him?"

"None. Nothing. Guy's a ghost. How do we know he's not in a car by now, driving away?"

"My gut says no," Savage replied. "He can avoid CCTV but ANPR cameras are a different matter. If someone sees him get in a car, ANPR cameras can track him. Plus, he'd need to transfer the doped-up child into a vehicle, and that's going to be tricky. I don't think he'd risk it. I think he's making his escape on foot."

"Hope you're right because I've got nothing."

"Where are you now Savage?" asked Vikram.

"Nearly at the end of Manor Avenue."

"Okay, take a right into Lewisham Way. All the way down. Into Lloyd Villas."

"Got it."

"This is bullshit," said Tannaz. "He's going to get away. We've blown it. We've lost our advantage."

"Course we haven't," said Savage. "We can still catch him."

"Minchie will have spooked him. He'll lie low now. Disappear."

"We don't know that," said Savage. He needed to keep her positive, even though he knew she was right. By now Archangel would know someone was on to him. His unblemished record of disappearing without a trace was now sullied. Even if it was an incompetent thug who had barged into him, it would be all he needed to retreat into the shadows without a trace. They may have lost him forever. And with that, any chance of finding Callum and the others. "Come on, Tannaz. Are you going to let this guy beat you? You're better than him. I know you are. Come on. Breathe. Recalibrate. Deliver."

"Stop doing your SAS Jedi mind trick," she shouted down the phone. "It won't work. Face it, the guy's disappeared with another kid. We failed."

"Tannaz! Breathe. Recalibrate. Deliver."

Breathe. Recalibrate. Deliver. was an SAS mantra used to reset a soldier's mental attitude when things weren't going to plan. Almost Buddhist in its approach, you take a second to still your mind, be calm, allow your brain to think, even if hand grenades are coming in through the windows.

Savage spoke calmly back to her. "Reboot your brain. Drop that negative attitude. It's no good to you. Now, figure out a way of finding this guy. I know you can do it. You said it yourself you're smarter than he is."

"I said I was a better hacker," Tannaz replied. "Not necessarily smarter. And I'm just being realistic. We've lost him."

"We lost him on CCTV," said Savage, jamming the gear stick into second. "Think. How else can we find him?"

"Without CCTV we're blind. And you driving around the area trying to spot him is relying on pure luck."

Savage spoke with resignation. "Okay, Tannaz. Seems like you're doing him a favour. On his side. Want us to give up. Let him have an easy ride."

Much swearing followed. She called Savage all the names under the sun and invented a few new ones.

Once she'd exhausted all the expletives she could think of, Savage said, "Feel better now? Come on, together we can figure this out."

"Savage, where are you?" asked Vikram.

"I'm on the main road now, Brookmill Road, crawling alongside the park. Stuck behind a bus, not going anywhere. It's chocka with buses."

"Buses?" asked Tannaz. "Did you say buses?"

"Yeah, it's a major bus route. You'd think they'd put in a bus lane. Place is snarled up with them."

"Vikram," said Tannaz. "Get me the number of every bus that goes along Brookmill Road."

"What for?"

"Just do it."

Though Savage was on the other end of the phone, he could almost feel Vikram flinch at Tannaz's command.

"What do you have in mind, Tannaz?" Savage asked.

Through a flurry of typing sounds, she said, "I think he may have slipped up. I'm hoping he has."

"How?"

"Guy's an expert at manipulating CCTV, old-style CCTV. The kind that are fixed, screwed to walls and lampposts. But there's another kind of CCTV, and I'm betting my reputation that's he's either forgotten about it or, more likely, hasn't got the skills to manipulate it, because these cameras keep shifting and the technology's more modern, which means it's out of bounds to him."

"What is it?"

"Dash cams," said Tannaz. "Every London bus has them and you said there're loads of buses."

"Tons."

"If he's crossed over the road, and the traffic's moving slowly, there's more than a good chance a dash cam has caught him. I'm hacking Transport for London, specifically CentreComm. It's their emergency command hub, a complete network for monitoring the operation and GPS position of every bus in the capital, including—Yes!—the feeds of every bus's dash cam. Vikram, have you got the numbers of the buses on that route?"

Vikram rattled off a list of numbers. Six of them in total.

"Okay, I've just pulled up their dash cams in real time," said Tannaz. "Got six video feeds on screen."

"Anything?" asked Savage.

"No, not yet. That would have been asking too much to spot him instantly. Right. I'm going to wind back the feeds, slowly."

"Anything?" Savage asked again.

"You'll be the first to know."

The phone went quiet. No noise, not even any static. Savage sat in the traffic queue waiting patiently, moving at a glacial pace.

A minute passed according to the clock in Savage's VW. It felt like an hour.

Savage heard a slap of palms on the table. Followed by a stream of swearing. "There's nothing Savage," Tannaz said. "Nothing."

"Are you sure?"

Savage got hit with a baseball bat of more swearing from Tannaz. "What do you think we've just been doing?"

"Tannaz, calm down." Savage knew it was a stupid thing to say. Nothing like angering someone even more than by telling them to calm down. He quickly changed tack. "If you lose your temper, that smart brain of yours will be no good to us. Breathe. Recalibrate. Deliver. Come on, Tannaz. You can beat this guy."

The traffic queue slowed to a halt. It would have been quicker going in reverse, thought Savage. That gave him an idea. "Tannaz," he shouted at the phone. "Buses also have rear-facing cameras. Pull up their feeds."

The click-clack of keyboard buttons.

"Got the rear-facing camera feeds now. Just winding them back..."

"There he is!" exclaimed Vikram. "Hipster beard pushing a large pram, crossing behind a bus."

Savage punched the air. "Yes! When was that?"

"Just two minutes ago," said Tannaz. Let me cross reference that with the bus's GPS at that time. Get you an exact location." More tapping of keys. Savage willing her to go faster. "Bus would've been adjacent to... Lind Street."

"That's behind you," said Vikram. "You passed it earlier."

Savage thought about pulling a U-turn and driving back the other way. A pointless exercise, seeing as how the traffic going the other way was equally slow in its progress. Instead, he pulled over and parked by the kerb illegally, next to double-yellow lines that had the extra yellow kerb strip to emphasise that leaving your car here really wasn't on and was an even bigger sin than leaving it on regular double-yellow lines. He'd get the inevitable ticket or clamp, that was for sure. Maybe if he caught Archangel, he could pull a few strings with DI Roberts and they'd overlook it.

Savage killed the engine, grabbed his phone and the compact umbrella he kept in the door pocket. For an impromptu weapon, he usually went for the hefty Maglite in his glove box, but today he thought he might need his umbrella.

Savage began to run back down along Brookmill Road, phone to his ear constantly in contact with Tannaz and Vikram. By contrast to the traffic, the pavement was deserted, a mostly residential area, bereft of shops apart from a barber's and a pub. He could see why Archangel chose this place. There were very few passers-by to witness him.

"Keep looking at the bus-camera feeds," said Savage. "Just in case this guy decides to double back."

"Already am," Tannaz replied.

"Where are you?" asked Vikram.

"Just entering Lind Street."

"What do you see?"

"Nothing, just a nice clean road of overpriced London terraced houses. I'm jogging down to the end."

"Okay, that's good. You'll be on Albyn Road," Vikram informed him. "That's a stroke of luck. South end of Albyn Road is a dead end, so he must have gone north."

When Savage reached the end of the street he followed Vikram's instructions and went north. There was no sign of anyone. The road was deserted and went on as far as the eye could see. "There's no one here."

Savage Children

"There's a bridge over the railway up ahead," said Vikram. "St John's station is on the other side."

"Damn it," said Tannaz. "He's got on a train. That was his escape route. We've lost him."

"Not so fast," said Savage. "This guy wants to stay off the radar. Avoid CCTV. Train stations are littered with cameras. Modern ones. He wouldn't have gone there."

"Well, where else would he have gone?"

Savage stopped jogging, thought for a moment. What would *he* have done? Definitely avoided public transport—that was asking for trouble. Savage looked at his phone, pulled up a map of the area. It was a network of little back streets. Archangel was safe if he stayed in the back streets, zigzagging his way along them. If he crossed over the railway bridge he'd be heading for Lewisham Way, the A20. A busy road full of shops and people. That decided it.

"I'm heading towards St John's Vale," Savage announced. He began jogging again.

"But that's almost doubling back on yourself," Vikram replied. "What would be the point of that?"

"Exactly," said Savage. "It's erratic. That's the best way to avoid being followed. Be unpredictable. And if we think this guy's smart, that's what he's thinking too."

"I think this is a mistake," said Vikram.

"Me too," said Tannaz. "He's gone to St John's station. Quickest way of getting out of there. I'm hacking into their cameras now."

Savage increased his pace, breathing heavily into the phone. "He won't want to get caught on their cameras, I tell you. He can't pull his CCTV magic trick because they'll be too up to date."

"There are ways of avoiding CCTV," Vikram explained. "He could just keep his head down, buy a baseball cap."

"Yes," said Savage. "I know about that, but he's pushing a pram. It's a giveaway, plus, prams are clumsy to control. What if the train's busy? He's got a drowsy ten-year-old bunched up in there, he'll want to avoid any close contact with people. He won't take that chance."

Tannaz joined in. "John, you need to go to the train station."

"No, I'm going with my gut. I'm just turning into St John's Vale now."

"Savage, don't waste your time," said Tannaz. "I've hacked into the CCTV at the station. Let me and Vikram examine the feeds, see if we can spot him."

"You don't need to," said Savage. "I can see him up ahead."

He hung up.

CHAPTER 31

IN THE DISTANCE HE SAW the back of a man, halfway up the road, walking away from him, pushing a big, bulky, old-style pram, heading back towards the main road. Clever, thought Savage. Those retro prams were becoming trendy again. They were only bought by those with plenty of disposable income, and no one would suspect a guy who pushed one. They were the perfect abduction device, big enough and strong enough to conceal a small docile ten-year-old, especially with those vast hoods making it impossible to see who lay beneath.

Up ahead, the guy gave a cursory look over his shoulder. That was when Savage saw the hipster beard. A positive ID.

The instinctive reaction was to run after him. Embark on a foot pursuit. Chase him down. Incapacitate the guy. Save the kid. Be the hero.

Foot pursuits were never a good idea. The guy was younger than him for a start, and even with the added burden of the pram, Savage reckoned he'd be outclassed. This led Savage on to his second reason, and the most important reason, why he didn't want to start a foot pursuit. This Archangel, or whoever he was, had a hostage. A young abducted child. Savage couldn't allow any harm to come to that child. If it did, he'd never forgive himself. While Archangel had the child, he had the advantage. Savage would have to figure out a far more subtle way of approaching this. One where the child was put in the least amount of danger.

Savage's hand was then forced even more. While Archangel was checking behind him, he glanced at Savage, locked eyes with him. The only other person on the road. The guy was already spooked, he couldn't allow him to get spooked any more and think that someone was following him. Savage turned around and walked away. Best way to convince Archangel he wasn't being followed was to not follow him at all. Savage made it to the corner of the road and disappeared from view.

As soon as he did, Savage sprinted. Ran as hard as he could. He remembered the words of Sun Tzu's *The Art of War*, "Attack him where he is unprepared, *appear* where you are not *expected*." That was what Savage would do. Archangel had seen a man walking away from him, threat level diminishing with every step in the opposite direction, convincing him that Savage was a nobody. What he would not expect is for Savage to sprint hell for leather around the block to get in front of his target. If the road Archangel was walking up formed one side of a square, then Savage would have to sprint around the other three to get in front of him. He would have to run until his lungs burst, and get to the main road before Archangel did, a classic outflanking manoeuvre.

Savage made it to the second side of the square. Still plenty of energy in the tank.

By the third side of the square he was panting heavily. He was on the main road now. No sign of Archangel, and the traffic jam had ended, cars and buses flowing nicely past him.

Savage took a deep breath and held it, in a bid to slow down his breathing and his heart rate. He did this once, twice, as he edged his way to the corner where St John's Vale met Brookmill Road. Just before he got there, only two or three metres away, he saw the nose of the pram appear. Savage would keep this simple. Gripping the end of the umbrella hard, he'd give the guy a straight whack to the mouth. Not leave any broken bones or life-changing injuries, just enough to shock and incapacitate him, bloody his mouth. While he was reeling from the blow, it would give Savage enough time to secure the pram, get a look inside. Check they'd got the right guy and not some random stranger that Minchie had picked on. Savage could then check the kid was okay. And maybe give Archangel a hard jab in the stomach to wind him and stop him running away.

As Archangel rounded the corner Savage knew he was onto him.

Savage Children

The guy turned and pushed the pram towards Savage with his left hand, his right casually draped behind his back, hiding something. Usually it was a move people used to conceal a knife so they could get up close then drive it into your belly. At least Savage knew it wasn't a knife. It was a can of pepper spray. Savage had never been so happy to have his umbrella with him.

As Savage closed the gap between them, he saw the guy's right arm move, bringing it round in front of him, pepper spray clutched in his fist.

The second that happened, Savage flicked the release switch on his umbrella. He'd chosen that particular brand of umbrella because he liked the swiftness of the mechanism, and it was strong and guaranteed never to blow inside out. Savage liked foolproof products. In a split second, it had automatically unfurled in one slick motion. A makeshift shield. He held out in front of him.

Savage heard the hiss of the pepper spray. None of its contents reached him, the umbrella protecting him. The hissing didn't last long. Having emptied most of its contents on Minchie, Archangel's attack was made up of whatever was left in the can, and it wasn't much. As soon as the hissing stopped, Savage charged forward, barging into Archangel, using the umbrella like a riot shield. Not hard, just enough to shove him. Savage hit the button on the umbrella, which automatically folded back.

Archangel still had one hand on the pram. With the other he threw the spent pepper-spray can at Savage. It bounced off his head, doing no harm.

Savage got his first proper look at the child abductor, the so-called Archangel. Not what he had expected. Surprisingly young-looking and trendy, with a check shirt buttoned up to the top and slicked back hair and that neatly trimmed hipster beard, he looked more likely to be running a microbrewery than snatching kids. Tattoos covered what flesh he could see, on his neck there was a dramatic weeping angel inked just below his right ear. Savage looked him in the eyes. They were blue and full of melancholy.

"Let go of the kid," said Savage. "And I promise I won't kill you."

"I'm already dead," he said humourlessly.

Savage gave him one more chance, then he'd step in and whack the guy in the mouth with the umbrella. "Come on. Let him go."

"Whatever you say."

Archangel heaved the pram into the fast-moving traffic and into the path of an oncoming bus.

"Noooo!" shouted Savage.

Despite the best efforts of the driver, the bus ploughed into the pram crushing it under one of its wheels. What was left of it became stuck between the tarmac and the front wheel arch, getting dragged along the road until the bus finally came to a screeching halt.

Savage rushed into the road. The driver got out too, traumatised that he'd just run over a baby. Savage got to the mangled pram first. Just a mess of twisted metal and torn fabric and foam.

There was no child.

Was there ever a child? Minchie had said there was. Savage's best guess was that Archangel had dumped the child when Savage had lost sight of him, to lighten the load, but kept the pram to cause a distraction. It had certainly worked.

Savage turned. Ran back on to the pavement, just in time to see Archangel sprinting off down St John's Vale. He gave chase, still not fully recovered from his last exertion. Though his lungs burned and his heart thumped against his rib cage, he at least kept his prey in sight. Archangel didn't turn off or deviate from his course, just ran straight to the end of the road towards the bridge over the railway line. A narrow road bridge painted dull grey, it had solid metal sides reaching up to about shoulder height. No attempt had been made to secure the bridge with safety measures such as covered-in mesh or high-sided metal grilles.

As Savage neared the bridge, he heard the pre-recorded message from the loudspeaker system of St John's station below. "The train now approaching platform two does not stop here. Please stand well clear of the edge of platform two."

Archangel slowed as he reached the middle of the bridge, turned and faced Savage. He smiled. Savage slowed his pace too, down to walking, then to a stop. With his hands outstretched by his sides, Savage tossed away the umbrella to signal to Archangel he wasn't a threat.

"You know," said Archangel. "They should've just given me a chance, then none of this would have happened."

"Where's Callum?" asked Savage.

"This is the gatekeepers' fault."

"Course it is," said Savage. "Just tell me what you've done with Callum and the other kids. Are they alive?"

"I'd never have done this if it wasn't for the gatekeepers."

"Who are the gatekeepers?" asked Savage.

Archangel snorted derisively. "They're everywhere. They're the ones who stop you, who say you can't do this or that, they say you're not good enough or worse they ignore you completely. Hit you with that big bubble of apathy."

Archangel's answers were cryptic at best. Savage tried to make sense of them while trying to think how this scenario was going to play out. One thing was for sure, he had to keep this guy talking.

"You know that cult sci-fi TV show *The Prisoner*?"

"I do," said Savage. "Watched it the first time it was on TV. Showing my age a bit."

"Remember how every time the prisoner tries to escape, and he thinks he's going to make it, that big bubble thing comes after him and squashes him. That's like the big bubble of apathy they squash your dreams with. Every time you think you're getting somewhere, think you're going to make it, this big nothing comes after you. Knocks you flat. And you keep trying and they keep knocking you flat. Squashing your hope with a big nothing. That's what the gatekeepers do. They kill hope. And without hope what are we?"

"Okay," said Savage. "Some assholes have ruined your dreams. I get that, I really do. But is it really necessary to take it out on these kids? They're innocent. You can let them go. The kid you had in the pram, where is he?"

Archangel ignored him, turned and lifted himself up onto the guard rail of the bridge, swivelled back around and perched with his backside on top and his legs dangling down.

"What's your name?" said Savage. "At least tell me your name."

Archangel swung one leg over then the other. He now sat with his back to Savage. Nothing but the railway line beneath him. Savage wanted to run over and try and grab him. Big mistake. Had to talk the guy down. Get him to see reason.

"Tell me more about these gatekeepers," Savage said. Misery loves company, thought Savage. Maybe if he could empathise with him, create a bond. "I've met loads of gatekeepers that have held me back. Who held you back?"

Archangel looked over his shoulder at Savage, smiled. "I see what you're doing. Bit of trust building. Makes it harder for me to do what I'm about to do. It's okay, you don't need to patronise me, I know the psychology."

"You're right, that's exactly what I'm doing. Look, I'll be honest with you. I'm just concerned about the kids. This one kid in particular. His name's Callum. Callum Leighton. I just want to get him back to his parents alive. Could you tell me if he's okay? Where is he?"

Archangel looked blankly at him, nonplussed.

Savage chanced edging closer, scuffing his feet inch by inch along the ground. He held his hands together in a mock prayer. "Please. His mother's worried sick. Just tell me where Callum is and the other kids. Just a clue. A lock-up maybe, a basement. Anything you can give me would really, really help."

Archangel's numb stare shifted gradually to a look of stone-cold terror. "I've done terrible things," he said. "Terrible things."

"Please, just an address. A postcode. Anything."

The pain on the abductor's face relaxed into a look of peace, almost serene. "But I'm going to atone now. I'm going to join the angels. Be one of them."

The Archangel pushed himself off the bridge just as Savage heard the fast train come thundering through St John's station. Several screams rose up from the platform below. Savage ran over, lifted himself up on the edge of the bridge to look down on the tracks below.

Archangel's days of abducting children were over.

Slowly, Savage lowered himself down again, leant his back

against the smooth metal of the bridge and slid down until he was on his haunches. He called DI Roberts and told her where they could find what was left of the man they called Archangel. He hung up before she had a chance to tell him to stay put and not move a muscle.

He got to his feet and retraced his steps along St John's Vale, the road that Archangel had pushed the pram up when he was briefly out of sight, and then had been chased back down again without it. The road was lined with smart, symmetrical, Georgian terraced houses, centred with brightly painted doors and black railings at the front. Some were lucky enough to have front gardens, only very small ones with neatly trimmed hedges. Savage figured Archangel must have dumped the kid somewhere along this route. He searched the first house he came to with a garden, then moved onto the next, and the next. When he reached the fourth house with a garden, he got down on his knees and looked under the hedge. Lying almost asleep was a young boy, a plastic lolly stick dangling out of his mouth, accompanied by some dribble. Savage reached in and pulled out the lolly stick and tossed it on the ground. The boy's weary eyes opened slightly. "I want to go home now," he said.

Savage smiled as tenderly as he could. In a soft voice he said, "Of course, let's get you home, but first we need to get you out of that hedge. I'm going to take your hands and pull you. Is that okay?"

The boy nodded his head slowly. Savage grabbed hold of his hands and as gently as he could, tugged until the small boy emerged from the bush. Savage sat him up straight on the pavement and brushed some of the dirt off his face and the twigs out of his hair. The boy kept toppling over, the fentanyl still affecting him. "I feel sleepy," he said.

Savage sat next to him so the boy could lean into him for support.

"Can you tell me what your name is?" Savage asked.

"Ralph, I think."

"Ralph. That's brilliant. We're going to get you home. Now, can you remember your second name."

Ralph strained to remember. Two thick tears made dirty tracks down his face.

"That's okay, Ralph. We don't need to know. I'm going to call my friend. She's a very nice police officer and she'll help you remember. Get you back home to your mum, okay."

More fat tears ran down the boy's face.

Savage called DI Roberts again.

CHAPTER 32

Ever since Tannaz had intercepted a text from Roberts, naming Archangel as a man called Dylan Harper and revealing his address, she'd been digging online, trying to find more about him and any clue as to what he'd done with Callum and the other children. She hadn't unearthed much. The guy had no social-media presence whatsoever. A true loner, he had no friends, no one who could shed any light on his personality. All she discovered was a trail of rejected applications for every fine art course he had applied for. Starting in his hometown of Brighton, he'd been an unsuccessful applicant for every art school in the area, sometimes several years in a row. Then he'd switched his sights on London, a city brimming with art schools and colleges. Every application had ended the same way with thanks but no thanks. Whether it was lack of talent or personality, or both, Tannaz could find no clue in the application records as to why he was so unsuitable. They just didn't keep that kind of information. Then it had stopped abruptly nine years ago. For some reason he'd given up his pursuit of painting and switched to installing CCTV systems.

From his little speech on the bridge to Savage, and his consistently unsuccessful art college applications, it didn't take a genius to work out he'd built up a serious case of rejection. 'The Gatekeepers' as he referred to them, clearly being all the people who had kept him from his dream of being an artist. Years and years of being turned away had festered inside him, fuelling his bitterness, nurturing a desire for revenge. But there was no indication why he'd decided to take his frustration out on children. Surely these 'Gatekeepers' would have been a more suitable target. And what did the angel drawings mean?

"I got something," said Tannaz, sitting at her laptop. She'd hacked Dylan Harper's bank account, and had been going through every item meticulously.

Savage was at her side. "What is it?"

"Long story short, he's tried to hide a payment. Done a good job of it too. Sent me on one hell of a wild goose chase. But I've tracked where the payment goes."

"Where does it go?"

"Place called StorUStor. One of them self-store places. It's in South Lambeth"

"Can you get into their system? Find out which unit it is?"

"Piece of cake."

A couple of minutes later, Tannaz had the information. "It's a big unit. Eight-hundred footer."

"Okay let's check it out."

They pulled up opposite the forecourt of StorUStor. It was big, bright and ugly with large signs everywhere announcing units from as little as £2 a day, which sounded cheap, until you added it up into months and years.

From what they could see, only one guy manned the small reception area.

"So how are we going to play this?" asked Tannaz.

"Keep it simple. You go into reception and talk to the guy, keep him distracted while I sneak in through the loading bay and take a look inside Dylan Harper's storage unit. Once I'm done, I'll ping you a text. Signal that I'm out and we can go."

"Sounds like a plan."

Savage reached into the glove box and pulled out his wallet of lock picks. They left the VW parked out on the road and went their separate ways.

Once in the loading bay, Savage sprinted up the stairs to the second floor where he found unit twenty-two. Dylan Harper's. Like all the other units, it was secured with a large garage-style roller door, each one identical to the next, save for a metallic number bolted on the wall. Below, along the bottom of the roller door was a keyhole. Savage pulled on some nitrile gloves, got to work with his picks and had the lock open in seconds. He lifted up the door with a whoosh.

He was immediately confronted by a timber stud wall across the entire width of the opening, set back by about two feet. Constructed from a four-by-two wooden frame covered in chipboard, and hand sawn by the looks of the wonky cuts. On the left side, a makeshift door had been fitted into the stud wall, attached with rough, silver-coloured hinges, secured by a padlock. Dylan Harper wanted extra privacy even when the roller door was up.

Savage made short work of the padlock.

He pushed the wooden door gently inwards, only to be confronted by another wall immediately in front of him. Made of opaque thick white polythene, it hung from the top of the high ceiling of the unit, reaching all the way down to the floor where it curled inwards. It too had a door, accessed by a zip that ran all the way round the edge, like the opening of a tent. Savage unzipped it and stepped in. Then zipped it back up. The air inside made him gasp and gag. Chemicals. Strong ones. At a guess, he'd say disinfectant and something foul that made his eyes water. Inside was a unit of freestanding metal shelves, containing stacks of canisters and bottles. Large water bottles were piled on the floor, the kind that fit into water coolers, and next to them was an old bath propped up to waist height on bricks like a car that had had its wheels stolen. Savage recognised a couple of large white rectangular dehumidifiers on castor wheels. Hanging up on the end of the metal shelves were a rubber apron, goggles, Wellington boots and a painter's mask. He took the mask and the goggles and put them on. His eyes and breathing felt marginally better, allowing him to take in his surroundings in a little more comfort. The polythene completely enshrouded the space, like a large white bubble, forming the floor, walls and ceiling, like being inside a giant cloud. Savage had a closer look at what was stacked on the metal shelving. One shelf held a row of bottles containing a pretty pink liquid. The one below was filled with a mint-green liquid. There were also bottles of blue, dark brown and clear liquids. The labels had been torn off all of them, but to Savage they looked like something you'd drizzle into a bath to make bubbles. Next to these sat several bottles with spray nozzles screwed to the top. Savage pulled down his mask and chanced a sniff. The pungent aroma of disinfectant. There were also large tins of paint and white spirit, mixing buckets and a pot of brushes ranging in size from the kind you'd use to paint toy soldiers to ones for painting the side of a house. A toolbox sat on the floor next to the shelving. Savage flipped open the two catches and lifted the lid, expecting to see a mess of tools and cutting instruments. Instead, it was filled with cosmetics of every kind—blusher, lipstick and foundation, plus brushes and small pyramid-shaped sponges to apply it all.

Savage got a sickly feeling in his stomach.

He moved round the back of the shelves where the sickly feeling became worse.

Coils of medical tubing lay on one of the shelves along with little drawers full of scalpel blades and handles, plus an array of needles, some straight and some curved. On the shelf below were long lengths of steel cable, together with a drill and small fixing bolts. Next to this sat a small electronic machine that looked like a food mixer with a larger glass cylinder on the top and a dial at the bottom to measure pressure in PSI, and two knobs beside it for adjusting pressure. It had a single length of surgical tubing hanging out the side. He had a pretty good idea what it was.

Savage felt a bad taste forming in his mouth, and it wasn't just the chemicals seeping in through the edges of the mask.

He looked around. Something else wasn't right. Tannaz had said this was an eight-hundred-square-foot unit. There was no way the space he was standing in was eight hundred square feet. Half that, maybe. Savage walked over to the opposite side of space and found another tent-like zip entrance in the polythene wall. He unzipped it and stepped through.

He got the sense of a space on the other side but couldn't quite make it out as there were no lights, just a dense, inky darkness. He got out his phone and used it as a torch.

Savage Children

As far as he could make out, in front of him were three more walls, which had been arranged in a U-shape. They'd been decorated to make them look like a blue sky with puffy white and pink clouds. Then he shone the light upwards.

Savage dropped his phone in horror.

CHAPTER 33

Savage fumbled around in the dark on his hands and knees, eventually retrieving the phone he'd dropped.

He pinged Tannaz a text.

He turned and stepped through the polythene wall and zipped it back up. Unsteadily, he made his way across the unit, and stepped out through the opening on the other side, zipping it back up behind him.

He relocked the wooden door in the stud wall with the padlock and pulled down the roller door until it clicked and locked.

Savage sprinted down the stairs and out of the building, dumping his mask and goggles in the nearest bin. He joined Tannaz back in the VW beside the road.

Breathlessly, he sat in the driver's seat and pulled off the nitrile gloves.

"You okay?" Tannaz asked. "You look like you've seen a ghost."

"I've found the kids."

"Wh—Are they alive? Are they okay?"

"No."

Savage relayed to Tannaz exactly what he'd initially found in the storage unit, and then what he'd seen beyond the polythene wall.

It looked like an art installation. Three plasterboard walls had been erected in a square shape, missing the fourth wall, similar to a piece of stage scenery in a theatre. Every inch of plasterboard had been painted by an expert hand. An almost photo-realistic representation of a sky with small puffy clouds. It would have been idyllic, almost soothing, if it wasn't for what were suspended from the ceiling to look as if they were flying through that sky.

Each missing child that Dylan Harper had abducted had steel cables attached to them in vital part of their bodies—the ankles, hips, shoulder blades and top of the head, suspending them in mid-air, about ten feet off the ground, the overall effect making them appear as if they were flying or hovering like a humming bird, their legs out behind them.

The children had been draped in white silk, dramatically wrapped around their waists to preserve their modesty. White wings had also been added to their backs. With blissful, wide-eyed expressions on their faces, they looked like a three-dimensional cherubic painting by Raphael. Baby-faced angels in mid-flight, frozen in time.

Tannaz gasped then swore, not aggressively, but in a sad, melancholic way. "Those poor kids. Evil bastard. So he was abducting them so he could preserve them. Then turn them into angels. Into a work of art."

"Now we know what the drawings meant," said Savage. "He was telling us what he planned to do with them. Literally showing us their fate in coloured pencil."

Tannaz shook her head in disgust. "Angels are also heralds in mythology. Announcing something bad's about to happen. The angel drawings were heralds."

"Seems like it. Can you send Roberts an anonymous text?" asked Savage. "She needs to know about this. Just say that Harper has a storage unit, paid for out of a secret bank account. That should be enough to get her over here."

"Sure," said Tannaz. She got out her phone and began thumbing away.

"There's one other thing."

"What's that?" asked Tannaz.

"There was no sign of Callum in that unit."

"What?"

"Leo Bright, Olive Foley, Sally Woodrow and Rhianna Pullman

had all been turned into angels, but not Callum. He was the only one missing."

DI Roberts and DCI Sutcliffe stood outside the home of Dylan Harper, a rented flat in Stockwell. Dylan Harper's landlord was with them, a short, squat little man with a large bunch of keys and two phones. A full forensics team, decked head to foot in white coveralls and masks stood by.

Sutcliffe wasn't in a good mood. Made worse by the fact that Roberts had been first on the scene at the railway station and had later made the call to the missing boy's mother to tell her they'd found her son alive and well, just a bit groggy. As senior officer, that was supposed to be his thing. Get the glory. Sure, everyone knew it was a team effort. But the officer leading the case usually got the pat on the back. He couldn't walk through the station next to Roberts without people coming up and congratulating her. Made him sick to the core. It wasn't even her. It was that pain in his ass Savage who had caught Archangel before he committed suicide. Savage wasn't interested in taking any glory, neither was his little sidekick, Tannaz. Together they had somehow deduced how Dylan Harper was operating. Information that they should've shared with the police but hadn't. He'd deal with them later. But first he had lots of bitterness and loathing to wallow in. Because Roberts, the smug little cow, was getting all the glory for putting a stop to the Archangel. He'd deal with her in due course too, but first they had to find the missing kids. Something that would be a hell of a lot easier if this Dylan Harper were still alive. At least they had found out where he lived.

"You're not going to smash the place up are you?" asked the landlord, "Dylan is a good tenant, always pays on time, keeps it clean. Very hard to find people like that in this area."

Sutcliffe looked around. They were standing on a narrow metal walkway three storeys up, overlooking a filthy, graffiti-ridden concrete skateboard park laden with perpetual puddles. Sutcliffe hated those places at the best of times. How did anyone live where there was the constant whine of polyurethane wheels on filthy cement?

"We need to search the property and gather evidence, and that might mean some disturbance," Roberts said diplomatically.

"What's he done?" asked the landlord.

"We can't divulge that at this time."

"Must be something serious." The landlord nodded in the direction of the forensics team.

Sutcliffe sighed impatiently. "If you could just open the door, please."

The landlord rattled his big bunch of keys in a bid to find the right one. He flipped a few over then selected a couple, a key for the cylinder lock and one for the deadlock. Then he stepped forward and opened the door.

The forensics team went in first. Sutcliffe and Roberts waited outside. After five minutes, one of the forensics team re-emerged and whispered in Sutcliffe's ear, "Nothing."

"Nothing?"

The forensics guy shook his head.

"Okay, keep going. Get what you need. Tell us when it's safe for us to enter."

The guy nodded and went back in. Sutcliffe took Roberts aside out of earshot of the landlord and the uniformed officer who stood guarding the door to the flat. "There's no sign of the kids, which is what we expected. Just got to hope this Dylan Harper has left some clue as to what he's done with them."

"How likely is that?" asked Roberts.

Sutcliffe frowned at Roberts. "Well, he's not exactly going to leave us a Post-It Note and directions, is he? Keep up, Roberts. This is where the real police work begins, and I'm not sure whether you've got the stamina for it. Sure, you got the glory finding Archangel's butchered body on the train tracks, but I think it might have gone to your head, dulled your senses."

"Sir, I called and texted you as soon as I heard."

"Course you did."

"I did, Sir. You can check the logs on your phone."

"Listen, Roberts. You need to realise it's not all handing-lost-kids-back-to-their-mums hero stuff. There's the nasty stuff too. We might never find these kids. Then you'll have to have some very difficult and dark conversations with the parents."

"I do realise that, Sir. And I have done that sort of thing before, breaking bad news…"

"Not like this, Roberts. This is big-league stuff. Have you got the stomach for it?"

Just then, Roberts' mobile phone pinged. She ignored Sutcliffe's bitter little speech and read the text on her screen.

Sutcliffe's face twisted into an angry gurn. "I'm trying to give you some advice and you'd rather read a text. I really do worry about your abilities, Roberts. I really do. And I'll be making some recommendations and they won't be good—"

"Shut up," Roberts blurted out.

"What did you just say?"

"Sorry, Sir. I'm really sorry. I apologise for my outburst. But this text says Dylan Harper had a secret payment going out of his bank account."

"Who told you that?"

"Don't know, it's anonymous."

"Anonymous? Let me see." He tried to snatch the phone. Roberts pulled away.

She continued reading. "Says it was a direct debit for a storage unit in South Lambeth, place called StorUStor."

"Who sent you that text?"

Roberts gave him a puzzled look. "I just told you, it's anonymous." She showed him the screen.

He read and reread it. "We need to find where that text came from. Trace who sent it. They could be working with Archangel, an accomplice."

"Sir, don't you think we should get over there now?"

"We'd need a warrant, and warrants take time, Roberts. This is basic, day-one stuff. Keep up."

"Not if we believe the kids' lives are in danger," she replied. "He might have imprisoned them there."

"Come off it, Roberts. In a storage unit. Bit public for that sort of thing. No, we wait for a warrant. Do it by the book."

"But, Sir. The kids might be in there."

"Are you challenging my authority?"

"No, Sir."

"Good. Just remember that."

Roberts turned her back on Sutcliffe for a moment. He saw her hand grip the edge of the balcony. Her knuckles went white. Then she turned to the landlord and said, "Where's the nearest place I can get a coffee to take out?"

"Gino's. Street behind this one," said the landlord.

"Sir, would you like a coffee while we wait for forensics to finish?"

"Decaf latte," Sutcliffe said without looking at her, preferring to stare into his phone's screen. That was more like it. She should be fetching him coffee, not questioning his authority. He watched her walk away. His dislike of her subsiding slightly.

"Could you get me one, sweetheart?" said the landlord.

"Get it yourself," said Roberts.

Roberts got into her car, parked in one of the visitor spots on the opposite side of the flats, out of Sutcliffe's sight. She started it up and drove off in the direction of StorUStor in South Lambeth.

Sutcliffe was being a prick. He was losing it. Any other senior officer would've been on this new information like a ton of bricks. She knew Sutcliffe's reluctance was down to the fact that the information hadn't come from one of his sources, it'd come from her. That meant he didn't want to act on it, or at least wanted to put the brakes on, so she wouldn't make another breakthrough if that was the case. He'd put in for the warrant, so he could turn up and make the grand discovery, even if there was a chance that kids' lives were being put at risk. Who knew what she would find there? A prison. A torture chamber. Or nothing at all. Maybe just a load of old CCTV cameras and a workshop that Dylan Harper had used to figure out how to make himself disappear from camera footage. Roberts had a feeling it would be the latter, and her insubordination would get her knocked down several paygrades or even kicked off the force. But she knew she had to check it out. Waiting around for a warrant was a waste of time.

CHAPTER 34

After the anonymous tip-off and the macabre discoveries Roberts had made in unit twenty-two at StorUStor, the police had the unenviable task of informing the parents. Roberts and Sutcliffe had driven away from Frank's flat after giving him and Julie the bad news that they'd found four dead children. Except for Callum.

This had been their fifth stop on what was undoubtedly the hardest part of being a detective and working a case—telling a victim's family what had happened to their loved one. Roberts and Sutcliffe had sat on the parents' couches declining the offer of tea, to sit them down and explain the grisly end their child had come to at the hands of a deranged and dangerous psychopath. The fact that he had taken his own life, under the wheels of a train, was of no consolation whatsoever.

They'd watched the tears, the disbelief, the horror.

The killer had left four sets of parents to mourn their beloved children. Children who'd been transformed into a hideous art installation. Years of heartache and grief would follow for the parents. Piled up high it would never diminish, only get heavier and more overwhelming. But at least they had that mountain of grief to cling to. Frank and Julie had nothing. No closure. Just a Mobius strip of never-ending worry and wondering what had happen to little Callum. The only child not accounted for. Was he lying in a shallow grave? Had Dylan decided at the last minute that Callum wasn't right for his vile composition, that he didn't fit with his artistic vision? Or had he created some other monstrous art installation with Callum as the centre piece, yet to be discovered. They might never find the answer. The police had turned over Dylan Harper's flat, taken away his computers, and bagged and tagged every item in the storage unit. Followed every new lead and found nothing. No sign or indication of what he had done with Callum.

Tannaz had tried to help. She'd got lucky with tracking down the hidden payment to rent out the storage unit, sending the anonymous tip-off to Roberts. But now the trail had gone cold. Nothing digital or otherwise linked Dylan with Callum Leighton or any clue as to where the little boy was.

At least Lev had been freed. A small consolation that meant a lot. An innocent man hadn't been punished for the crimes of a complete and utter madman.

Savage and Tannaz heard the sobs coming through the wall that separated his flat from Frank's. Julie bawling her eyes out. Every time Frank tried to comfort her, her grief would turn to rage. "This was all your bloody fault," she shouted. If you'd hadn't let him go up that park, he'd still be with us."

"And what about Savage?" Frank shouted back. "If he hadn't chased Dylan Harper, the guy would still be alive. Police could've questioned him. Found out where Callum was."

"You bloody idiot," shouted Julie. "Dylan Harper has killed four children in a storage unit. Do you think he's keeping Callum alive, all nice and cosy? He's already dead because you let him go up that park."

"You don't know that."

Savage spoke quietly to Tannaz, "I think we better go out. Leave them to it."

"Good idea." She got out from behind her laptop and was about to fold it up and put it in her bag when they heard someone knocking at Frank's front door.

"Well, I'm not spending another minute here," Julie shouted. "That's my mum, she's taking me back home. Can't stand the sight of you any longer." Stomped footsteps followed. The door slammed. A car sped off.

Savage Children

No more sound came from Frank's flat.

Then, from next door, they heard the TV come on, turned up too loud. Explosions and gunfire. Frank was playing *Call of Duty*. Normally Savage would bang on the wall. Tell him to turn it down. Savage had had his fill of explosions and gunfire, even if they were make-believe. But not tonight, not after the trauma Frank had been through.

Savage listened hard. Over the noise of simulated warfare, he could hear crying. Frank had the game on to drown out the sound of his tears.

"Come on," said Savage, "let's move into the kitchen, quieter in there."

Tannaz carried her laptop through into the tiny kitchen and sat at Savage's equally tiny kitchen table. He put the kettle on. She peered into her screen.

"So, it's still not over then," said Savage.

"Nope. Can't rest until we find out what happened to Callum and where he is. Question is, where do we start?"

Savage placed a black coffee in front of her and sat down opposite with his tea. "That's a good question."

"I think we start back at the beginning. With the video of him going into the park."

"Tannaz, we've watched that video like a hundred times."

Tannaz chuckled.

"What's funny?"

"You said 'like'. You sound like a teenager."

Savage smiled. "Okay, you got me. But do you know what I mean?"

"There you go again, sounding like a teenager. So what if we've watched it a hundred or a thousand times. Doesn't matter. And this time, I've got some image-enhancing software Vikram lent me."

"How will that help?"

"Clean up the image. Give more detail. I'm going to go through every frame with a fine-toothed comb."

"Didn't Vikram already do that?"

"Not to the level I'm planning on. I'm going real deep. Wanna help?"

"Is there any point? What else is there to see? We'll just end up seeing cigarette butts and discarded condoms in all their detailed glory."

"Look," said Tannaz, "do you want to help or not?"

"Sure. Why not."

"Let me get you a spare laptop. I'll have to teach you how to use the software first."

"Okay. But surely this is a fool's errand. We know Dylan Harper took himself out of the picture. Deleted himself from CCTV. How's this going to help us find Callum?"

"That's the thing, I don't think he did delete himself. Sure, he did with the other four kids, but not with Callum. Remember, the data traffic? It spiked on all four cameras, except Callum's."

"Maybe he'd perfected his software by then so it didn't show up."

"Then why did it spike when he took the last kid, the one you found under the hedge? It set off the alert. If he'd perfected it there'd be no alert. Also, I've been looking at the data traffic from the warehouse camera. No matter what I do, it won't spike. I've tried everything, and believe me, if it was there, I'd find it."

"What does that mean?"

"If there's no evidence of a spike, he didn't hack the camera by the warehouse."

"That's puzzling. But I still don't know how this helps us."

"There's something different about the way Callum was taken. Remember how we thought Archangel had tried to set Vikram up. We wondered why he took Callum, another kid from a sports club, even though Vikram had been cleared. Archangel didn't need to. It's a risk he didn't have to take. Callum's abduction is odd. It's just a gut feeling I have."

"Okay," said Savage. "Gut feelings are usually right. Load me up with knowledge."

After an hour of Tannaz's tuition, Savage had the basics down and could clean up a frame, examine it in more detail. Once he'd mastered it, Tannaz put him to work.

"Okay, what am I looking for?" asked Savage.

"I don't know."

"That's not very helpful."

"You'll know it when you see it."

"That's even less helpful."

Savage took a deep breath and began the gargantuan task. Sifting through the CCTV footage one frame at a time, cleaning it up and examining each one for any anomalies. It was like emptying a swimming pool with an eye dropper.

The yawns Savage had been stifling were getting closer and closer together.

"Savage, go to bed," said Tannaz. "I'll carry on. I'm getting into this."

"You sure?"

"Positive."

Savage didn't need telling twice. He wanted to help and normally he would, but going over footage they'd seen a hundred times, that Vikram, a video expert had examined and couldn't find anything wrong with felt like a fruitless exercise.

He said his goodnight and retired to bed, put his head on the pillow, closed his eyes.

The image of Dylan Harper leaping off the bridge into the path of the train popped into his head.

"*Frank was right you know,*" said Jeff Perkins.

Savage groaned. He hadn't heard from Jeff for a while. But then, Jeff's kryptonite, Tannaz, had been pretty much at Savage's side since this horrible business began.

Savage resigned himself to the fact he would probably get no sleep tonight. He wasn't so worried about that. What troubled him was the fact that Tannaz was just in the other room, but it didn't seem to be having any effect on Jeff's ability to pop into his head and berate him. Usually Tannaz's presence kept him at bay. Maybe Jeff was right, maybe he was getting stronger.

"I know what you're going to say," Savage replied. "If I hadn't intervened, Dylan would still be alive, and so would our chances of finding Callum. But look at it this way, I also saved a life. Stopped him abducting another child."

"Sure, whatever you say. You know I'm right. I'm your conscience. Can't you feel the guilt prickling away at you."

"Thing is, Jeff. I had no idea that would happen. It was out of my control."

"You know it's funny. Ironic even," said Jeff. "You banging on to Carl Cooper's men about restraining Dylan Harper if they found him and not hurting him and that lives were at stake, yet you were the one who cocked it all up. Killed the guy."

"He took his own life."

"Yeah, because you were chasing him through the streets of London with an umbrella."

"Okay, what would you have done?"

"Not that. You should have called the police. Got backup. But you had to be the hero, didn't you?"

Savage ignored him. "One thing I don't understand is that Dylan Harper committed suicide."

"Yeah, and?"

"Where were you, Jeff? You said you love that sort of thing. Said suicide makes you stronger. Your voice is always a lot louder when terrible things are happening to people or to me, especially suicide. Yet, you were quiet. In fact, you've been quiet throughout most of this business with Callum."

"Ah, I'm glad you noticed. I was just coming to that..."

Jeff paused.

"Coming to what?" asked Savage. Jeff didn't reply. "I said, coming to what?"

Jeff had gone quiet.

Savage heard a gentle knock. The door slowly opened. Tannaz poked her head in. "Savage, who were you talking to?"

"Oh, er. Just thinking out loud."

"Okay. Listen, I think I might have something."

CHAPTER 35

Savage flopped into the chair at the kitchen table in his dressing gown. Rubbed his eyes with his fists. The clock on the cooker told him it was midnight. "I need tea first," he said.

"Tea can wait," said Tannaz. Savage felt hurt. Starting anything new was always easier with a mug of tea in his hands. "What do you know about trainers?"

"The shoes or the personal ones?"

"The shoes. Sneakers."

"Only that you put them on your feet."

"Okay, you need educating. Trainers are a big deal, fashion-wise. Lots of brand loyalty. Some people only wear Nike others will only wear Puma..."

"Yeah, I get it. Got to have the right pair to fit in."

"In gangs, even more so."

"Okay."

"So here's our gang going into the park after Callum went in." Tannaz swivelled the laptop round to show him a CCTV freeze-frame of the entrance to the park. A group of lads, hoods up. One of them pushing a BMX, another sitting on the handlebars, legs dangling down. They'd seen it dozens of times. "From the angle of the camera we can't see their feet, apart from the one sitting on the handlebars. He's wearing Adidas trainers, retro ones. Now I've cleaned up the image, checked them out, pretty sure they're Adidas Gazelles." She pulled up a Google image so Savage could examine it.

"Like Run DMC," Savage offered.

"Good effort," said Tannaz.

"I only remember it because of their song, 'My Adidas'."

"Right make, wrong shoes. Run DMC wore Adidas Superstars, a seventies basketball shoe. White leather, black stripes. This guy sitting on the handlebars is wearing Adidas Gazelles."

"How can you tell?"

"Details, Savage, details. Adidas Superstars have a rubber toe, Adidas Gazelles don't. Tiny details are very important when it comes to trainers, as you'll see. So Adidas Gazelles aren't cheap, set you back nearly a hundred quid."

"For a pair of trainers!" Savage exclaimed. "I could buy five pairs of Dunlop Green Flash down the market for that."

"And that's why you're not in a gang. But that's a good point, not everyone can afford that money, but they want to wear a cool brand. Shoe companies know this, so they always have a cheaper alternative."

Tannaz pulled up another image of some Adidas trainers, almost identical. "These are called Adidas Pace, almost the same but less cash. Now, to differentiate them from Gazelles, Adidas Pace has a super-thin pin line around the tops of the soles. With me so far?"

Savage nodded.

"Now you and I, well, mostly you, wouldn't be bothered about a tiny detail like that. Probably wouldn't give it a second thought. But that pin line is there so the trainer *connoisseur* can tell them apart, otherwise what would be the point forking out the extra money for Gazelles? It's a kudos thing, but it has to be ultra-subtle, because on the other hand, no one would buy Adidas Pace either. They'd be the poor alternative."

"Yep. Where's this all going?"

"Okay this is the image of the guy on the handlebars going in wearing Gazelles."

"And this is him coming out, still sitting on the handlebars." Tannaz opened another window, an almost identical image but reversed. The guy going in the other direction, leaving the park, still sitting on the handlebars, hood up, feet hanging down.

"It looks the same," said Savage.

"Wait a second." Tannaz adjusted some of the software filters and enlarged the image so the kid's trainers filled the screen. It was grainy and blurry and black and white but there in front of Savage was a clue.

"It's really faint at this size, even with the filters cleaning it up," said Tannaz. "But if you squint you can just about see the pin line around the sole. They're different trainers."

"Okay," said Savage. "So it's a different gang member sitting on the handlebars going out."

"I don't think so. Gangs all tend to wear the same trainer. It's part of their identity. The infamous MS-13 gang in America all wear Nike Cortez, and The Cripps in LA used to wear British Knights trainers—the logo "BK" stood as an acronym for "Blood Killer", The Bloods being their rivals. Gangs always adopt a certain type of trainer as their trademark. It's important to them just like tagging where they've been with a marker pen. I don't think this is a gang member. I think this might be Callum. Does he wear trainers like that?"

Savage looked at Tannaz. "He definitely wears a pair of Adidas, but I couldn't say if they were Gazelles, Pace or what."

"I know it sounds slim and tenuous but it sort of makes sense."

"How?"

"Remember the guy in the red Adidas T-shirt? Another mystery. He comes out after the gang, but we never see him go in, no matter how far we rewound the footage."

Savage nodded.

"Okay. I think he's a member of this mystery gang, and I think he's the one sitting on the handlebars when they go in the park. Look at it this way. Gang goes in. Once in there, they intimidate Callum. Don't know how, younger kids are always intimidated by older kids. Threaten him. Or give him a fentanyl lolly to soften him up. Say he's got to come with them. Callum agrees because he's scared or stoned or both. They tell him to sit on the handlebars of the bike. One of the gang members takes off his hoodie, gives it to Callum, says he's got to wear it, hood up to cover his face, because they know there's a CCTV camera by the entrance. The gang leaves same as they come in with Callum, except they leave a member behind. The one with the red Adidas top who's given his hoodie to Callum. I remember you said Red Adidas Top was small for his age. His hoodie would fit Callum without drowning him. He hangs around in there for a while, so it doesn't look like he's part of the gang when he leaves because he also knows the camera's watching him."

"Okay," said Savage. "Let's assume you're right. They did a switch in the park to smuggle him out. I don't understand what this has to do with Dylan Harper. Frank and Julie got an angel picture drawn by Callum through their letterbox. Why would a gang do that, and how would they know about it?"

"Don't know, maybe they were working with Dylan Harper."

"Doubtful."

"Or maybe he hired them to bring him kids. Paid them to get them from parks where he knew he couldn't hack the CCTV cameras. Who better to snatch kids than other kids? Scary gang-member kids. Archangel keeps himself out of the loop. They just bring them to him, like he's Fagin and they're Artful Dodgers."

Savage shook his head. "Again, doesn't make sense. He wouldn't need to. He's got hundreds of parks to choose from with out-of-date CCTV where he can be invisible, swoop in and out undetected, take a kid without anyone seeing him on camera. He wouldn't need to take that risk."

"Okay. I agree. It's not watertight. We don't know the whys and wherefores. But the explanation of how Callum left the park on the handlebars is the only one that makes sense."

"That's true. Okay, let's put your theory to the test."

"What are you going to do?"

"Wake up Frank."

Tannaz and Savage knocked quietly on Frank's door and waited.

They heard a noise from behind the door. "What do you want?" Frank demanded.

"It's me, Savage. And I'm with Tannaz."

"Haven't you done enough harm already?"

Tannaz stepped closer to the door. "Please, Frank. It's important. We may have some information about Callum." Not exactly the truth but they needed him to open the door.

Frank went silent.

They heard chains and bolts slide back and then a latch turn. The door opened a crack with Frank's unshaven face in it, reminding Savage of Jack Nicholson in *The Shining*. Though not so much scary as smelly. A stagnant waft came from within his flat.

"What do you know about Callum? Is he alive?" In the dim light, Savage could see Frank's eyes were raw and red-rimmed.

"We don't know," said Tannaz. "We've found a clue."

A small flicker of light came on in Frank's dull eyes. "You know where he is? Tell me, please."

"Frank," said Savage holding his hands up. "At the moment, it's just a tiny clue. But it might lead to something else."

"You better come in."

They sat in Frank's living room. Tidy for once, probably down to Julie staying there for the last few days, but there were signs it was quickly returning to its old ways. An empty pizza box here, a discarded cup there, and a scattering of biscuit crumbs over the table.

Savage filled Frank in about what they'd seen on the tape, and the possible switch-around.

"That's how we think he disappeared from the park," said Tannaz. "At the moment it's just a theory."

"A good theory," Savage added. "It'd be a whole lot stronger if we knew exactly what trainers Callum wore."

Frank sat back, rubbed his stubbled chin. "Well, I know they're Adidas. Grey ones. That's about it."

"Would you have the receipt?" asked Savage.

"Look around," Frank replied. "Do I look like the kind of guy who keeps receipts?"

"What about pictures of Callum wearing them?"

Frank looked ashamed, stared at the carpet. "I'm not big on taking pictures." He went quiet. Covered his face with both palms as if he were a child trying not to see something scary. He sat like that for a minute, in complete silence.

Tannaz and Savage looked at each other, at a loss to what he was doing. Then they heard a tiny whimper and it became apparent. His hands were covering his face to mask his sobbing.

"I've been an awful father," he said through his fingers, wet tears filtering between them. "Shouldn't have let him go up that park. None of this would've happened."

Savage sat next to him. Put an arm round him.

"I've been an awful person," Frank added. "Done really bad things."

"We've all done bad things," Savage said.

Frank mopped his eyes with his cuffs and said, "I was the one who contacted Carl Cooper. Tried to blame it on you. I'm a coward, see. Couldn't handle the blame. Much easier to put it on someone else. I'm so sorry. I'm really sorry."

"Okay, well, that was a bit of a dickhead thing to do," said Savage. "But then I've also been a dickhead. That stuff I said about you making Callum disappear for the money. I'm really sorry too. That was a terrible thing to say. But what's done is done. Exceptional circumstances and all that, so let's just forget about it. Concentrate on seeing if we can get Callum back."

Frank nodded. Sniffed back a couple more tears.

"One thing, though," said Savage. "Did you plant that football in my back garden?"

Frank stared at Savage. "No. No way. That wasn't me, I swear."

"Okay. Can I have a look in Callum's bedroom?"

"What for?" asked Frank.

"The box," Savage replied. "I remember when I was ten, if I bought anything cool like a Matchbox or Hot Wheels car, I couldn't bring myself to throw away the box. I'd keep it, put pennies in it or little knick-knacks. Maybe Callum kept the shoebox his trainers came in."

"That's a good point," said Tannaz.

Frank stood up. "This way."

Down the hallway on the right they came to Callum's bedroom door. It was covered in football stickers. Inside, it was spotless, bed made, everything put away, wall posters straight, carpet vacu-

Savage Children

umed—more of Julie's handiwork, no doubt. Savage went straight for the wardrobe and opened the doors. All Callum's clothes had been neatly hung up and in the bottom his shoes arranged in a line, but no shoeboxes.

Tannaz got down on all fours and looked under the bed. "Got it!" She slid out a blue box branded with an Adidas logo and overflowing with football cards.

Tannaz spun it round until she found a rectangular label with a barcode stuck on one end. She smiled and held it up to Savage.

He read it out loud, "Adidas Pace. Colour: Grey. Good work, Tannaz."

"Is that good?" asked Frank.

"It is," Savage replied. "Hope is back on the table. Not much. Just enough."

They left Frank in a slightly better mood than they had found him. Instead of returning to Savage's flat they headed straight up to the park where Callum had been taken.

"This puts that mystery gang squarely at the centre of Callum's disappearance," said Savage. "We'll check in with the Mojos, see if they have any information for us. Anything that will point us to who they are. Someone must know."

When they arrived at the park it wasn't the Mojos in residence. The Red Crew were back.

At first the whole gang rose from the one park bench to confront whoever had dared to enter their kingdom at this time of night. Primed and ready for a fight. But when their leader Snake Eyes saw it was Savage and Tannaz, his expression changed to one of welcome. His foot soldiers all joined in.

"Savage, Tannaz. You legends!" said Snake Eyes, holding out his hand for a complex handshake that went on and on, which Tannaz could handle but Savage couldn't quite keep up with. He was slightly taken aback at Snake Eyes' friendly warmth. "We heard you taught the Mojos a bit of a lesson in knife fighting. Took their blades off them. Story's all over the neighbourhood."

"Well, they weren't as welcoming as you guys."

"Don't be humble, bruv. You got some skills."

"A few. So what happened to the Mojos then?"

"After we heard what you did. We got all inspired, like. We kicked them out. Gave them a good slap, I can tell ya. Tails between their legs, man. So what brings you two here?"

"That kid Callum who disappeared. Remember that mysterious gang, we showed you the CCTV footage of? We're pretty positive they took him."

"Yeah, I remember, and we've all been asking around. I swear, we've asked everyone. No one knows them, or has seen 'em since. They're ghosts, man."

Savage frowned. "That's a pity, we were hoping you might have something for us."

"We'll keep looking and asking," said Snake Eyes. "You need anything, you just ask, okay?"

"Thanks, we will."

"So, have you sprayed over all of Mojos' tags then?" Tannaz asked.

"Damn right," said Snake Eyes proudly. "Not one left anywhere. It's all Red Crew tags now, far as the eye can see."

"Tell me," said Tannaz. "Tagging's important for a gang. Like marking your territory."

"Damn right."

Tannaz continued. "But a gang will also mark where they've been in another gang's territory. As an achievement. Like planting a flag on a mountain top. Sticking a middle finger up to the resident gang."

Snake Eyes smiled and shook his head. "I know what you're saying. You're thinking that gang of ghosts tagged our park. We've been all over every inch of this park, there ain't any mysterious gang tags hiding nowhere."

"You sure?"

"Course. It's all Red Crew tags."

Tannaz pointed to the dog-poo bin. "Even in there?"

"You for real? No one's going to tag inside a poo bin." Snake Eyes screwed up his face. "If you wanna take a look, be my guest."

"It's a dirty job but someone's got to do it," said Savage. He walked over to the poo bin, accompanied by Tannaz. Essentially it was a red plastic box perched on a metal post with a flip-up lid. The same one he'd plunged Carl Cooper's head into a few days earlier. Such sweet memories. Nothing like submerging a racist's head in canine waste to warm the heart. It still hadn't been emptied.

Tannaz held the lid open while Savage got a grip of the plastic sack lining the bin. He managed to gather the edges together and clutch them in his fists. A few loose poop bags fell out. It took a bit of wiggling but eventually he managed to dislodge the sack and extract it, dumping it on the ground beside him.

"Want some hand sanitizer?" said Snake Eyes.

"Have you got some?"

Snake Eyes fished around in his jacket pocket and pulled out a small bottle containing a bluish gel. "Can't be too careful in the city. Germs everywhere, bruv."

It was the last thing Savage expected a tough gang leader to be carrying. He was glad of it and slopped some on his hands. When the gel had dried, Savage got out his phone and used the flash as a torch to shine into the bin. There at the bottom, squiggled in Sharpie pen, was a gang tag.

The Red Crew gathered round, staring down into the plastic box, an unpleasant stench rising up to meet their collective nostrils, even though the contents had been removed.

Snake Eyes was furious.

"We're gonna find out who did this. No one tags our territory. Going all freehand with a Sharpie like they been watchin' *Art Attack*. Literally, disrespecting our shit."

Savage liked the fact that Snake Eyes, unlike his Mojo counterpart Shankster, knew how to use literally in its proper form.

"Anyone recognise that tag?" asked Tannaz. It was the letter B, written in a Gothic font. Quite elegant for a gang tag, which are usually designed for speed rather than aesthetics.

"One way to find out," said Snake Eyes. "Everyone get a shot on your phones. Send it to your contacts. I don't care if it's your nan. Wake her up. Wake everyone up. Someone must know who these fools are."

One by one, the members of the Red Crew leaned over the bin and snapped a shot of the unknown tag, then sent it out to everyone they knew. Then they waited.

Tannaz pulled out a packet of cigarettes, took one for herself and offered them around. No takers from any of the Red Crew. A gang that used hand sanitizer and didn't smoke—young people these days, what were they coming to?

A phone pinged. Everyone looked round. The gang member who owned it looked up and slowly shook his head.

More phones pinged and alerts went off at random intervals. More messages. More negative shakes of heads.

"If this doesn't work," said Savage. "We hit the streets tomorrow. Show this tag to every kid in London until we find this gang."

A small lad leapt up off the bench, holding his phone up triumphantly like the Olympic torch. "I got it! They're the Blashford Boys from the Blashford Estate in Woolwich."

"You sure?" asked Snake Eyes.

"Positive. My cousin goes to Woolwich College. Says that tag is everywhere in Woolwich."

"I think we need to pay these Blashford Boys a visit," said Savage. "One other thing. Where would we find the Mojos at this time of night?"

CHAPTER 36

Follow the River Thames downstream and eventually you come to Woolwich, one of London's eastern-most towns. Famous for its ferry and a foot tunnel that dips beneath the Thames like the approach to an underground lair of a super villain. The town had recently undergone a much-needed makeover. With millions to play with, the local council had torn down ugly tower blocks and flattened undesirable housing estates, replacing them with modern, bright and airy apartment buildings, all except one. The Blashford Estate hung on defiantly, like a boil that refused to pop, a big brutal reinforced concrete carbuncle. Or was it that the local council simply didn't have enough money to demolish every single eyesore. Probably the latter, as Woolwich still had pockets of dingy, industrial areas, left disused and decaying.

With a U-shaped footprint, the Blashford Estate was a giant cul-de-sac comprising of five storeys accessed by dreary concrete walkways along its length on every level, overlooking a large courtyard below. "Courtyard" was too generous and glamorous a word; "litter-strewn concrete death trap" would have been more apt. From their position in the van Tannaz could see a gang hanging out, around fifteen lads. Sitting on concrete benches, under the streetlights, drinking, being noisy and obnoxious. Throwing bottles and resigning the neighbours to being locked up tight behind their doors after sundown, many of which were secured with metal cages.

Tannaz snapped off several shots of them with her phone. She had a better camera than the one on Savage's, with plenty of zoom. One guy stood up on the bench, mucking around, pretending to dance. Holding her finger down on the button, she captured rapid fire shots of his feet, then scrolled back through her shots, selecting the clearest one. With her fingertips she enlarged the image focusing on his footwear. It wasn't the best shot in the world. But it did its job. Adidas trainers, suede ones. Gazelles.

The guy dancing on the bench got knocked off and someone else took his place. Tannaz repeated the exercise and got the same result. Gazelles again.

From across the other side of the road came two more gang members. One riding a BMX, the other sitting on the handlebars. Tannaz got more shots as they passed. The two guys with the BMX joined the others. Savage and Tannaz examined the image of them. Both wore Gazelles. She snapped off a few more shots just to be sure. There was no doubt. Gazelles all the way.

"If the shoe fits," said Savage. "The Blashford Boys is our mystery gang."

"Shall we go talk to these goons?" Tannaz asked.

"Give it a few more minutes, just to be on the safe side."

They waited.

Savage's phone pinged. He glanced at it. "Okay, we're good to go."

They left the VW Caddy and approached the courtyard. As soon as Savage and Tannaz got closer, The Blashford Boys went on high alert. Those who were sitting stood, hands reaching behind them, probably for knives. Getting into their fighting stances. They relaxed a little when they saw it was a young girl and an older man.

"Nice night for a walk," said one of the guys. He wore a red Adidas top. Savage recognised him from the video and from when he and Celia had bumped into him as he was leaving the park.

"*Terminator*," said Savage.

The gang looked confused.

"It's a line from *Terminator*, the original movie..."

Savage was just about to launch into one of his movie explanations when Tannaz elbowed him to get on with it. They had more important things to discuss than the merits of classic movie lines. Savage got the rather large hint.

Savage Children

"Relax, guys," he said. "We just want to ask you some questions."

Red Adidas Top approached him, followed by the rest of The Blashford Boys. He swore. "Who do you think you are? Coming in here, telling us to relax. Best be moving on. Or we'll take whatever you've got, phones, cash. Then maybe we won't stab you." He was a little guy with a big mouth on him.

Savage ignored the threat. "There's this kid who went missing in a park near me. I think you guys might have had something to do with it. No, actually, I'll rephrase that, I'm *sure* you had something to do with it. So I'm going to ask you nicely, where is he?"

Red Adidas Top started laughing. "Oh my. You're some kind of special-needs guy, ain't ya? Coming in here, making demands and shit. Accusing our asses. Now, most folks run a mile when they see us. Cross over the road and that. Turn and walk the other way. But you must definitely be a special-needs case. Is she like your carer or something?" He pointed to Tannaz.

"Nah, he can look after himself," said Tannaz. "But I bet you still need your mum to look after you. Tuck you up in bed."

"Hey, old man. Keep that bitch in line or you'll be carrying your guts out of here."

"She can say what she likes, especially when she's talking to a dimwit like you. Now answer us. What have you done with Callum?"

"After we're done shanking you, we're gonna rape her. All of us. And I'm going first."

Tannaz stepped forward. "Why don't you shut that sphincter mouth of yours and give it a try."

Red Adidas Top looked around at his mates in disbelief. A girl and an old man coming on their turf, challenging their authority. Some laughed. Others shouted out despicable things that they wanted Red Adidas Top to do to Tannaz. Jeering him on.

"What are you looking at them for?" said Tannaz. "Need their permission?"

He looked back, his face darkened. He pulled a knife out from the back of his waist band. Rushed at her. Tried to stick it into Tannaz's midriff. She saw the move coming, darted left, kicked him hard in the ankle of his leading leg. A whopping great roundhouse kick, super low. Not to inflict damage, more to change the angle of his body. Shifted him by about thirty degrees, deflecting the knife away from her. This left his right flank—his ribs—exposed. Tannaz grabbed his knife arm, held it tight with her left hand, then with her right she hit him with an unmerciful hooking punch to the bottom of his ribs. Specifically, his floating ribs. Last one on the rib cage, so called because it doesn't attach to the sternum. Prone to fracture. Once, then twice she hit him. Third was the charm, cracking his bone. He kinked over to contain the pain. He dropped the knife. She kicked it away. It was then that Tannaz noticed she'd sustained an injury. Before she'd kicked his ankle, her opponent had taken a nick out of her arm.

"You okay?" asked Savage.

"Yeah, tis but a scratch."

Before Savage could point out a Monty Python movie reference, Red Adidas Top said, "So the little bitch can fight." He held onto his side with both hands, wincing. Remaining defiant. The rest of the gang closed in around Tannaz and Savage. "My boys here are going mess you up now. You're crazy. Coming in here. Outnumbered. Alone."

"What makes you think we're alone?" said Savage.

From behind them, down the street where Savage had parked his Caddy, two large separate groups appeared from around the corner of the Blashford Estate. Walking rapidly towards them, they converged, as one, easily numbering over forty. The combined forces of the Red Crew and the Mojos. Marching into the courtyard, they fanned out across its entire width, sealing it off, and any chance the Blashford Boys had of escaping.

"I'd like you to meet our friends," said Savage. "On the left of me we have the Red Crew, and on the right, the Mojos. Now, they're here to discuss some territorial issues with you. Seems like you've been straying onto their turf, and they're really not very happy about it."

"Normally," said Snake Eyes. "Red Crew and the Mojos hate each other. We're rivals round our way."

"But what we hate more," said Shankster, "is some jumped-up little gang from Woolwich, coming into our territory, acting like it's theirs."

Red Adidas Top straightened up, tried to look more dignified. "Nah, you've got it wrong. Made a mistake."

"No mistake," said Savage. "We've got you on CCTV."

"That's someone else."

"No, it's not," said Tannaz. "And you stupid idiots had to go and leave a tag didn't you? Couldn't help yourself. Had to tag where you'd been, it's like a compulsion."

"So we've got your tag, we've got you on CCTV and you all wear Adidas Gazelles," said Savage. "But before our friends here discuss you trespassing on their territory, there's a small matter of a child you abducted."

"That wasn't us," said Red Adidas Top desperately, all the menace gone from his face. "I swear."

"Let me beat the truth out of him," said Snake Eyes.

"Yeah, I'll help you," said Shankster.

"No, wait," Adidas Top pleaded. "Someone hired us."

"What?" asked Savage.

"Paid us, he did. Guy knew everything about us." The rest of his gang nodded their heads rapidly. "He knew all our names. Families. Addresses. All the bad stuff we'd done. Everything. Said he had a job for us."

"Go on," said Savage.

"He said he'd pay us five hundred upfront. And five hundred once we'd taken the kid. Gave us specific instructions how we were to do it."

"How did he tell you?" asked Tannaz.

"Through Strangerly."

"What's Strangerly?" asked Savage.

"An anonymous app," Tannaz replied. "Lets you talk to strangers. No profiles or usernames. Perfect for sending instructions for kidnapping a child. Give me your phone," she said to Red Adidas Top.

"It won't do you any good," said Red Adidas. "Messages have all been deleted. No names on them any ways."

"Give her the goddam phone," said Snake Eyes.

Red Adidas Top handed it over with shaking hands. Tannaz immediately went to work, thumbing away on the phone's screen, hacking into the app.

"And who was this guy?" asked Savage.

"Never said his name."

"What did he look like?"

"Never met him. We got the money through dead drops."

"How did you get Callum to go with you?"

"Not difficult. Look at us, we're a gang. Little kids are scared of us. Plus when we got the first drop of money, he left some lollies with drugs in them. Gave the kid one. Made him easy-going, you know."

"Then what happened?"

"We were told to take him to this abandoned warehouse. Inside was an old, beat-up caravan. Told us to handcuff him to the wall and leave him there. Put the key under some rubble outside."

"So you abducted a young, ten-year-old boy, drugged him up and locked him in a caravan?"

"Yeah," said Red Adidas Top. "Well, for a grand."

Snake Eyes swore. "Can we mess these fools up now?"

Savage held him back. "One last thing before I let these guys beat the crap out of you. Where's the warehouse with this caravan in it?"

CHAPTER 37

THE WAREHOUSE WASN'T VERY FAR from the Blashford Estate. Savage drove while Tannaz continued to hack Red Adidas Top's phone. Towards the most eastern edge of the town, the address they'd been given took them to the abandoned docks that once teemed with ships and boats offloading goods by the ton from every corner of the world. Now only relics of a bygone era still stood, their windows smashed and their roofs leaking, the council's redevelopment budget not stretching this far.

"How are you doing with the app?" asked Savage.

"Yeah, got the deleted messages back," Tannaz replied. "He was telling the truth. All the instructions are here. Giving him the fentanyl to soften him up. Right down to my theory about them switching hoodies with Callum and getting him to swap places with the guy sitting on the handlebars. I'm just trying to get into the account details."

"Won't it be anonymous?"

"Possibly. I've never looked into this app before but I'm hoping you'd at least need a mobile number to set it up on your phone. Surely it's got to be Dylan Harper. Just taking a different approach."

"Yeah, I agree. I still don't understand why he'd risk hiring a gang to abduct a kid when he can do it perfectly well without getting anyone else involved. Seems unnecessary."

"Who knows? Guy obviously wasn't in his right mind. Or maybe he needed a fallback, just in case people got wise to his masking software. I mean we did, right?"

"That's true," Savage remarked.

"Perhaps this was a test run. A first attempt to see if it worked.

If it did, he's then got his backup strategy in place, ready for when people catch up with his stealth software."

"Maybe. Let's just hope we find Callum alive."

Savage drove slowly, until they came to the warehouse Red Adidas Top had described. A two-storey brick building with a flat roof. What few metal windows it had were smashed and broken. Gutters full of moss sagged from its eaves like bunting that someone had forgotten to take down. Savage noticed a large metal sliding door on its front side, easily big enough to accommodate a caravan. Next to it was a small access door.

Savage pulled up. Turned off the engine then reached over to the glove box and pulled out his leather wallet filled with tools for picking locks and his hefty Maglite. They both slipped on nitrile gloves, got out of the car and hurried over to the access door where Savage began picking the three locks that held it shut.

The last lock popped open, and they both entered the warehouse. It was almost dark inside apart from some light pollution leaking in through the broken windows and the many holes in the roof. The place felt damp, the moisture hanging in the air like mist. Savage flicked on the Maglite and swung it in a wide arc around the space. Empty.

They would have searched but there was nowhere to search. The old abandoned warehouse was one big space. A single, double-height building, apart from a stud-walled partitioned office that had long since splintered and given way to the pull of gravity. Nothing left but dust and the stench of rats.

Savage shone the torch on the dirty floor, searching every inch of its surface. When he got to the middle, he saw what he was looking for. A couple of small rusty parallel gouges about two hand widths apart. Keeping the torch aimed on the floor, he swung it over to the left and found two more.

"What are they?" asked Tannaz.

"A caravan was here. Red Adidas Top said it was an old beat-up caravan. If Archangel was using it to hold Callum, I doubt he'd be bothered to keep the tyres pumped up, which meant it would have been resting on its rims. The weight of the caravan pressing down has gouged marks into the concrete floor. Been taken away, along with Callum, I presume. Question is, where?"

Savage shone the torch down on the floor again, near the gouges. Thick lines could clearly be seen where the dust, dirt and grit had been disturbed. "Not exactly tyre marks," said Savage. "But you can see a truck's been in here and taken the caravan away."

"Damn it," said Tannaz. "Every time I think we're getting anywhere, we're either too late or we hit a brick wall. Do you think Callum is still alive?"

"Doubtful. But we can't give up hope."

They scoured every inch of the filthy floor, both of them bent over. Savage with his Maglite, Tannaz with the light from her phone, searching for anything that would help them. Something discarded or left behind. Anything that would help point them in the right direction to the caravan's whereabouts.

"There are only two possibilities," said Savage. "The caravan with Callum in it has been relocated to another secure location and Dylan Harper did this just before he died. Or Callum has been taken somewhere else, and the caravan has been taken away, the evidence moved, possibly to destroy it, by someone else."

Tannaz straightened up, stretching her back. "Then we need to get out of here. Get back to yours so I can begin searching traffic cameras and CCTV round here. Surely a caravan being moved is going to need a big truck. It'd be easy to spot in traffic. I'm sure I could follow where it's gone. Camera by camera."

Savage straightened up too, a few joints in his back popping. "Yeah, good point. It hasn't been dragged out of here and we know it's got no tyres, so it must've been lifted. Hoisted on the back of a flatbed, probably."

Tannaz flicked off the light on her phone. "We better get back. Make a start on hacking cameras. Maybe wake up Vikram. Get him to help us."

"Okay, but first we clean that knife wound."

They left the warehouse, Savage re-locking it, jumped into his van, stripped off their gloves and headed back to Savage's flat. All the way there, Tannaz kept hacking into Red Adidas Top's phone, hoping to get any more clues out of it. Even if it was just to confirm their suspicions that Dylan Harper had set this all up.

The sun had well and truly risen when Savage pulled into his road. They'd been up all night and now his bones longed to get into bed and sleep it off. That wouldn't happen. Not yet, and not for a long while. They still had work to do.

Halfway up the street, a car sped past them, overtaking on a road that was far too narrow for overtaking. Savage was about to call the driver a maniac when he recognised it as Julie's car. Up ahead it screeched to a halt, smearing two black tyre marks along the tarmac. She beeped the horn several times. It was not like Julie at all to be making a noise at this early hour of the morning. That was more Frank's style.

Savage pulled up behind her. He and Tannaz got out onto the pavement outside Savage's flat to be confronted by Frank, bursting out of his door, fully dressed for once, a big beaming smile splitting his face in two.

"Savage!" he shouted. "They've found him. They found Callum."

CHAPTER 38

"Wh-what?" said Tannaz and Savage simultaneously.

Still sitting in her car, Julie wound down her window. "They've found him. He's alive." Happy tears tracked across her cheeks. "We're off to the hospital now."

"Is he okay?" asked Savage.

Julie's words were ecstatic and fast. "Yes. Still don't know the full story. Found him yesterday evening. Wandering around outside King's College hospital. In a daze. He'd been drugged but he's healthy, unharmed. Untouched. Hospital didn't know who he was or anything. Couldn't identify him until just now when he managed to remember his name. He's a little upset. Disorientated. Asking for me and Frank. We're heading there now."

"Oh, that's amazing news," said Savage. "He's been found."

"That's the best news ever," Tannaz added.

"Thank you. And thank you for all your help," said Frank, hopping into the car. Julie executed a rushed three-point turn, bashing the tyres against the kerb each time, and then they were off, speeding back down the road.

Tannaz looked at Savage. "Well, I wasn't expecting that."

"Me neither. He's safe, that's the main thing." Savage's eyes were far away, fatigued and unfocused.

"You okay, Savage? This is a good thing, right? Callum's been found. You don't look very happy."

Savage's body had crumpled slightly now the pressure to find Callum was off. "It's amazing he's been found. I just feel shock and a bit of disbelief. I'm not sure I buy it."

"Buy what? You think it's not Callum?"

"No, I'm sure it is, but come on. A kid who's been missing suddenly turns up wandering around outside a hospital of all places. I mean, don't get me wrong, I'm so relieved he's been found safe. So happy for Julie and Frank, they've got their little boy back. But the circumstances. I smell a rat."

"Maybe Dylan Harper had him locked up somewhere and he managed to escape."

"They said he'd been found drugged and disorientated. Probably up to his eyeballs with fentanyl. You know what I think? Whoever's been holding him captive in that caravan has got scared and released him. Got rid of the caravan somehow. Maybe just before we got to the warehouse. And we know it can't be Dylan Harper because he's dead, so it must be someone else."

"You saying Dylan Harper had an accomplice?"

"How else could Callum have been released? Dylan wasn't working alone. I can't see any other explanation. Come on. Let's get you inside. Clean and dress that knife wound."

After Savage had disinfected and wrapped Tannaz's arm in a fresh white bandage, she got straight back on the phone she'd taken from Red Adidas Top, still hacking into the Strangerly account.

"Shouldn't we get onto hacking traffic cameras?" asked Savage. "See if we can spot that caravan being moved. Track its whereabouts?"

"I just want to see if I can get a number off this account. It may belong to the accomplice we're looking for."

Savage slurped tea and watched Tannaz work. His weary mind trying to slot in this new piece of the puzzle. The possibility that Dylan Harper hadn't been working alone, if that was the case. New avenues to be explored flashed through his head. Dylan Harper may be dead, but his partner was not. And if the guy was still out there, he needed to be caught. Savage still couldn't figure out how it all fitted together. The gang and its technique for snatching kids seemed at odds with the way Dylan Harper operated. It was haphazard and clumsy compared to Dylan Harper's highly sophisticated CCTV hacking approach. The guy took no chances. Operating alone would've suited his profile. Having a partner did not. Savage could be wrong, of course. It just didn't feel right and his gut was telling him so.

"There may be another explanation," said Savage.

"What's that?" asked Tannaz, not looking up from the phone.

"Could be a copycat. Someone found out about Archangel, the drawings, the fentanyl. Decided to have a go themselves."

Tannaz stopped what she was doing. This new revelation was distracting her from her work. She thought for a moment, digesting Savage's new theory. "You know, that would make sense. If it was a copycat, they'd definitely lack the technical knowhow to do Dylan Harper's CCTV hack, or maybe they didn't even know about it."

"That would explain why there was no spike in data traffic," said Savage. "And no hack on the camera by the warehouse. It wasn't Dylan Harper. It was someone who has nothing to do with him. Someone Dylan Harper didn't even know."

"Yeah," Tannaz agreed. "But whoever it is, he's smart enough to know he needs to avoid the camera. So he hires a street gang to snatch the kid for him. Gives them specific instructions so it looks like Callum has disappeared like the other abductions."

Savage clicked his fingers. "That's just made me remember something. Didn't think anything of it at the time. Just before Dylan Harper jumped off the bridge, I pleaded with him to tell me where the missing kids were. Asked him what he'd done with Callum specifically, used his name. He stared back at me blankly. Almost puzzled. I thought he was doing his cold-hearted psychopath thing. You know, all unemotional. Now I think about it, it could've been because he had no idea who I was talking about. I think we could be onto something here."

Tannaz's brow knotted in confusion. "But if it's a copycat, how would they know about the Archangel, the drawings, the intimate details of this case? It's not public knowledge. The press has been fobbed off."

"Maybe not public knowledge, but there are plenty of people who would know about it. All the coppers working the case for instance."

"You think it could be a copper?" said Tannaz.

"That would be my first assumption."

"I thought coppers weren't supposed to talk about ongoing investigations."

"In an ideal world," said Savage. "I'm sure some do, though. And whether it's a copper or not, or someone linked with the case, we still have a child abductor at large."

"But not a murderer."

"No, Callum's alive, so he hasn't killed yet. Unless he was just biding his time."

Tannaz looked unsure. "Again, seems a strange thing to do. Hold a child captive, then let him go unharmed."

"Unless his motivation was to put the fear of God into Frank and Julie. I mean, he's succeeded doing that."

"It's also risky. Leaving a child alive as a witness."

"A very drugged-up child. That's the thing. If Callum's been continually fed fentanyl, I doubt he'll remember anything. And let's hope it stays that way. You wouldn't want a ten-year-old remembering that part of his life."

"Damn straight," said Tannaz. "So what do we do now?"

"Well, we've got another bad guy to catch. Have to start again. Find whoever took Callum. But first I need another cup of tea. You want coffee?"

"Always."

Savage took himself off to the kitchen, his brain wired but his body running out of charge. He wished he still had Tannaz's youthful stamina.

He filled the kettle with shaky hands and a grumbling stomach. Plugging it in, he then pulled a slice of wholemeal bread from the cupboard and slathered it with Marmite. Took a bite and felt marginally better.

The kettle huffed and was about to reach its ideal temperature when Tannaz shouted his name from the living room. She shouted it again. This time it was verging on a scream. Not a fearful one, more an excitable one.

Savage sprinted down the corridor, back into the lounge.

Savage Children

"What?" he demanded.
She held up Red Adidas Top's phone.
"I know who set up this Strangerly account."
"Who?"
"Sutcliffe."

CHAPTER 39

Savage glared at the screen. A bunch of code stared back at him. Meaningless.

"What am I looking at?" he asked.

Tannaz pointed to a line about halfway down the screen. In amongst the code was a long string of numbers.

"Is that a mobile number?"

"Yep, it's Sutcliffe's. I recognise it from Roberts' texts. You need a mobile number to set up the Strangerly account. Course, it never appears in any messages, I had to do some deep digging but it's definitely his. Savage, he's the one who took Callum."

"Hold on a second. Let's not jump to any conclusions."

"Savage, it all makes sense. We were just talking about how it could be a copper. I mean, who else would know about this case? He's made it look like Archangel to cover his tracks. Then when Dylan Harper died, he's let Callum go."

Savage shook his head. "Sutcliffe is a nasty, bitter old burnout, and much as I'd like him to be the bad guy in all this, one thing I know, he isn't stupid. He wouldn't use his own number to set up a Strangerly account to communicate with a gang of kids he's using to abduct a child. Is it possible someone's set up an account with his mobile number, hacked his messages without him knowing?"

"Anything's possible."

"But would you need to be an IT guru to do that?"

"No, not really," said Tannaz. "There's a guy on YouTube who shows you how to hack a Strangerly account in a minute. More likely, this person's set up the account with Sutcliffe's number then used an intercept so he never receives any notifications. He'd be oblivious. So yeah, anyone could do it. Don't need to be a techie."

"Maybe Dylan Harper did it. Set him up before he died, to drop Sutcliffe in it. A bit of inverted poetic justice. A final attack on the guy who was trying to catch him?"

Tannaz thought for a second. "A posthumous act of revenge. Sounds like something an artist would do. Yeah, definitely possible. But if that's the case, who released Callum?"

"Unless Sutcliffe really was working with Dylan Harper. I mean, what better way to avoid detection than having a copper on his side, protecting him. And if he was holding Callum when Dylan died, he had no choice but to release him."

"Doesn't make sense," said Tannaz. "If Sutcliffe was in cahoots with a child killer I doubt he'd let Callum go, leave a witness alive. He'd want to silence him for good, surely."

"Okay. Either way, this isn't over. Whether it's Sutcliffe or someone trying to make it look like Sutcliffe, we need to bring Roberts in on this. If there's the remotest possibility that Sutcliffe had something to do with Callum's disappearance, she needs to know."

"Do we trust her? How do we know she's not the one who took Callum and is setting Sutcliffe up, making it look like he did it?"

"We don't."

The two of them went silent. Thoughtful.

"We need to be really careful here," said Savage. "Can't trust anyone."

Tannaz's big brown eyes brightened. "I think I might know a way to be sure."

"How's that?"

"A very special kind of hack called a tower dump. I harvest data from the nearest cell-phone tower to the abandoned warehouse where the caravan was. Whoever held Callum there would've had to go back and forth to check on him, keep him drugged up, watered and fed etcetera. Every time a phone connects to a tower its number gets recorded. A tower dump will tell us every phone number that's been in that vicinity. Once I get the data, I can run a check through the numbers, see if Sutcliffe's or Roberts' phone is amongst them. Their number would show up regularly."

"That's a great idea," said Savage. "But what if Sutcliffe or Roberts left their mobile phone at home or at the station so it didn't tie them to the warehouse? They're coppers, remember. They use cell-tower positioning all the time to finger criminals."

"True, but unlikely. A senior police officer being away from their phone for that amount of time—that would take some explaining."

"That's a good point."

"Do detectives carry radios?"

Savage shook his head. "No, but they have them in their cars. But a detective would still be expected to be contactable by phone, to receive and respond to text messages, they can't rely on the radio in their car. If one of them had left their mobile phone behind and made the drive over to Woolwich, that's a round trip of at least an hour. Plus, say, another half an hour to get in the warehouse, check on Callum, then lock it back up again. They'd be out of phone contact for over an hour and a half."

"Yep, that's too long. A lot can happen in an hour and a half."

"You're right. They would have some serious explaining to do. No, whoever did this would've had to take their phone with them. How long will a tower dump take?"

"All day to hack and harvest the numbers."

"And what's the accuracy like? How small an area can you get it down to?"

"In a city, accuracy is good. I can get down the radius to fifty or a hundred metres of the abandoned warehouse."

"So how many numbers will it generate?"

"Can't say for certain. I mean, how many people would come within a hundred metres of that ugly old warehouse? Not many. It's not exactly Oxford Street."

"What can I do?"

"Keep me fuelled up with caffeine and biscuits."

"Right you are," Savage got to his feet, groaning, knees popping.

"I tell you what," said Tannaz. "Leave the drinks. You get some sleep."

"You sure? It's no trouble."

"You look like you need sleep more than I need coffee. Go on, get your ass into bed."

"You say the sweetest things." Savage wasn't going to argue. He took himself off to bed and was asleep within seconds of closing his eyes.

Savage could hear someone calling his name, gently tugging him from his slumber. He thought it was Tannaz, come to tell him she'd finished the tower dump, until he heard the words, "*Savage, you utter moron.*"

His eyes flicked open. There, sitting on the end of the bed was Jeff Perkins, as real as the age spots on the backs of Savage's hands.

Savage pulled the duvet up to his chin like a scared child. He'd never seen Jeff Perkins before. Sure, he'd heard him and his berating monologues, he'd almost got used to them. However, this was Jeff in the flesh. A stern-looking fellow with long Basil Fawlty legs and a shiny bald tonsure to match, a black wrap of hair below. He also had a moustache that kept twitching. His eyes were completely black, no whites in them at all, like two lumps of coal on a snowman's face. Dressed in a pressed white shirt and a red tie, tight as a noose, Jeff looked as if he worked in a high-street bank, the kind that relished making you fill out a ton of forms, then would tell you off for getting them wrong.

"*Well, what do you think? I'm quite dapper, aren't I?*"

Savage swore. "What are you doing here? How come I can see you?"

"*Well, I always get to you when you're at your lowest, which is now. You're tired. Haven't slept. Haven't solved the case either. Callum's been found and it was nothing to do with you. You could've stayed in bed and the outcome would've been the same.*"

"I found Archangel, that had something to do with it."

"*Correction. You killed Dylan Harper. That's your solution to everything.*"

"That's not true."

"*I have hundreds of dead souls, your victims, screaming in my head who'd beg to differ. Wanna hear them?*"

Jeff opened his mouth unnaturally wide, like a snake unhinging its jaws. Out of it came a wind, a tornado of screams that had weight and power. Savage felt like the old lady in the Aphex Twin video, pure pain and torment flooding out of Jeff's mouth, shoving Savage back against the headboard.

Savage clamped his hands over his ears and scrunched his eyes up tight. The torrent of howling, unending.

"Make it stop!" Savage shouted. "Make it stop!"

The roaring continued. Went on and on. Savage thought he might explode, he was unable to contain the misery flooding through him.

And then silence. Savage slumped forward, the ordeal draining him of not just his energy, but carving out and removing a large chunk of his spirit. He felt emptied.

Slowly, he opened his eyes. Jeff sat there in front of him, legs crossed. He spoke calmly, as if what had just happened was a mere triviality. "*I told you I was getting stronger, so I thought it was time to make a live appearance. In the flesh, baby.*" Jeff gave a shark-like grin. "*That's what I was trying to tell you the other day, and why you hadn't heard from me in a while. I was conserving my energy. Reserving it for this appearance. And when Dylan Harper committed suicide, well, that filled the tank right up. Gave me what I needed. Just had to bide my time, until it was right, comfortable.*"

Savage felt his stomach come free and drop like it had fallen down a mine shaft.

"*You can't keep a good man down, especially if he's made from your miserable psychological issues all rolled into one.*"

Jeff got to his feet, standing to his full height, easily seven foot and skinny as a chopstick. He sauntered over to Savage's wardrobe and began admiring himself in the mirror. "*I look rather good. A little on the svelte side, but I'll fill out as I get stronger and you become smaller.*" He turned and fixed Savage with those two, small full-stop eyes, coming closing to peer at him. It was then Savage realised they weren't black eyes; Jeff didn't have any eyes at all. They were holes in his face, black and bottomless. *"Oh, you do remember my prediction for the future, don't you? I hate to be the one to toss the electric fire into the bath, but my temporary residence in your messed-up bonce will soon be permanent, and then I'll take over proceedings proper. You'll be where I am, and I'll be where you are. In charge of that ugly little body and brain of yours. Not the nicest prospect but it's a small price to pay."*

Savage sat up. "No, no way." His determination and resolve returned. Yes, he felt afraid, but he'd been trained to use fear, control it, feed off it and turn it back on his enemies. Whatever the circumstances.

Jeff feigned worry, putting his long claw-like hands up to his mouth. *"Oh no, you're not going to hurt me, are you?"*

"Hell yeah," said Savage. "Remember me saying I wished you were real so I could punch you in the face? Well, now I'm going to get the chance." Savage flipped back the covers, ready to leap out of bed and pummel the lanky ghoul right between the place where his eyes should be.

Savage looked down and gasped.

He had no legs.

"You're in my world now, Savage," said Jeff, relishing every syllable. *"And what I say goes. I suppose you could try clicking your heels like Dorothy to try and get you home. Oh wait, you haven't got any heels. Just like your daughter when she exploded, except she didn't have any arms or legs either. Didn't have much left of anything. You could've buried her in a sandwich box."*

"Tannaz!" Savage screamed. "Tannaz! Help me!" Jeff cackled like a strangled hyena. The room spun on a wash cycle to the sound of Jeff's maniacal laughter mixed with the cacophony of moans from Savage's victims.

He squeezed his eyes tight again. Hands firmly clamped over his ears. It made no difference. He could hear every diabolical utterance. His own screams mixing with theirs.

Soon he felt himself being rocked back and forth. Through

blurry, tearful and terrified eyes he saw the blessed sight of Tannaz. Her hand on his shoulder, trying to wake him up.

"Savage, it's okay. I'm here."

His breaths came heavy and sharp. A man drowning in the horrors he'd accumulated throughout his life. Not the strong, tough, resilient Savage, who always knew what to do, but a broken one. A corrupted file of a man.

She sat him up. Cradled his head. His sobs coming thick and fast.

"It's okay," she said. "Just a nightmare. Just a nightmare."

Savage shuddered. He didn't know how to tell her it wasn't a nightmare. It was a traumatic, psychotic episode of the worst magnitude. Jeff Perkins, the voice in his head, had become real. He now had visual as well as audio. A hallucination, yes, but as real as Tannaz was. Soon he'd be more than that. The demon who lodged in his head now wanted to be the landlord and it was only a matter of time before Savage got evicted.

"I'm here," she said. Her voice should have soothed him like honey, calmed the storm in his mind. Tannaz had been there to save him. But he knew Jeff was right. A day would come when Tannaz would not be there to chase the demon away. Or her presence would not have the same kryptonite effect on him. That day, that zero hour, was coming, and Savage had no idea how to fight it. How do you fight an enemy who was your own self?

Savage straightened up, cleared his throat, sniffed back the tears and dabbed away the ones on his face with the corner of the duvet. "I'm sorry you had to see that," he said quietly.

Tannaz shook her head. "Savage, stop being the tough guy. You had a nightmare. People do. It's nothing to be ashamed of."

Trouble was, Savage's shame was causing his living nightmare. "I feel better now," he lied.

"Bullshit you do. You were shaking when I came in. Shaking with fear and screaming my name. You need to talk to me about this."

"Like you said, it was just a nightmare. He swung his legs out of bed. Savage was still dressed in his clothes apart from his socks.

He sat on the side of the bed and put them on one by one. Taking a modicum of comfort from the fact that he still had legs.

"How did you get on with the tower dump?" he asked.

"Forget the tower dump, that was some nasty stuff you were going through. I was frightened for you."

He turned and faced her. "It was just a nightmare."

"A pretty terrifying nightmare. Do you get them often?"

"Look, Tannaz. I'm touched you're worried about me, really I am, but I think we have bigger problems to worry about."

"Okay, fine," said Tannaz getting to her feet. "I'll tell you everything. But first you need to tell me who Jeff Perkins is."

CHAPTER 40

SAVAGE SHRUGGED. LOOKED BLANKLY BACK at Tannaz. "Jeff who?"

"Jeff Perkins." She sat down on the end of the bed. "Was he someone in your unit? Did you lose a mate called Jeff Perkins? He doesn't sound like someone who'd be in the SAS."

Savage shook his head.

"You were screaming out his name, telling him to stop."

"I don't know any person called Jeff Perkins." It was a kind of truth. Sort of. He didn't know anyone real called Jeff Perkins. But, then again, if Tannaz had said do you know a persona that embodies all of your guilt consolidated into a berating presence known as Jeff Perkins, he'd have still said no.

Tannaz raised her dark eyebrows, as if to say *"Really?"*

"I don't know anyone who walks this green earth known as Jeff Perkins." Again, another truth—ish.

"Well, I don't like this Jeff Perkins. Don't like the effect he has on you."

He doesn't like you, either, thought Savage. "Now can we get on with the tower dump? Is it finished?"

"It is, and I've triple-checked the numbers, neither Roberts' number nor Sutcliffe's number is among them. So we're safe to call Roberts."

"You still think it was Sutcliffe, don't you?" asked Savage.

"Damn right. The guy's been a pain in the ass all through this. He arrested you, remember?"

"He was desperate for a conviction."

"So what? I'm desperate for lots of things. Cigarettes, most of the time. Doesn't mean I can just march into a newsagent and demand they give me them."

"Desperation makes you do weird things."

"You seem like you're defending him. His number was on that app so he's suspect number one as far as I'm concerned. You're always telling me to follow the logic."

"Yeah, you're right. I'll make the call to Roberts."

Savage got hold of Roberts and said they needed to set up a meeting urgently, with her and her alone. Roberts promised to get away as soon as she could but with Callum being found—the only victim of Dylan Harper to survive—she was pretty tied up. Savage and Tannaz had to sit tight and wait.

They waited all day. Savage still tired, but too frightened to cat-nap just in case Jeff decided to materialise in his dreams. He hadn't figured out what he was going to do about him. He had to sleep sometime, but he couldn't risk another episode. The lack of shuteye made him feel delirious, the thought of seeing Jeff again producing an anxious sickness in his stomach. He'd never been so glad to have Tannaz by his side, keeping his demon at bay. He knew he should tell her. She'd kick him for not doing so, a big, scything roundhouse kick to his head to knock some sense into him. He would tell her soon. Maybe after all this business with Callum was properly over.

At nine p.m., there was a knock at the door. Savage opened it. DI Roberts stood there looking exhausted but happy. Her hair was lank and her skin as pale as a White Walker's—Savage knew the feeling. But her eyes held a sparkle. There was an energy spurring her on, the result of getting some sort of closure on a case that had so far outfoxed her.

"Please come in," he said.

DI Roberts entered the hallway. Savage led her into the lounge where Tannaz sat behind her computer screens.

"Would you like tea?"

"No, I'm good. Had enough tea and coffee to sink a battleship."

Savage offered her a chair, she declined. "No, I'm worried that if I sit down I'll never get back up again."

"Long day?" asked Tannaz.

"Yes. Just come from the hospital."

"How's Callum?"

"He's okay. Bit early to tell. Doctors won't let us question him for very long, not in the state he's in. Lucky for him he doesn't remember anything. Unlucky for us trying to piece together what happened. But at least Dylan Harper won't be taking any more kids, thanks to you."

Savage frowned. "That's what I'd like to talk to you about. This might not be over yet."

The tired optimism on Roberts' face fled, causing her features to sag. "Oh, and why is that?"

"We think someone else might be out there," Savage replied. "I mean, you must think it's odd that Callum was released after Dylan Harper got hit by a train. Who did that? It couldn't have been Dylan Harper."

"Well, we're keeping our options open until we have more information." Police shorthand for they didn't know. "It's all dependent on how much Callum remembers, if he remembers anything at all."

"Well, we think we've discovered something." Savage picked up Red Adidas Top's phone, and held it up. "We took this phone off a gang member in Woolwich. They call themselves the Blashford Boys because they hang out on the Blashford Estate."

"Never heard of them," said Roberts.

"Well, you have seen them before and will be interested in the schedule of events I'm about to show you." Savage fingered the phone and pulled up the deleted thread of anonymous messages from the Strangerly app. Ping-ponging back and forth, the messages Tannaz had managed to salvage, highlighting the money, the dead-drop locations, the warehouse and, most importantly of all, the specific instructions for taking Callum, right down to putting a hoodie on him and swapping places on the handle bars of the BMX, and giving him the fentanyl lollies to keep him quiet.

Roberts took the phone and slowly scrolled through each message. Then she shot a look at Savage, then at Tannaz, then back to Savage. He could sense a shift in her world of plate-tectonic proportions. The look of someone who thought they had almost everything figured out, neatly sewn up, only to find it quickly unravelling like a Primark jumper.

Her lips went to form a word, then snapped shut again. She pondered briefly, as if her brain were resetting.

"So this is how Dylan Harper abducted kids? He used a gang? Then held them in a warehouse in Woolwich?"

"No," said Tannaz. "We think Dylan Harper used sophisticated software to mask his presence on CCTV. That way he could just go into a park, ply a kid with fentanyl lollies, soften them up, stick them in a pram and walk them out again without being detected. Obviously, avoiding any eye-witnesses."

"How do you know all this?"

"We figured it out," said Savage. "Well, mostly Tannaz over there."

Tannaz gave a weak smile and waved. "And a friend of ours who's pretty hot with CCTV." She would've mentioned Vikram by name to give him credit but there was no point muddying the waters, especially as Vikram had been an early suspect.

Roberts' inquisitive face became stern. "You should have come to me with this information."

"Sorry," said Savage. "I know, and I apologise—"

"Hold on a minute," Roberts interrupted. "If Archangel had software to get past CCTV cameras why did he use this gang to take Callum?"

"That brings us onto our second bombshell of the evening," Savage continued. "We believe Callum's abductor wasn't Dylan Harper. It was someone else, making it look like him. A copycat. They didn't have his software skills to do his CCTV disappearing act so they got resourceful, used a gang."

Roberts put her hands on her hips, the anger not subsiding. "And how do you know this little nugget of very important information?"

Tannaz took a deep breath and took the phone back off Roberts. Pulled up another screen, the one covered in code. Held it up for Roberts to see. "This is the backend code of the Strangerly app, this copycat used it to communicate with the gang. It's basically the code supporting the sign-up page. You need a mobile number to make an account." Tannaz pointed to the phone number halfway down. "That's the number used."

Roberts swore.

"It's Sutcliffe's number, isn't it?"

Roberts nodded. "But there has to be some mistake."

"No mistake," said Tannaz.

Roberts wobbled a little, pulled up a chair and collapsed into it.

"Would you like that cup of tea now?" asked Savage.

"Yes, please." Roberts' voice sounded young and unsure. Savage returned with drinks for all of them. Roberts took a long draught, not worrying about the scalding hot tea burning her mouth. "I find this all difficult to believe," she said. "I've worked with DCI Sutcliffe for over two years now and, yes, he's an old-school misogynist copper. But to take a kid and use a gang like that. I just can't believe it."

"I think you're being too generous," said Tannaz. "He's a burnout who doesn't care who he arrests as long as he gets someone in custody. Doesn't matter if they're innocent or not."

Roberts remained defiant. "That is not true."

"Oh, come on," said Tannaz. "He arrested Savage and then he arrested Lev. You knew he was clutching at straws and you went along with it."

"Hey, don't speak to me like that. He's my superior. There's a chain of command."

Tannaz locked eyes with her. Neither prepared to back down.

"A chain of command that you ignored when it suited you," said Tannaz. "I sent you that tip-off about Archangel's lock-up and you jumped on it like a dog humping a cushion. Where was your chain of command then?"

Roberts flinched slightly. "You sent me that tip-off?"

"Yep."

Roberts stood up. "And how did you acquire that information?"

"Okay stop," said Savage. "None of this is important. Dylan Harper is out of the picture, but we still have a second player at large who needs to be caught. There's a good chance it's Sutcliffe…" Roberts went to speak. Savage held up his hand to allow himself to finish. "... Might not be Sutcliffe at all. Could be someone setting him up. But surely he's the number-one suspect and we need to investigate so we can rule him out if it's not him." He looked at Roberts.

"Okay, you're right. But I'm telling you Sutcliffe's a good man. A bit overwhelmed, but a good man. Good at his job."

"Maybe once he was, about a million years ago," Tannaz muttered.

"Okay, Tannaz," said Savage. "That's enough." He turned to Roberts. "You have everything you need to close the net on this guy, if you're assuming it's not Sutcliffe."

"Pretty sure it's not," she said.

Savage continued. "You have the phone, the messages and the location of the warehouse where Callum was held. Unless this person was wearing a hazmat suit when he entered it, it'll still be covered in his DNA. If it's Sutcliffe, his DNA will still be there. If it's not, you can at least run it through your database."

"You'll have to rule out ours, of course," said Tannaz. "We've been in there."

Roberts' face became enraged. "Wait, hold on, you've been in this warehouse? Contaminated an important crime scene? I don't believe this!"

"We had to," Tannaz replied. "This is before Callum had been found. We thought Callum was being held there. We had to check it out as soon as we knew."

"You should've called me first." Roberts swore. "You know, Sutcliffe was right. You two are a pair of well-meaning amateurs. Stomping around like pissed elephants, getting in the way and ruining evidence."

"If it wasn't for us, Dylan Harper would still be out there," said Tannaz. "Kids going missing, and you with your thumbs up your asses."

Roberts didn't reply. She stood up and retrieved a small clear evidence bag from inside her jacket, opened it and snatched the gang leader's phone out of Tannaz's hands and dropped it in. "This isn't over," she said. "You will have some serious questions to answer about interfering in police business, I promise you that. And I'll see myself out."

She turned and marched out of the lounge, slamming the door behind her.

"That went well," said Savage.

"She's just pissed we've had to do her job for her. And that her boss might be a copycat child abductor. Probably not the best day she's ever had."

They heard the front door of Savage's flat open and close, followed by a loud bang, something heavy hitting the floor like a concrete block being dropped.

"What the hell was that?" asked Tannaz.

Savage immediately went to investigate.

Out in the hallway by his front door, Roberts was lying unconscious with a thick line of blood running from her hairline down her forehead.

CHAPTER 41

Savage was by Roberts' side in a second, crouching down low, checking her vitals. She was still breathing.

Tannaz bundled into the hallway, saw Roberts's crumpled body. "What happened?"

"Think she collapsed. Hit her head. Call an ambulance," Savage shouted back.

Tannaz disappeared back into the lounge to get her phone.

Savage sensed movement behind him. Looked over his shoulder. It was at that moment he knew he'd made a mistake. A big unforgivable rookie error.

He'd got distracted by Roberts lying there. Should've checked the property first for whatever or whoever had done this. Not assumed she'd collapsed.

From out of Savage's small bathroom under the stairs, Sutcliffe emerged. Face enraged. Extendable police baton raised. He must have followed Roberts here. Waited outside then slipped in when she opened the front door to leave. Cracked her over the head, then darted into the bathroom to hide.

Savage had no time to respond. No time to defend himself. His weariness and lack of sleep not helping his reaction times. It also didn't help that Sutcliffe was standing above him and Savage was crouched below. His enemy had the high ground. Sutcliffe swung the baton down on top of Savage's head. Once, then twice. Savage could feel consciousness slipping away. A third blow would seal the deal.

Tannaz emerged from the lounge, phone at her ear. She dropped it the second she saw Sutcliffe, her eyes darting to him then at Savage on the floor, his head lolling over to one side, eyes half-lidded. Almost out of the game.

The old copper now turned his attention on her. Baton held in the ready position, up by his shoulder as if he were a tennis player holding a racket about to serve. His other arm was outstretched, palm up, ready to shove Tannaz back.

"Two beats one," Savage croaked at her.

Tannaz looked confused momentarily. Then her eyes flashed with understanding.

She darted back into Savage's lounge and reappeared in the corridor holding a metal poker in one hand and metal tongs in the other, acquired from the brass set of fireside implements he kept hanging by his fireplace.

Sutcliffe had one weapon. She had two. Two always beats one.

Sutcliffe advanced forward. Slow as a tree. But definitely stronger and more powerful than her. By contrast, Tannaz bounced up and down on her toes. Light, agile, blurringly fast. No fear in her face, only determination. Savage had always taught her Bruce Lee's poetic philosophy for fighting; "Be like water... flow and crash." To that he'd added his own less elegant philosophy—fight dirty. If someone picks a fight with you, they've just given up all their rights to fair play. Tannaz was about to unleash a big crashing waterfall full of dirty crap on the guy.

Sutcliffe swung his baton from his shoulder down and across diagonally, catching Tannaz hard on her thigh. Advancing again, Sutcliffe did the same on the other side. Shoulder-height strike, smashing into her other thigh. Savage heard her whimper. It was a textbook police crowd-control move. Hit them in the thighs while moving forward. Thighs are a big easy target. Once they're battered and bruised, you can't move and you can't fight. Plus, it hurts like hell.

Tannaz would not be caught out again.

As Sutcliffe swung a third blow to her thighs, his baton met Tannaz's poker coming the other way, blocking his strike, preventing it from finding its target. Momentarily distracted by this, he didn't see the tongs in her other hand, as she slammed them into his neck, hitting him right on the carotid artery. He staggered back, dazed. Took a breath and regained his composure. Came at her this time with a jab to her sternum. Tannaz tried to dodge backwards but not far enough. The jab pushed her back, giving Sutcliffe time to set up another attack. He did his swinging technique again, not to her thighs but her arms. He hit her once on the bicep. Tannaz nearly dropped the poker. He tried again on the other side. Tannaz blocked him with the tongs, they clanged as they struck his baton. He quickly withdrew his weapon, bringing it up to his chest to protect himself. Tannaz read the move and feinted an attack to his torso. Just what he expected. At the last moment she dropped low and whacked him hard on the side of his creaky knees.

Sutcliffe staggered back, the ferocity of Tannaz's last attack forcing him to limp. By contrast, she danced forward, light and agile. He aimed a blow to her face. She easily parried it away with the poker. For his trouble, she gave him a hard whack on the side of the ear with the tongs. A second later a trickle of blood issued out.

Tannaz raised both weapons high in her hands as if she were going for a double blow to his head. Sutcliffe bought her charade, held his baton up to protect himself. Instead she kicked him hard in the shin with her DMs, in the same leg he'd been limping on. The guy kinked over to one side, that leg now losing its ability to support him. Tannaz spotted a target. His left flank was exposed. Unmercifully, the poker slammed into his rib cage. He kinked over the other way in pain.

His hands were low now. The baton hanging down by his waist, weakly, being held more like a dog lead.

Tannaz knocked it with the tongs. Sutcliffe's grip wasn't strong enough and the baton slipped from his hand and onto the floor. He made a move to retrieve it, not thinking straight. As he bent down, she cracked him across the face, right on the nose with the poker.

Sutcliffe's eyes watered. Blood flowed from both nostrils. His eyelids fluttered, then closed. The old copper lost consciousness and was suddenly just a pile on the floor.

He could easily be faking, so he could grab her as she stepped over him to get to Savage. Just to be sure, Tannaz kicked him in the stomach a couple of times. Sutcliffe didn't groan or move. She prodded him with the poker, fairly hard. No response. Out of the fight.

Now she could safely get past Sutcliffe and get to Savage.

Savage's eyes were open, but dozy. She checked the top of his head. A couple of nasty bruises were already forming.

"Good work, Tannaz," he said woozily.

She shifted him into a more comfortable position.

"Savage, are you okay?"

"There's something you need to do," he said seriously. "Before anything else."

"What?" asked Tannaz. "What is it?"

"Stick the kettle on. I'm gasping."

"Yeah, you're okay," she said. "Tea can wait, mister. We need to get you and Roberts an ambulance. I'll get my phone." She stood to her feet and headed down the corridor to pick up her dropped phone.

"And then tea," said Savage.

CHAPTER 42

TWO DAYS LATER, DI ROBERTS sat in Savage's front lounge taking a statement from both him and Tannaz. Pad on her knees and pen in her hand, she wrote quickly, in neat little words, all in caps. Up by her hairline were three black stitches where Sutcliffe's baton had split her skin and knocked her unconscious. Looking at them made Savage's own injuries throb. He had two large circular lumps in the centre of his bald patch courtesy of Sutcliffe's attack.

"How's your head?" asked Savage.

"Fine," Roberts replied. "How's yours?"

"Good. Apart from looking like a skateboard park."

Roberts smirked. "I can't drink which is really annoying."

"That is annoying," said Tannaz.

Then silence. They'd run out of small talk. The only sound was the scratching of Roberts' pen against paper.

Tannaz went for the elephant in the room. "So, go on, tell us what's happening with Sutcliffe."

"As a police officer I'm not at liberty to discuss—"

"Hey, RoboCop," said Tannaz. "Stop with all that by-the-book stuff. If I hadn't stopped Sutcliffe he'd have probably beaten you to death, so I think you owe us some info. And we did try to warn you."

Roberts looked offended. Savage couldn't tell whether it was because Tannaz had called her RoboCop or that they had spotted Sutcliffe had lost it long before she had. Probably the former.

Roberts took a deep breath. "Well, being a police officer is generally considered a high-risk group for the development of mental-health problems. And I think Sutcliffe has become another statistic."

Tannaz laughed. "I think you can do better than that."

Roberts took a deep pull of air into her lungs. Let it out slowly, reluctantly. "You're right, he was fried, hadn't slept for months. Job had got to him. Got him down. Didn't let on, though. We didn't spot the signs. Just thought he was being a miserable bastard."

"So what's happened to him?" asked Savage.

"He's been sectioned under the mental health act. Because it's all tied up with the case, they're holding him in a secure forensic psychiatric unit. They're evaluating him as we speak."

Savage tried to look sympathetic. "Any clues yet for why he took Callum?"

"Well, that's just it," Roberts replied. "He denies the whole thing."

"So why did he attack you, attack all of us?" asked Tannaz.

"Says he was convinced I was after his job. Was delusional and paranoid. That I was trying to make him look bad to get him fired so I could get a promotion. And when you two tracked down Dylan Harper, he thought I was colluding with you both. That the three of us were working together to end his career. So he followed me here that night."

"Jeez," said Savage. He hated to admit it, but he did feel a tiny bit of empathy for the guy. Savage knew that could easily be him. Knew what mental-health issues could do if they went unchecked.

"But it's clear he did take Callum," said Tannaz.

"He's saying he didn't," Roberts replied. "Unless he's delusional and his mind has blocked out the whole episode."

"But surely you can prove he did it," said Tannaz. "What about the warehouse? His DNA must be all over it."

Roberts put her pen away. "We've searched the abandoned warehouse, forensics has been all over it, and while there are traces of Callum's DNA, there's nothing of Sutcliffe's, not a jot."

"How's that possible?"

"Well, it's not. Unless he was visiting Callum in a hazmat suit and mask. Thing is, he must have brought food and water on a regular basis, and those fentanyl lollies to keep him sedated. I don't know how he could get in and out of there without leaving DNA."

"Well," said Savage. "He was a copper, he'd have known how to do that. Maybe your first assumption is right. Probably donned a hazmat suit before going in."

Roberts looked doubtful. "Yes, but even if we assume that's what he did, which would make him highly conspicuous, there's still the problem of how he got over there. We checked ANPR traffic cameras and his car's never been anywhere near that warehouse, plus it's got a tracker, that came up negative too."

"He's an old-school cop," said Savage. "He'll know every trick to avoid detection. Borrowed a car, maybe."

"We're still waiting on his mobile-phone provider," said Roberts, "to give us data from the local tower. Will tell us if his phone's been anywhere near that warehouse."

Tannaz and Savage exchanged glances.

"What?" asked Roberts.

"You have to promise you won't get all RoboCop on me," said Tannaz.

"You're not withholding information from me, are you? Because this time I won't be able to turn a blind eye."

"We have the tower data," said Savage.

"What?"

"We've got the list of numbers from the mobile-phone tower nearest the warehouse."

"Wh—? How did you...?"

"Not important," said Tannaz.

Roberts stood up. "It is important. This is highly—"

Tannaz cut her off. "Sutcliffe's number isn't amongst them. Unless he left his phone behind when he went there."

"Impossible," said Roberts. "An officer couldn't be uncontactable for that amount of time. He'd have to have a pretty good excuse for not having his phone on him. No, Sutcliffe would have kept his phone on him. Are you sure his phone number doesn't appear?"

"Positive."

"I want to see it," said Roberts. "The list of numbers. And I want to know how you got them."

"Well, I can help you with first part, not the second." Tannaz got up and went over to the table where her laptop sat. "I'll ping the list over to you."

"No," said Roberts. "I can't have an electronic trail leading to me. I want a hard copy."

"Don't worry," Tannaz reassured her. "I can cover my tracks. No one would know."

"I'm sure you can. But I'd rather not risk it. A hard copy if you please."

"Fair enough." Tannaz hit a couple of keys. "It'll come out of Savage's printer in a second."

Down the hall they heard the clunk and whir of Savage's printer coming to life in his bedroom. Savage got to his feet. "I'll get it," he said.

He took the short walk to his bedroom where a single sheet of paper sat on the printer tray. Savage picked up the sheet and scanned his eyes down the three columns of phone numbers together with dates and times. It was the first time he'd seen them. He'd left Tannaz to check them for Sutcliffe's and Roberts' numbers.

Tannaz had narrowed the parameters down to only those that had come within a hundred metres of the abandoned warehouse, so there weren't that many numbers to start with. It wasn't exactly a place where people would be hanging out drinking lattes; mostly people passing by on their way to work, taking a shortcut past the shabby, derelict buildings. The same numbers kept repeating themselves at the same time of day, once in the morning and evening. Definitely people on their way to and from work.

One of the numbers caught his eye. Kept popping up erratically. Turned his blood cold because he knew who it belonged to.

It was a number he knew well. And it had nothing to do with Sutcliffe.

CHAPTER 43

JULIE SAT DRINKING HER COFFEE, nervously. It was just the caffeine giving her the jitters, she told herself. But she knew that it was far more than that. How she'd held it together with everything that had gone on she'd never know. But held on she had, and was proud of herself for getting through this.

A little glimmer of hope had told her, yes, you can make it. Everything is going to be okay. It couldn't get any worse, could it? But life is a bitch, especially when you tempt fate like that. Yes, things could get a whole lot worse. Were about to get a whole lot worse. She had Callum back, that was the main thing. Yes, she had her beloved son back. And now she was about to lose something else she held dear. It had to be done, even though it hurt like hell.

She'd been through all the different levels of grief and tears and denial and pain and anger when Callum had disappeared, and then she had gone through them all again. Mostly sheer disbelief and anger. She'd cried hateful tears, something she didn't think was possible. How can you be angry and sad at the same time? It had all come out in a torrent, after she'd stopped trying to deny it. The evidence was all there. Even a fool could see it. Now all that was left was why. Why had this been done to her and her family? She'd get answers. Demand them if she had to.

She glanced at her watch. Ten minutes late. That wasn't helping. She just wanted this over and done with. Then she would start work on shutting it out. Blocking the memories, or better still erasing them like they do on those sci-fi shows. She wished such technology existed. Maybe she'd try hypnotherapy. Anything to get rid of the history in this particular part of her life. The whole of her life, for that matter. A tear fell from her eye. She swiped it away. Had to be strong. Now wasn't the time for weakness or getting emotional.

At that moment the door opened, and her mother Celia bumbled in, with far too many bags, letting the warm spring air into the stuffy café. She smiled at the guy behind the counter and ordered a cappuccino and a large slice of Victoria sponge. Beaming brightly, she joined her daughter at the small round table by the window. Her daughter didn't return the smile.

"So, this is nice," said Celia. "We don't usually get time together. Just hurried chats at work or at home."

Julie didn't reply. Just gazed out the window at the busy south London road, cars parked in every available space. People bustling past, heads down, engrossed in their phones. She wondered if their lives were any easier than hers.

The waiter came over and placed a generous slice of Victoria sponge in front of Celia and a frothy cappuccino sprinkled with chocolate dust. Celia took a fork and sliced off an edge of cake and popped it in her mouth, then washed it down with coffee, getting a milk moustache. She quickly wiped it away with a napkin.

"Why did you do it?" asked Julie.

"Do what, dear?"

"Take Callum."

Celia's next fork of cake stopped midway, her mouth hanging open, as if she'd been put on pause. Her head jerked back in shock. "What are you talking about?"

Julie slammed her hand down on the table, making the cups and plates jump. A few people looked round. "You took Callum, didn't you?"

"What's wrong? Are you feeling okay, dear?"

Julie swore. "No, I am pretty far from feeling okay. I know what you did. Now I just need to know why. How could you do such a thing? To me? To your own grandson?"

"Oh, sweetheart. I think this has all been too much. The stress has got to you. What an ordeal you've been through. It's got into your head. That's understandable. Trauma has a way of skewing reality. Making you see things that aren't real."

"Stop psychoanalysing me. You know what you did. I know what you did. I just don't understand why. Why would you punish me and Callum like this?"

Celia reached across the table to grip Julie's hand. Julie pulled it away. "Listen, dear, it was that horrible detective Sutcliffe who took Callum. I never liked him from the start. Nasty, bitter man he was. Had it in for that young DI Roberts. Typical misogynist. Frightened that a woman could do his job better than he could."

"That last bit is true. But he didn't take Callum. He's always denied it."

Celia laughed. "Oh, come on, Julie. You believe him? The man's delusional."

"Mum, why don't you just admit it. You took Callum."

"Because there's nothing to admit. This is crazy talk. I was with you all day Friday, the day Callum was taken, remember? Never out of your sight. How could I have taken him? We were at work the whole time together. Don't you remember? Maybe you need to have a lie down."

"I'm feeling fine apart from the fact that my son was kidnapped by his own grandmother."

"How can you say such a thing? Accuse me of taking my beloved grandson."

"Because your DNA was found in an abandoned warehouse in Woolwich where Callum had been held."

Celia waved away the comment as if it were worthless. "You've been watching too many of those crime shows. They're always so far-fetched. It's probably because some of my DNA was on Callum's clothes, that's all. You know how I'm always hugging the lad."

"Mum, you know that mobile phones can be tracked don't you? Even if they're off." Julie studied Celia's face for her reaction. Her expression was unflinching, like a granite cliff face. But then there was a fleeting indicator of doubt. A minuscule twitch, not more than a flicker at the corner of her mouth. "Maybe if you'd watched a few more crime shows, you'd know that mobile-phone towers track the position of phones. Your DNA and your mobile phone showed up in that abandoned warehouse. You were there. It's pretty damning evidence."

Celia regained her stoicism. "Well, that doesn't mean anything. I probably drive past it on the way to work. We both do."

"What at four a.m.?"

"There must be some mistake."

"No. No there's no mistake. In fact, your phone shows up there at all sorts of weird times of the day. You were checking on Callum, weren't you? Giving him more of those hideous lollies to keep him sedated."

"You're quite mistaken. How would I get hold of drugs like that?"

"We work for social services for crying out loud. We look after vulnerable people, many of them with drug habits. I'm sure you found a way."

"That's a good point. We work for social services, with loads of good counsellors, who I think you need to pay a visit to. A bit of counselling's what you need. Getting things off your chest."

Julie swore again. More heads turned in her direction. "Just shut up, Mum. Actually, you're no longer my mum. I disown you."

"You? Disown me? What a horrible thing to say. After everything I've done for you. Everything I've sacrificed. I gave up my career to bring you up. To give you the perfect, storybook childhood. You know I could've been the head of my own department. Had the respect of my co-workers. Been invited to speak at conferences and had my opinions listened to and written about in journals and blogs. Been a trailblazer in my profession. But no, I chose to be a mother because bringing you up and spending time with you was more important to me. Was the right thing to do." Celia sat back, took a slug of coffee and slammed it down again, she wasn't done yet. "I thought I'd done a good job with you. Led by example and all that. Thought you'd do the same for Callum. Be there for him. Sacrifice your career prospects so you could be a full-time mother just like I did. But no. You chose your career over him. You were never there. Always working late. Always promising to be home, to be at school plays and open evenings but you never showed up

Savage Children

because the job was more important. You turned into a cliché of a working mother. Always saying, 'Oh, next time I'll be there.' And you never were. That's why Frank got custody of him. I mean, on what planet would that idiot ever get custody, apart from one where you neglected your son. You're not a mother, you're cold and ambitious. And you got what you wanted, didn't you? Head of Children and Families. But at what cost? You lost custody of your own son. How could you? I would've never done that to you as a child. I gave up my job to give you the best start in life. Don't you think I wanted to rise through the ranks and be where you are now? Course I did. But I gave it up and put you first. Thought I'd set you off in the right direction, give you a good moral compass. But you didn't want to spend time with Callum."

Julie's eyes became tearful. "Yes, I did."

"No, you didn't, you left him with that fool of a father. Shame on you. It's a wonder he's turned out like he has. No thanks to you."

More tears arrived at the corner of Julie's eyes.

"Oh, stop your crocodile tears," said Celia. "It's too late for that now." Celia leant forward and added venom to every word. "Yes, I did take him. You needed to learn a lesson. A lesson in what happens when you put your career first."

"How could you?" Julie said quietly. "How could you do that to Callum?"

"It's your fault. You needed to learn a lesson. Learn the value of having a child, of having a family, and you only know the value of something when it's taken away."

"You're insane. Callum already has been taken away from me. He lives with his father, remember?"

"Not like that. You can see him whenever you choose. I mean what it feels like to permanently lose someone."

"You did all this to teach me a lesson. Put me through hell. Kidnapped my son and held him prisoner. Drugged him. You're a monster."

"I'm not a monster. You needed teaching. Bit of tough love."

"You are a monster. If it wasn't for Tannaz and Savage I'd never know anything about it. You had no intention of telling me. Wanted to make it look like Dylan Harper had done this, didn't you? Or Sutcliffe. Or Savage. Did you plant Callum's football in his garden to get him arrested?"

Celia nodded. "Well, had to cover my tracks. I couldn't let you know it was me. Wouldn't have the same effect. You wouldn't have taken it seriously. I wanted you to remember this forever, that actions have consequences."

"The trauma and stress you've caused me. Caused everyone. I'm ashamed of you."

"No, I did this out of love for you. That's what mothers do."

"Lots of mothers work. That's just modern life. You can't punish me for providing for my family. How else do you think I put food on the table and buy Callum new football kit? It's certainly not Frank doing that. His benefit cheques just about keep the lights on. If it wasn't for me working, they'd both starve."

"You can justify it how you like, doesn't make it right. A woman's place is at home looking after her children."

"Only if that's what she chooses to do. Other women take a different path. You know what, you're a psychopath. No better than that Dylan Harper."

"I am nothing like him. He was a monster."

"Oh, yeah, well why did you choose to copy him then? And how did you know about him?"

"From work. Information-sharing protocol with other agencies. I just kept my eyes open until I intercepted something on the system from the police that fitted the bill. I had the name of the officer in charge, Sutcliffe and his contact number, and the details of the case—the Archangel, the fentanyl, the drawings. I simply copied his approach, to camouflage my actions, make them look like his. Then when Savage chased him to that bridge and he threw himself off, it forced me to cut things short and release Callum. I was always going to release him, dear. You must realise that."

"You make it sound like I should be grateful. And what about the gang?"

"Well that was the tricky part. No one could figure out how Archangel was taking the kids. So I had to improvise. Get resourceful. Being a social worker, I know lots of older, desperate kids. I could use them, I thought. I knew all about the Blashford Boys. Had been their social worker on and off, knew them from little kids, knew everything about them. So I set up a Strangerly app, using Sutcliffe's number, as a bit of a red herring. Set up a divert on my phone so any messages came to my phone and not his. Then I could message them anonymously. Started sending them little individual texts, telling them I knew stuff about them. That one of them wet the bed until he was sixteen or that one of them was gay. Got their attention. Offered them cash to take Callum. Gave them specific instructions, swapping hoodies while one of them stayed behind to make it look like Callum had disappeared into thin air. Told them to take him and leave him at the warehouse."

"You told a violent gang to kidnap my son and lock him in a warehouse."

"He was never in any harm, I made sure of that. Told them they wouldn't get paid otherwise. I checked him over. I checked on him every day to make sure he was okay. Several times a day, in fact. He's fine, doesn't remember a thing. Like having a long sleep with all that fentanyl I gave him."

"He doesn't remember anything at the moment. But that could be temporary. The consultant warned us it might be a while before any trauma appears. There's a fifty-fifty chance he'll have flashbacks. Can you imagine what that will be like? Remembering he was chained up alone in a caravan in an abandoned warehouse. Do you have any idea what you've done?"

"I did what needed to be done," Celia said innocently.

Julie rose from her seat, feeling the bile rising up her throat at the same time. She had wanted to hear her own mother say these words, to confess them out loud. And now that she had, she felt as if she'd stepped into some weird parallel universe where the mother she loved and respected had become a hideous and unrecognisable child abuser. She had to get out of there, away from this strange, inhuman woman who bore no resemblance to the loving parent she once knew. Insanity had clearly gripped her, fed by years and years of bitterness from watching her daughter's success. If she didn't get out of that café fast, she feared she might be sick, or worse, pick up a fork and thrust it into this woman's face.

"Where are you going?" asked Celia.

"Goodbye," Julie said without looking at her. She weaved her way through the tables towards the door, gathering speed as she went, knocking into the odd chair or two. A few customers tutted.

As she left the café, across the road several men and women got out of parked cars—DI Roberts and her team. They crossed over and met Julie on the pavement.

DI Roberts put a reassuring hand on her arm. "You okay?" she asked.

"No. I don't think I'll ever be okay," Julie replied. "But I will feel a little better when she's behind bars."

"Well, that's something we can help you with," said Roberts.

"Lock her up and throw away the key."

"My pleasure," said Roberts. She gave the signal. She and her team of police officers entered the café to arrest Celia.

CHAPTER 44

Nine years earlier

THE EDGE OF THE BLACK art portfolio collided with another person as Dylan Harper negotiated his way onto the steep escalator of Pimlico underground station.

"Sorry," Dylan said, even though it wasn't his fault. A guy had cut in front of him in a rush to get a foot on the escalator first, not noticing the cumbersome black art case that was the size of a family dining table. He didn't even give Dylan a backward glance, let alone an apology. Every second counted when you were in London and had somewhere important to be. And everyone seemed like they had somewhere important to be, crisscrossing this way and that, as if the world would end if they didn't save an extra second by shoving in front of someone else. Since arriving in the capital that day, his bulky portfolio containing his precious artwork had been bent, pulled, crushed, stepped on and caught in the closing doors of the underground train he'd just travelled in. Out on the pavement in front of the station, he gave his portfolio a once over. Glad he'd paid the extra money for a better-quality product. The stiff, black vinyl casing seemed to be holding up to the punishment of another trip across London.

Dylan checked his bearings, got out his dog-eared A to Z of London. The busy road he stood beside was undoubtedly the A3213. Forgettable modern office blocks mixed with expensive Georgian terraces with white stucco exteriors, and in between the two rows of buildings, three lanes of hectic traffic bled into Vauxhall Bridge Road, in a rush to make it across the River Thames.

Dylan slotted his A to Z into his jacket and followed the congested road, crossing over a set of traffic lights into a quieter back street with a pub on the corner. More stuccoed buildings lined his route with car-parking spaces out front. Strict authoritative signposts placed every couple of steps announced that these parking spaces (rarer than winged pigs in London) were for residents only and that you had to display the correct permit or risk getting towed away.

Dylan took a right, then a left, then another right and found himself staring at the imposing sight of Chelsea College of Art. Imposing, not just because of its reputation, but also because it used to be the Royal Army Medical College. Its military past still intact, three handsomely proportioned turn-of-the-century four-storey blocks stood, boxing in a wide square parade ground. And if that wasn't enough, facing all this on the other side of the road, the Tate Britain Art Gallery presided over the whole ensemble. Dylan was surrounded by internationally renowned art institutions. The butterflies went haywire in his stomach. Not least because he was running out of options. He'd had interviews with every art college in London, as well all the art colleges in his hometown of Brighton. The result was always the same. Rejection. He'd had so many rejection emails and letters clogging up his inbox and landing on his doormat that rejection now defined who he was, overshadowing every aspect of his life. He'd always suffered from low self-esteem, but it had gone into negative equity. There seemed no escape from this cancerous feeling, pulling him down every second of the day and sucking the confidence out of him. His only hope was that Chelsea College of Art would see something in him that the others had not. Everything hinged on this one interview. He daren't think what he would do if they also rejected him.

Dylan took a nervous step forward onto the parade ground, which was filled with students hanging out and chatting, or on their way to lectures. Desperately trying not to look like someone coming for an interview, he sought out the main entrance, eyeing each building for clues to an access point. The intimidating façades, full of columns and red brickwork and elegant arches gave no hint as to how you got in the place.

"Are you looking for reception?" a voice said from behind him.

Dylan swung around nearly whacking the pretty girl, Laurel-and-Hardy style, with his sail of a portfolio. She was achingly trendy, peroxide blonde hair cut short in a pageboy bob with a severe fringe, and a red bandana tied across the top, land girls' style. The look was perfected with a denim bib and braces, the hems of her trousers rolled up revealing scuffed-up para boots. The kind of girl he would normally shy away from. The kind of girl that made him feel invisible.

"Y-yes," he said.

"Got an interview?" she asked, her mouth lined with blood-red lipstick.

Dylan wondered if she was setting him up for humiliation. Would laugh at him for even attempting to get into the Chelsea College of Art. He studied her eyes. They were soft and blue and held no trace of malice.

"Er, yes, I have. Fine art."

She smiled. "You'll be fine. I remember I was so nervous at my interview I could barely speak. But then that's the good thing about art. The work does the talking."

"Thanks," said Dylan.

The girl pointed to the building behind him. "Main entrance is round the side of that block, out on the road. Can't miss it. Fine art is on the second floor, and good luck." She flashed him another perfect smile and took off across the parade ground.

He smiled back, felt his confidence lift a little. A pretty girl had talked to him. Not just talked to him, befriended him. Made him feel like he mattered. Like getting a place here wasn't an impossible dream.

Dylan set off, bouncing with every step, heading towards the main entrance. The receptionist directed him up to the second floor, through a matrix of high-ceilinged white, echoey corridors that buzzed with students. Dylan caught their abbreviated conversations, none of it about art, all of it about their social life, where they would eat and where they would go out that night and how much they would drink, and that they couldn't really afford it, but they would go anyway. From their sound-bite chatter, it didn't sound like they were taking this seriously, like it was just a stop gap, a way of filling time until they got a proper job. He wondered if he joined their ranks, how he would fit in with these people. How would his seriousness conflict with their superficiality? He wanted depth, to talk about meaning, about life and death, and how art hovered somewhere in between. Not beer and burgers and DJ sets.

Up ahead he saw three bright-orange plastic chairs arranged in a line outside of a door, just as the receptionist had described. He'd arrived at the office of Professor Gerald Chambers, Fine Art Course Leader. The man who would decide his future in this place. The plastic chairs were a temporary measure, said the receptionist, while the professor held his interviews. A holding place for prospective students to wait until they were called in. Dylan parked himself on the first seat closest to the door, placing his precious portfolio between his legs to stop it falling over. When the corridor quietened down, he could hear the booming voice of the professor coming from within. He couldn't make out whether he was angry or enthusiastic. Dylan leaned in, eager to get some morsel of sound, a clue as to the professor's mood or what he liked and what he didn't like.

The door burst open.

Out backed a tall, lanky lad, nearly having to duck to get his head under the lintel of the door. Curiously, he had no portfolio under his considerably long arms. Instead, he had one of those new iPad thingies. Dylan didn't think they would catch on, surely they were a con. Just a large iPod. A way of making more money with existing technology, just, well, bigger. In his head, Dylan scoffed. Clearly the professor's booming voice had been because he'd been angry at this guy for turning up to an interview without a portfolio and with a gadget. An overpriced electronic gimmick. This was good. A bit of *schadenfreude*. This guy's downfall would work to Dylan's advantage. He'd breeze in with a proper portfolio. Artwork in the flesh that you could touch, see and experience.

The previous interviewee got a hearty handshake. Briefly his eyes alighted on Dylan, then he turned and sauntered off down the corridor, clutching his silly iPad.

Professor Gerald Chambers curled his neck round the door. He had a beard, sprawling out in every direction, and hair to match, but his eyes were small and piercing, bright and intelligent.

"Dylan Harper?"

Dylan stood. Hefted his large case full of work. Followed the professor into his office.

He saw Dylan struggling. "See that lad I just interviewed? Had all his work on one of those new iPads. Very clever. I could just swipe through it all. Forward and back. I could even enlarge it with my fingers, zoom in close. I like that kind of thinking. That's creative. Using digital technology and art together. That's the kind of thinking I want on this course. We need to push the medium. Explore paths. Mix digital with traditional. Like that guy did." Dylan immediately felt on the back foot. Why didn't he think of that? He could've put his work on an iPad. Could've done it easily. He was good with technology, especially video. Brilliant in fact. In his mind, Dylan hit himself around the head for not coming up with that idea.

"Take a seat," said the professor. His office was just how Dylan imagined the office of an art college professor to be. Cluttered. Piles of papers and bookshelves bowing under the weight of hefty volumes on art and art theory. Walls were papered with hastily scribbled notes, Polaroids and prints. His desk similarly covered in sheaves of paper scattered like autumn leaves.

"Okay, let's get straight to it," he said, gesturing to Dylan's portfolio.

Dylan heaved it on the desk. Unzipped all round its edge. Before he flipped open the top, Dylan began to speak, to explain the theories behind his work. "For me, the greatest unanswered question in life is death. Where do we go? What happens to us when this life ends and the next begins. Death is everything, has become my obsession..."

The professor put his index finger to his lips and shushed him.

"Let the work do the talking, eh?" The exact same words the girl had used on the parade ground. Maybe she was a student of his.

Probably on the same course. He was sure they'd made a connection, no matter how brief their meeting. Maybe after this, and after Dylan had got a place here, he could be proper friends with her, and they could discuss how she felt about death. Perhaps even be more than that. The possibility sent a warm glow across his belly.

Dylan silently watched as the professor turned over each plastic sleeve containing his beloved pieces. The result of hours and hours of work. Painstaking, long-suffering work. Work he'd agonised over, often tearing it up and starting again, and again, and again. Dylan was the archetype of the tortured artist.

Watching as each piece flipped over, the professor seemed to speed up, flicking through them faster and faster like they were the pages of a brochure. Rather too flippantly for Dylan's liking. Not pausing over any of them to take in Dylan's mastery with a brush. His control of colour. The emotion and heartache he'd poured into each one, to create pieces of great melancholy and meaning.

The professor came to the last one. His eyes barely skimming over the painting in front of him. Leaning back in his chair the professor groaned and rubbed his eyes with his fists, as if this were the most agonising task he'd had to do today. Dylan shifted in his seat and gulped, waiting for the professor's verdict. Deep down, a growing demon of pain rose up from the lowest pit in Dylan's stomach. Deep down, he already knew the professor's verdict. It would be just like all the rest. Like all the other pompous gatekeepers he'd encountered.

The professor sat up straight and looked Dylan in the eye. Smiled. Not a confident one, but a sympathetic one. "Tell me, Dylan, what else do you? What other things interest you?"

Dylan thought for a moment, wondering if this were a trick question. If the professor were setting a verbal trap for him. "Nothing really," Dylan said. "I love painting. It's my life. Everything."

The professor leaned forward, rested his elbows on Dylan's portfolio and laced his fingers together.

"There must be something else you do. I mean, what do you do when you're not painting?"

"I quite like playing with video. You know, editing things. Doing special effects."

The professor closed Dylan's portfolio and zipped it up. "Then I suggest you do that, pursue a career in video. I don't know, I've heard videoing weddings is quite big these days. That involves lots of editing I bet."

Dylan couldn't hide the anger and crushing disappointment in his voice. "Why would I want to do that? This is what I want to do. To be here and paint."

Sitting back in his chair, the professor said, "I won't patronise you. There are two types of people who sit where you're sitting. There's the small, tiny percentage that have what it takes to get into The Chelsea College of Art. They have that rare quality. The 'X factor' for want of a better word. Like the guy who was in here before you. They've just got something. A spark about them. And then there's the other type who just miss out. Sure, they have talent, but they're just not quite good enough to get in here. But they usually find a place at another art college. Maybe not in the top five or even the top ten art colleges in this country. But they find somewhere to study. Now I'm going to save you a lot of time, and a lot of bother and a lot of disappointment. You, unfortunately, don't fit into either of these two groups."

"What group do I fit into?"

"One that shouldn't be pursuing art."

"Why not?"

"For a start, all your paintings are of angels."

"I like angels. I like how they represent fear and hope. Protection and damnation." Dylan's reply was turning into a rant. "They are outside of death. They transcend it. An angel is the ultimate creature. Free from death…"

"Angels are trite and overdone. But let's just imagine for a second, they're not. Where's all the rest? Installations. Sculptures. Experimenting with different media, different techniques. Where are your sketchbooks full of ideas? I'd like to see you push it more. I want to see angels made out of, I don't know, something surprising, crazy, unexpected or outrageous. I'd rather you shock me than bore me."

"I can do that. I can be shocking."

"No, sorry. You misunderstand. What I'm trying to say that a life as an artist is not for you."

"But why?"

"Quite frankly, your work is unmemorable. It's never going to get noticed. Never going to cause a reaction, create neither admiration nor upset. And as for your painting, well, I've seen ten-year-olds paint better than you."

The last sentence felt like a spear being thrust into Dylan's chest. Spreading a searing pain across his whole body. There was something permanent about this pain. A finality. Hope had well and truly been cut out by the root and concreted over, with the professor's last few, hurtful words scratched into the rough surface with a rusty nail. So he was no better than a ten-year-old.

Something shifted in Dylan's brain.

An irrevocable change.

Strangely, there was no anger or rage. He didn't want to suddenly smash up the professor's office, or throw a chair through the window. Quite the opposite. A calm resolve came over him. Almost dignified. The ambition to get into art college had evaporated. That now seemed small and insignificant. No. Dylan realised this world he had so long desired was beneath him. It was thin and frivolous. A game they played. *If you do this, then you can have this.* He looked down on the professor now. Pitied him. A man whose vision was limited. Conventional. Dylan would create his own art. A new art. Far beyond the comprehension of this small-minded man.

Dylan rose slowly to his feet. Smiled serenely. Turned and walked out of the professor's office and down the corridor.

"Excuse me, Dylan," the professor called after him. "You've forgotten your portfolio."

Dylan ignored him and kept walking.

He had plans to make. Big plans.

He'd show him. He'd show them all.

No more painting. No more angels.

Savage Children

Why paint angels when he could become an angel.
The most powerful angel of all.
An angel of death.

EPILOGUE

THEY SAT IN HIS GARDEN, slumped in a couple of deck chairs, letting the sun warm their faces and the birdsong fill their ears. Savage wore his comfort clothes, Crocs and those pale-blue elasticated waist trousers, plus his beloved Jam T-shirt, and slurped his bucket-sized cup of tea, nose deep in his book on ancient Rome. Tannaz sipped a black coffee, sunglasses on, playing on her phone.

"Did you know," said Savage, "where the word decimation comes from?"

"Sure, it means to reduce by a tenth," said Tannaz, not looking up.

"Yeah. But do you know where the word came from?"

"No, but I have a feeling you're going to tell me."

"It was a punishment in the Roman army. If a group of soldiers deserted or didn't follow orders or fell asleep at their posts, they were divided up into groups of ten. Each man would draw straws. Soldier who drew the short straw would get beaten to death by the other nine. Thereby reducing their number by a tenth. Hence, the word decimation."

"Harsh. Can't imagine that's the best military strategy, reducing your forces by a tenth every time someone does something wrong."

"That's why it never caught on."

Tannaz put down her coffee, reached into her bag and pulled out an apple.

"What are you doing?" asked Savage.

"Eating an apple. Want one?"

Savage screwed up his face. "After having a drink? No thanks.

Two wet things in a row. You can't have one wet thing followed by another wet thing. It just isn't right."

"Why not?"

"They just don't go together. It's like having beer and soup. It doesn't work. Soup and bread works. Or beer and crisps. Or tea and biscuits. One wet thing, one dry thing. They work together. Complement each other. Apples and coffee don't."

"I tell you what doesn't work," said Tannaz, turning her nose up. "Those blue elasticated trousers and Crocs."

Through the open door of the kitchen, Savage heard the doorbell ring. He leapt to his feet.

"Ah, that'll be my special delivery." He hurried into the kitchen and through the corridor to the front door. Opening it wide to find the smiling friendly sight of Lev, the Polish online retail giant, filling the doorway.

"Lev!" said Savage. "Good to see you. How are you?"

"Good, very good. Better now I am not in police station. This crazy guy thought I had stolen children. Had taken child next door. Is madness."

"I heard about that. They arrested me too."

"They did? What is this? I try to tell them. It is not me. You have wrong guy. They did not listen. Kept saying I did this bad thing. I get tears. They make me cry. I would never do this thing."

"I'm so sorry, Lev. Nobody thought it was you. We all knew you were innocent." Savage thought it best not to complicate things and tell Lev that it was his next-door neighbour's mother-in-law who had dropped them both in it. "Don't worry, though. They caught the guy. Well, I say caught. He committed suicide. Jumped off a bridge."

"Good, I say. Best thing for evil man like this."

"So what goodies have you got for me today?" asked Savage.

"No package, just small envelope you must sign for. Must be important."

Savage saw the markings on the envelope. "Oh, it is very important. A present for someone."

"Ah, someone special?"

"Very special."

Savage signed Lev's handheld device, took the envelope and waved goodbye. He closed the front door and re-joined Tannaz in the garden.

"Who was that?" she asked.

"Lev. A delivery. It's a present."

Tannaz perked up. Sat up straight. "Is it for me?"

"No."

Tannaz slumped back down again. "Oh, well, I'm not interested then."

"It's for Carl Cooper."

Tannaz became bolt upright again. Indignant. "Why the hell are you buying a present for Carl Cooper?"

"You know, for helping us out. Helping us catch Dylan Harper."

"He didn't choose to help us, we bribed him."

"Yeah, I know, but I like to repay a favour, even if he was coerced."

"I can't believe you bought that little racist prick a present. Are you mad?"

"You don't know what I bought him."

"Well, unless it's a brain or a better set of moral values, I don't think you should be giving him anything."

"Oh, I think you'll like what I've got him. It's very personal. Actually, you can't get more personal than this."

She went back to playing on her phone. "I don't want to know. Hope I never see the little creep's face again."

"Oh, I think you will want to when you find out what it is."

"No, I won't."

"Okay, well, just read the outside of the envelope." He waved it in front of her face.

She wouldn't look at it. "Not interested."

"Go on, just read the logo on the outside," he said.

She glanced up, just briefly. Did a double take. Read the name of the company on the outside of the envelope. "Find My Ancestors."

Savage Children

Her eyes lit up. "Is that one of those places that trace your DNA?"

"Yep."

"And it's Carl's?"

"Yep."

"Savage, you crafty devil. But how did you get his DNA?"

"Remember the pint glass I took from Bexhill Arms?"

"Oh yeah, I wondered what that was for."

"I took a swab of the inside of the rim. Sent it to them. And this is the result."

Tannaz jumped up and down in her deck chair. "Open it! Open it! Open it!" She tried snatching it out of his hands. "I gotta read it."

Savage pulled the envelope back out of her reach. "Now, now. Let's take our time."

"Savage, you're so annoying, just open it already!"

"Oh, okay then." He prised open a corner of the envelope and ran his thumb along its length, then extracted the letter and began to read it to himself. When he got halfway down, he burst into big belly laughs. Uncontrollable ones, the kind that make snot bubbles come out of your nose.

Tannaz whipped the letter out of his hand and read the results of Carl's DNA ancestry out loud, "Seven percent North African. Ten percent British. Twenty-six percent Romany Gypsy. Fifty-seven percent Persian." Tannaz did not look happy, like she wanted to spit out something she hoicked up from the bottom of her lungs. "Fifty-seven percent Persian! Persian! You mean to tell me that little prick is mostly Iranian. Like me. Makes me ashamed to call myself Iranian."

Savage wiped a few tears from his eyes. "Oh, that is beautiful. The man leading the fight against immigrants is mostly an Iranian Gypsy by way of North Africa. I think he really needs to know this."

Tannaz giggled. "I suppose it is pretty funny. I mean, the irony."

"Come on. Let's hop in the van and give him the good news."

"Oh, yeah. I can't wait to see his face. Do you think he'll believe it?"

"Don't care. I'll pay to do another test, if he doesn't."

They left the house, not bothering to fold up the deck chairs. Savage locked up and they walked down his front steps towards the little VW, Tannaz keeping a tight hold of the envelope and its contents. Probably, the first time the thought of visiting the Bexhill Arms had put smiles on their faces.

Giggling away, the pair who emerged from the flat seemed to be sharing a joke, oblivious to the fact that they were being watched by three men parked up the road on the opposite side. Two in the front and one in the back.

The girl was loud, cocky and over-confident. They caught brief snippets of their conversation.

"I can't wait to see Carl's face," she cackled loudly. "Hey, we should give Vikram a call. He'd love to see this."

"Great idea."

The man accompanying her, in his late fifties or early sixties, had a big grin on his face. He wore a T-shirt that said 'The Jam' on the front of it. Apart from that he was plain and unremarkable. Hair receding, not much of gut on him, his arms were toned and muscular. He was in good shape, rare to see on a guy of that age.

By contrast, the girl was attractive, young, middle eastern, decked out in black. Not fashionably, more alternatively.

The pair of them looked odd, an unlikely coupling. Definitely not romantic, you could tell that by their body language. A friendship, although it seemed more business-like than a friendship. Work colleagues perhaps?

The man sitting in the front passenger seat held up his smartphone on camera mode. He kept his finger down on the button, snapping off rapid-fire shots of the couple as they climbed into the small VW van. As soon as they were inside, he stopped taking pictures and turned to the other two, shuffling through the shots, selecting the clearest one he could find. He enlarged it with his fingers.

The man in the back took out a creased and crumpled shot and

Savage Children

held it next to the image on the smart phone. All three men leaned in to get a better look, to compare the two images.

"That's a positive ID," said the man in the back.

Down the road, the VW van started up and pulled away from the kerb, driving away from them.

"Shall I follow them?" said the man in the driver's seat.

"No," said the one in the back. "We have what we need."

If you've enjoyed this novel, why not read the first one in the series, *SAVAGE LIES* or the second one, *SAVAGE GAMES*.

There's also a **FREE** short-story prequel you can download from Prolific Works called *SAVAGE*.

Thank you for reading *Savage Children*. I'd love it if you could leave a review on AMAZON and recommend it to your friends. Your opinion makes a huge difference, helping readers discover my books for the first time.

You can also drop by for a chat on social media.

Facebook: **PeterBolandWriter**
Twitter: **@PeterBoland19**

OTHER BOOKS BY PETER BOLAND INCLUDE:

Savage Lies
Savage Games
The Girl by the Thames

ACKNOWLEDGEMENTS

Writing isn't easy. It's complicated, long-winded and nerve-wracking. You're constantly second-guessing everything you do and wondering whether it's good enough. And the fact that most of it is done alone isn't healthy for the festering paranoia that grows with every sentence written. So it's extremely reassuring to have brilliant people who support you throughout the process, not just telling you everything will be alright, but also being honest and setting you straight about anything that's amiss.

This is the first novel where Savage has had a brush with the law, and that involved police procedure. I was determined to get this right. So I enlisted the help of Samantha Smith, a full-time police officer who patiently answered all my questions and enlightened me about how the police go about doing a very difficult job. It also helped that Sam is a writer herself, letting me know when, and when I couldn't, get away with a bit of artistic licence. Sam's input into *Savage Children* was invaluable and I'll be calling on her knowledge for the next Savage novel (yes, I'm already planning it now).

Once again, I am massively indebted to the great editorial skills of Lauren Finger who always does a brilliant job of smoothing out, polishing and pointing out where I can tighten things up. I'm also very blessed to have an amazing team of beta readers whose attention to detail simply astounds and impresses me every time. They include: Deanna Finn, Terry Harden, Kath Middleton and Suze Clarke-Morris. Suze also provided a lot of reassurance throughout the writing process, giving great advice and support. I also have to give massive thanks to my go-to proofreader Loma Halden, who is always quick and highly professional.

The amazing Sarah Hardy who runs her blog tours like a well-oiled machine, ensured plenty of people got to hear about my new book. Massive thanks to every one of the bloggers who took part in it, you guys do an awesome job. And thanks to Helen Boyce from The Book Club who had the gargantuan task of sending out all the ARCs for review. Thanks to everyone who took the time to read and review *Savage Children*.

Big thanks also to Simon Tucker for his graphic design skills on the front cover, and Glendon Haddix for his pristine formatting.

And to my lovely wife, Shalini, thank you for supporting and keeping me sane every time I write one of these thrillers.

www.ingramcontent.com/pod-product-compliance
Lightning Source LLC
Chambersburg PA
CBHW022058090426
42743CB00008B/648